T'RIFIC

T'rific

MIKE REID

with Peter Gerrard

PARTRIDGE

LONDON · NEW YORK · TORONTO · SYDNEY · AUCKLAND

TRANSWORLD PUBLISHERS
61–63 Uxbridge Road, London W5 5SA
A division of the Random House Group Ltd

RANDOM HOUSE AUSTRALIA PTY LTD
20 Alfred Street, Milsons Point, Sydney
New South Wales 2061, Australia

RANDOM HOUSE NEW ZEALAND
18 Poland Road, Glenfield, Auckland 10, New Zealand

RANDOM HOUSE SOUTH AFRICA (PTY) LTD
Endulini, 5a Jubilee Road, Parktown 2193, South Africa

Published 1999 by Partridge a division of Transworld Publishers Ltd

A catalogue record for this book is available from the British Library.

ISBN 085225 2774

Typeset in 11/14pt Times by
Phoenix Typesetting, Ilkley, West Yorkshire

Printed in Great Britain by
Clays Ltd, St Ives plc

1 3 5 7 9 10 8 6 4 2

For my wife, Shirley, who has been behind me all the way.
For my family, because that's what my life has been all about.
And
in memory of our son Mark and granddaughter Kirsty Anne.

ACKNOWLEDGEMENTS

I would like to thank Tony Lewis for looking after my interests over the years, not only as a manager, but as a friend.

CHAPTER ONE

I CAME INTO THIS WORLD ON THE 19 JANUARY 1940 IN THE HACKNEY Hospital, east London. And being what they call a breech birth, I was a pain to my mum through a long delivery, and nothing really changed for the rest of her life.

What with young Reidy deciding to come into the world arse first, it meant a lot of tugging and pulling, and so I ended up with a dislocated shoulder. Today things are different. When a woman has a baby she goes home in two minutes. In the days I'm referring to, they stayed in hospital for about a fortnight. For those two weeks all the nurses called me Little Hitler, because I was this comical little figure with a bandaged arm stuck up in the air giving the *Sieg Heil* salute.

I think the family home was somewhere in the East End, but as soon as they got me home, Mum Helen and Dad Sid moved to South Tottenham. Then, a short time later, we moved out to Ruislip, which was virtually on the border of Greater London and Hertfordshire. Considering they were both townies this was quite a move, because that area then was right out in the sticks.

Remember, this was bang in the middle of the war, and perhaps Dad's idea was to get his family away from the bombing and all that, but if that was the case he made a little error of judgement.

Dad never actually went to war because his job came under the heading of essential war work, and that was driving the basic skeletons

9

of army lorries from one factory to another, where they'd be kitted out with cabs, bodies and what have you.

The place we moved into was a flat in a block that was one of five – they were one of the first to be built in Ruislip. Anyway, he was doing one of his deliveries not too far from home when he looked up and saw German bomber planes heading into London. As they passed overhead, up went our boys in their Spitfires and started shooting the crap out of them. Those heavy bombers couldn't take on our nippy little fighters, so they turned tail and headed back the way they'd come – though not before they did what was called a tip. That is, they jettisoned their payload of bombs to gain extra speed.

Imagine how Dad felt watching all this, knowing that those bombs were heading towards his wife and little baby. He could see and hear the explosions in the distance, no doubt every one tearing his heart out.

By the time he got home it was all over. Every block was razed to the ground, except one that was badly damaged but still standing. The police wouldn't let him through, but with him screaming for his wife and son they let him cross the cordon, where he found Mum being treated for badly cut legs, still holding me tight in her arms. What went through his head at that moment he never ever said, but it doesn't take much imagination to guess.

When the first bomb went off close by I was in my pram in the middle of the room. Mum grabbed me, stuck me under a big old table just as two more exploded, bringing down a glass chandelier that cut Mum's legs to pieces. A split second earlier, and it would've fallen dead centre into my pram.

Loads of people were killed that day and our block was declared unsafe, so we were on the move again.

This time to 38 Vicarage Road, Tottenham, where we lodged with Mum's parents Nan and Grandad Ives. Straining my head to go as far back as I can, my earliest memories go no further than this house. And it's here that one incident stands out in my mind, and it must have happened not long after we arrived at Nan's.

I must have been young, because I remember lying in a cot listening to this strange buzzing noise that got louder and louder. Then suddenly it stopped, and at the same time my mum, who must have been in the room, gave a loud scream and pulled me out of the cot. I can see it as though it was yesterday. My head was over her shoulder, then there was a great bang. The bedroom door seemed to float across the room, and then smashed into the wall at the same time as the window went out. A doodlebug had come down in the road right outside the house. I suppose that incident was so traumatic for a very young child that it became etched on my mind. But other than that, I have no recollection of people, places or things that happened to my family until we moved into Beaufoy Road, just round the corner from Nan's. Though I'm told that before we settled there, we lived in Enfield, Edmonton and Ponders End. I don't know why Dad didn't get a gypsy caravan because we were like bloody nomads.

As I said, though, none of that's in my head, and as far as I'm concerned life began for me when we finally put down roots in Tottenham. I must have been about four then.

My second memory is of a street party in Vicarage Road. This was the end of the war, and I may or may not have understood what it was all about. All I know is that there were tables laid out from one end of the street to the other, piled with cakes and sandwiches, and everyone was singing and dancing and, overhead, planes were flying in V formations.

Even at that age I was a bit of a loner, and loved nothing better than to go off roaming by myself. I wasn't at school yet, but I'd slip out of the house and go off and do my own thing. This was nothing to do with irresponsibility on my mum's part. Times were different then. I mean, nowadays you're frightened to let your kids out of sight, but then we could disappear all day and nobody worried, within reason.

At first, the farthest I'd go would be round to Nanny and Grandad Ives, because from my house that was just up Church Road, across Tottenham High Road then into Vicarage Road, just opposite the Spurs Football Ground.

Even now I've only got to get a whiff of embrocation, White Horse it was called then, and I'm right back in Nanny's bedroom. I hated it. The whole house stank of it, but I put up with it because I was always guaranteed a few sweets or a piece of cake, and every now and then a penny when I showed up.

My nan was a great big woman and seemed to spend most of her life in bed. She probably wasn't in good health, but I wasn't aware of that.

Grandad was a big man too, but my memories are of him hunched over the fire, winter and summer. He rarely spoke. I'd walk in the room and he'd look up and say, 'All right, boy?' and that would be it until the next time I saw him.

Like a lot of his generation, the First World War crucified grandad. I'm told he volunteered for the war full of himself; outgoing and always ready for a laugh. Four years on he was a broken man, only fit for seven years in a mental institution.

I would have loved to have known him better, but there was no getting through to him. I'd chatter away about this and that, like kids do, and it was like I wasn't even there. He wasn't a mental case or anything, just sunk into himself.

It was only in later years that I realized his behaviour wasn't normal. At the time I just accepted that's what grandads were like.

My other grandparents I didn't really know at all, because they lived in Benfleet, Essex and we hardly ever saw them. Nanny Reid was an opera singer and a very, very good one at that. Perhaps she passed on a few genes to me. I know her game was a bit more high-brow than what I do, but at the end of the day it's all entertainment.

My grandad was a pianist to concert standard, but what held him back was that he couldn't keep away from the bottle. He was very talented in another direction, too, as he was something to do with colour mixing for fabric dyeing – one of the few people who could actually do it. So from that he earned a tremendous amount of money, but as Dad told me, eventually pissed it all up the wall and ended up smoking and drinking himself to death.

So my dad's legacy from him was a love of the piano and a reasonable skill at knocking a tune out, which made him a very popular man in the pubs or at parties.

Every house had a piano in those days, whether you could play it or not, so when we were indoors or visiting the shout would always go up, 'Come on, Sid, give us a tune', and he didn't have to be asked twice. Up he'd get and start belting out 'Tiger Rag' or whatever, then one would get up and sing, then another, so wherever Dad was it always turned into a party.

Like I was saying, I started to spread my wings at about four years old. As my confidence grew, those visits to Nanny's gave way to more adventurous trips.

Just round the corner and over Church Road was Bruce Castle Park. As its name suggests, there was a smallish castle stuck in one corner, and me and my little mates grew up thinking that that was where Robert the Bruce sat and watched the spider going up and down. We'd sit on the grass looking at it, thinking blimey, who'd want to sit in a place like that for weeks on end? In retrospect, the park was probably no bigger than a couple of football pitches, but what appeared to me at that age as an endless expanse of grass and trees was, as far as I was concerned, the countryside. I spent every day of the year searching for birds' eggs in the hedges before I learned that they could only be found in the spring. Insects, butterflies – you name them, I looked for them, all over the place. Give me welly boots and a jam jar and I was the happiest kid in the district.

Right behind our house was Tottenham cemetery, and that was even bigger than the park and equally as exciting a place for a young kid.

I said I was a loner but that didn't mean I had no mates. Of course I did, and we got up to all the things that, without exception, most London children of our generation did after the war. We collected treasure, like shrapnel from the bombs and that silver foil stuff the Germans used to drop to confuse the radar. We played on bomb-sites and rooted through wrecked houses, claiming bits and pieces to take home, always returning as black as arseholes.

Three things happened when I was five that stick in my mind. My brother Brian was born, Dad went into business and I started school.

I've already said that Mum was pretty easygoing as far as my disappearing went, but once she was tied up with the new baby I could virtually come and go as I pleased. As long as I was in for bedtime the day was my own, so I blessed Brian for that.

Now my old father was a clever man. I don't mean bursting with O levels, but with his hands there was nothing he couldn't do.

About this time he actually built a car. Starting with the chassis of an old Morris he begged, borrowed and I won't say stole all the parts, because unlike his eldest son in later years, Dad would rather cut off his hand than lift anything that wasn't his.

Anyway, he got together all the bits, and over the months put together what they now call an estate car. This wasn't some old banger tied together with bits of wire – it was the proper business, and for years we went everywhere in that motor. Without doubt he was mechanically competent, as was his brother George; the upshot being that they both opened a little car repair shop in Vicarage Road, just down from Nanny Ives.

Perhaps Dad was fed up with driving lorries all hours of the day, and thought this would be an opportunity to be nearer home so he could spend more time with his boys, because believe me, we were his life. Whatever the reason, him and George set up this shop, and from what I'm told it took off, and they were doing good business and keeping their heads above water. Then they had a falling-out – some financial problem, or whatever. Maybe it was over two bob or half a crown. It couldn't have been very much because we didn't have jack shit in them days. So Dad walked out and they didn't speak for years.

Young as I was, I can remember my dad saying to Mum: 'Helen, I'm finished. I don't want no more of that.' I don't think Mum ever forgave him. She had great aspirations for going up in the world, and quite simply he didn't, no matter how hard she tried to push him.

One of her greatest hardships was walking past a certain bungalow about a quarter of a mile down our road. She would've given her right arm to have lived there because it was brick-built, much bigger than her own place, nicely laid out and had a fair piece of garden. What choked her every day she lived in that street was the knowledge that they'd been offered this bungalow in the first place but that Dad wouldn't stretch to the seven-and-six rent, as opposed to six bob for the prefab she ended up with. Not a week went by without Mum having a dig about what might have been.

Growing up, I was never one for analysing people or situations, but looking at it from where I am now, Mum and Dad were like the characters in that TV series *Keeping Up Appearances*. The old man doing anything for a quiet life, and the woman basically working class, but desperate to aspire to something much better. That was my mum.

I might unintentionally give the impression that I didn't have any time for Mum throughout my life. That would be wrong. I loved her, and in her own way I know she loved me, but for some reason we always clashed. We rubbed each other up the wrong way, and I can hardly think of an occasion until the day she died where our relationship wasn't strained.

Who can really look at themselves honestly? As far as I was concerned, every bit of aggravation, every bit of friction I laid at my mother's door. Perhaps there was an annoying side of me that I've completely forgotten about. She might have tried to get through to me, failed, then given up. I really don't know. One area where I do know I was at fault, but not when I was a youngster, was what I perceived as her meanness, that bordered on the miserly. This came to a head one time and I had a go at her. It was over her keep taking my fags. I mean, I was offering them, but she kept taking them, bang, bang, bang, one after another even while one was burning in the ashtray. I said, 'Mum, I don't believe you, you're as tight as they come.' She just looked at me and said, 'Michael, if you'd known hard times like your dad and me, you'd be a bit more careful with your money.' That should have given me something to think about, but I was young and it didn't. At least, not until many years later when I came to realize that Mum hadn't been as bad as the picture I carried in my head. But I suppose that's what growing up is all about.

Anyway, I'm five years old or so, and it's time to start school. Most of my little mates were dreading the prospect, but me, I couldn't wait. I think I would have gone at three if they'd let me.

The thought of new books and learning new things filled me with utter excitement. So while other kids were being dragged kicking and screaming towards Lancasterian School in Church Road, Mum had to hold me back.

I had this tremendous thirst for knowledge, and I still have. I think I've got to thank my father for setting me on the path. He always had time for me and Brian and the patience of a saint.

Like most kids I was inquisitive, or perhaps a bit more than average. 'Dad, what's this? What's that?' and he'd explain whatever it was without any fuss at all. By contrast, I might be in a mate's house and they'd ask something or other and their old man would go,

'Christ sake, boy, I'm reading the paper', and that made me realize Dad was a bit special.

Even before I started school he'd come home with a pile of knowledge books – probably paid coppers for them down the market – but they meant as much to me as a computer means to a kid today. If it was raining, I could sit at the table all day studying birds of the world or pygmies in the jungle, and it just fired me up. So what with all the pre-school learning I soaked up, those early years were a piece of piss.

There was one time I got caught out, though. I mean, my hand was up and down in question time like a bleeding yo-yo. The teacher asked, 'What is the heaviest? A ton of lead, a ton of gold or a ton of feathers?' Bosh, I'm there, because Dad often said how valuable and heavy gold was. 'Gold, miss. Gold.' 'Course, we all know the answer now, but at least I was on my own; the rest of the class thought the answer was lead.

As for those early school years, they just drifted by in a pleasurable daze.

Outside, though, even at that tender age, I'd started the ducking and diving that was to become a way of life for the next twenty-five years.

Money was tight at home, and if there was any spare Mum kept her fingers firmly round it. After his failed business venture, Dad had gone back to driving. Drivers were ten a penny, and I doubt whether he was bringing home much more than four quid a week. Makes you think, doesn't it – you can pay that for a cup of tea and a round of toast on the motorway these days.

So when I wanted money for sweets or Saturday morning pictures, I had to find it myself. Mum wouldn't part with it, and Dad didn't have it to give away, even if he wanted to. One of his stock answers when I did ask for a couple of pennies was, 'Son, if battleships were ten bob I couldn't afford a rowing boat.'

One of my earliest earners was selling firewood door-to-door at tuppence a bag. I was six years old. Getting the wood was no problem, because it was years before they got round to renovating bomb-damaged properties. I had a little old cart Dad had knocked up out of an old pram and a rusty meat cleaver with no handle.

Everybody had coal fires in those days, so I always sold out.

The best seller, though, was the tarry blocks they dug out of roads when they were relaying them. Whether these wooden blocks were some early type of foundation, I haven't a clue, or even if they reused them. Either way, those tight-bastard roadworkers wouldn't part with one. They stacked them behind wooden paling fences. So Reidy waited until they knocked off for the day, then did a bit of knocking off himself. Sometimes I'd make six trips in an evening. And did those things burn! Being full of tar, they didn't do the chimney much good, and I should think there were more chimney fires in my area than anywhere else, but that was one of the hazards of a good blaze.

When the firewood game went flat in the summer I had to resort to outright thieving to keep up my sweet ration, and as there were only two shops near my house, they both had to suffer.

One of them was Berry's, the off-licence, and the best I could do there was creep into the backyard, nick as many empty bottles as I could carry, then go into the shop from the front and collect the deposit money on them. Trouble was, I couldn't do that too often. But Gearing's on the opposite corner was a gold mine – for me, anyway.

I'm ashamed to think of it now because the ancient couple that owned the shop were two old dears really. But they weren't on the ball, and to us kids who were starved of sweets and other little luxuries, they left themselves open to being robbed blind. Old man Gearing had the biggest hooter I'd ever seen and permanently swinging from the end was this dewdrop we couldn't take our eyes off. Not only were these two about ninety years old, but they were both bent double and moved like snails. Didn't matter which one it was, if you asked for something on the back shelf, by the time they turned round you could have emptied the shop. Well, fill your pockets anyway, and I did regularly.

Another move, which, considering I was only a baby, showed I wasn't lacking in a bit of ingenuity, was to paint an old copper penny silver. I'd leave it overnight, then offer it to old man Gearing as a half a crown. Nine times out of ten it worked, and I got a bit of change. The few times he caught me out he'd tell me not to come in his shop ever again. Two hours later I'd slip back in. By then he'd forgotten all about it, so over the counter went another painted coin.

I'm always saying I have no regrets about anything I've done in my life. Now that's a bold statement, and broadly speaking it's true, but I have to admit there are a few times when I'd like to turn the clock back and go another way.

I'll touch on other bits and pieces as I come to them, but there's one incident in particular that still gives me a little twinge of pain fifty years later. My dad was the best in the world. Not once in my life did he raise a hand to me, and, thinking about it, his voice either, and God knows I must have asked for it a hundred times.

Over Bruce Castle Park there was a fair, perhaps a couple of times a year, and this time I was desperate to get myself over to the swings, carousel and everything else. But I was potless. Totally b'rassic. I ducked and dived and came up empty-handed, so I went down Dad's jacket pocket and dug out all that was there – two bob and three pennies.

I had my night at the fair, blew it all on nothing worth a light, then my arsehole went. I went home fearing the worst – nothing. All the next day I waited for something to be said – nothing. And it was never mentioned, not then, nor years later, either in jest or anger.

Being the way she was and no different from any other housewife in this respect, Mum would take his bit of wages then hand him back his grub money for work. So for a couple of days my old dad went without his lunch or a cup of tea because of me. He knew. He must have known where that money had gone to. It couldn't have been Brian because he was only about three, so he knew it was me and he chose not to say anything. Strangely enough, that said more to me than if he'd skinned my arse.

It wasn't too long after that that we nearly lost him. Then how would I have felt? As I said before, I was a great roamer and a proper nature boy, and I was bursting to see the world, or indeed anything that lay beyond our little corner of Tottenham. So when he suggested a trip in his lorry I can't begin to describe my excitement.

Things must have been a bit quiet as work went, because I know at that time we were struggling for money. Anyway, Dad applied for and got a job driving for British Road Services, and his first job was to deliver farm equipment to Scotland. This was on the eve of my ninth birthday. No – he was setting off then, so he must have sprung this on me a couple of days before.

He came into my bedroom and said, 'Son, tell you what. I'll take you to Scotland with me for your birthday. You can miss three days of school. I'll write a note and tell them you're sick or something.' I couldn't speak. I just remember nodding my head up and down. He might as well have suggested Africa or the moon, because it was all the same to me. The excitement filled my chest so I thought I'd burst. I was literally shaking for days.

Then on the afternoon before we were to set off I did something so trivial I can't even remember what it was. Bit of backchat, broke a cup, whatever, and Mum saying, 'You're not going.' I cried so much I thought I'd choke myself. I pleaded and made promises that would have turned me into a saint overnight, but she wouldn't budge. My last resort was that Dad would overturn her decision, but I should have known better. As always he didn't say a word, but the way he looked at me I knew it tore him up inside.

When he went off to Scotland he left me in a heap.

He'd never done any long-distance work before, and in the early hours of my ninth birthday he nodded off at the wheel, touched hubcaps with another lorry, smashed through a wall and over a viaduct with twenty tons of tractors right behind his head. Ninety feet he went down, and what saved him from being crushed to death was that the tractors were ripped off the back by trees. Even with this broken and that broken and a leg pulped to jelly, he managed to get out of the cab and crawl up the ravine.

When we eventually saw the photographs that were in all the Scottish papers, it was obvious that the part of the cab where I would have been sitting was totally destroyed.

I'd like to say that Mum had had a premonition of what might happen, but I can't. Using whatever I'd done to stop me going was pure selfishness on her part. Strange, when you consider that I spent every waking hour roaming as far as I could go, but I honestly believe that she couldn't bear me to be out of her sight for too long. Overprotective I suppose you'd say. Perhaps I'm being too hard on her, because I can imagine most mums out there going, 'What's wrong with that?' But you've got to let your kids spread their wings, no matter how you feel.

Dad spent months and months in hospital – some in Scotland and the rest nearer home, but in all, he never worked for about three years.

I said money was tight before he got that job. Well, it was almost non-existent in those following years, and we lived hand to mouth.

As young as I was, I did my bit to help out. If something wasn't screwed down I nicked it, sold it on for a few coppers and handed it over to Mum. She never questioned where it came from. I might come home with a pot of jam or a packet of biscuits I'd lifted from the shop and she'd say, 'Oh, you are a naughty boy', then wallop – it's in the cupboard. No more said.

The accident was a terrible thing, but what it did was give me and Brian endless and unlimited time with our dad. With most kids their dad is at work or tired after grafting all day, so they become distant. But with ours, we always knew where he was and in the first year or so, that was at the kitchen table with balsa wood, strange-smelling glue and a knife. And from that he turned out model Spitfires, Wellingtons and Lancasters. All in intricate detail, and so sought after he had a job keeping up with the orders.

I spent hours at that table with him while he talked about every subject under the sun, and instilled in me simple philosophies that I still live by today.

The total contrast between the relationship I had with my dad and the constant tension between me and Mum amazes me even today. I've got to stress that she was a wonderful parent and always did the best for her family. I loved her, but some of the time didn't like her very much, and no doubt the same applied the other way round. It's a strange contradiction but I'm sure a lot of people will understand what I mean.

This unexplainable tension was between her and me – no-one else. No doubt my Brian will get on the phone when he reads this, and demand to know why I'm digging out our mother. But his relationship with her was in total opposition to mine. I was never jealous of it, and I'm not bitter now. I accept we are different people, and our mum reacted to us in different ways.

To everyone else, Mum had a great sense of humour and was

invariably the life and soul, and I have to agree, she was a very funny woman. Without the telly, which basically killed family together-ness, in our house or round Uncle Fred's it always seemed to be party time.

Initially, these gatherings wouldn't set out to be a party, but one thing would lead to another, Dad would sit down at the piano and then it was off, and in no time at all we'd all be singing and having a good time. At the centre of it would be Mum, cracking everyone up. Yet even among all that laughter and carrying on, her and me would catch each other's eye and something unspoken would spark between us. I can't put my finger on it and I can't explain what it was.

Once Dad was able to get out of his chair and walk with the aid of a crutch or a stick, he'd take us out at every opportunity. We went all over the place. Epping Forest, Cheshunt, Cockfosters – all those beautiful country places. Two bottles of water and three cheese rolls, and we were set up for the day.

One of our favourite places was Hadley Woods. Not only for the wood, which was wonderful for us, but the main Northern Railway line ran through there, and we'd look out for and wave to the famous Flying Scotsman while Dad had a nap on the embankment.

Or better still, he'd take us inside the tunnels, and in my young mind they were miles long and we'd put pennies on the tracks then stand in the little offshoot of a workers' tunnel while trains roared past at a hundred miles an hour, flattening our coins to wafers. Mum would have had a fit, but we never told her.

He's been gone a few years now, but I still miss my dad and that big grin of his.

You might notice that I never refer to him as my old man, like most people from my culture do. I never have, and that stems from listening to my mates talking about their fathers at a very young age. They'd say, 'My old man's a bastard', or 'My old man's as silly as arseholes'. And that made me think, because my dad was none of those things. So whether to separate him from that sort of talk or because I wanted to stress my own individuality – though not consciously, because I wouldn't even have known what it meant – he was always Dad or my father, and I was proud to say it. So I spent many, many happy hours in his company, but that didn't mean I lived in his pocket.

Away from home I lived life to the full, what with my ducking and diving, raking around the fields, school and – very high on my list of interests – the opposite sex.

By the time I was four I'd worked out that girls were different, and I mean I knew their differences were more than having just longer hair and that they didn't pee up walls like us boys. I won't go into detail about what older kids told us of what to look forward to when the opportunity arose – suffice to say, it puzzled and intrigued me at the same time.

Little Lisa White was my first girlfriend at age six and for many years after. She was a pretty girl, and I can still see her frozen in time smiling out of an infant-school photograph in one of my albums. She was really just a mate, as was another girl, Alison Clark, who lived off Beaufoy Road, and God forgive me, we tormented the life out of her. I'm sure she grew up to be an extremely attractive woman, but then she was painfully thin, and being cruel little bastards we called her 'Infantile Paralysis'. That's what they called polio in those days, and no doubt it was often on our mothers' lips, so we picked up the word because it made us sound grown-up to repeat it, even though we didn't know what it meant. Making up our little team was Dave Butler and Dave Gurling, and the five of us got up to all sorts.

Talking of girlfriends reminds me of a time when I set my sights much higher than Lisa. I fell completely in love with my school-teacher. Although I was a very bright and enthusiastic pupil, for some reason I got stuck in the B or C group. Consistently I was in the top three, and often number one in class, which didn't mean I was Einstein; just that most of the kids couldn't find their arse with their hands behind their back.

Anyway, some of the teachers thought I should be upgraded, and they laid on a special competition, knowing I'd come out on top. Then they could justify moving me up. The incentive for me wasn't academic, but the fact that I could end up in the class of Miss Sail. She was beautiful, and even before I was in her class I used to look at her with amazement. She was twenty-one or so and I was eight. Not a huge gap when you're an adult, but beyond comprehension then.

I didn't know what to do to get a word or a smile from her, so I plied her with gifts – the old 'apple for the teacher' thing. Two presents stand out in my mind. One I had to travel miles for, to Waltham Cross. Out there was this tumbledown old mansion that I'd found on one of my trips, and out the back was a derelict swimming pool still filled with stinking black water. Dangerous place really, I could have drowned in there and not been found for months. Why I risked my life in that murky water was so I could catch and present Miss Sail with some great crested newts. They were green and orange with serrated backs, and I'm told they're quite rare today. To me they were like giving the equivalent of a gold necklace. I got a smile and a 'Thank you so much, Michael' that made my lower portions tingle because, believe me, eight or not I was well aware of what was moving about under that tight jumper and skirt. I've often wondered what she did with four slimy newts.

The other gift was a bit over the top. In the corner of our front room stood my mum's pride and joy – a china cabinet. And dead centre for everyone to see was a bone-china and silver cruet set – her equivalent of the crown jewels. Your mind's probably jumped ahead before I've told the story. Yes, Michael whipped it out, gave it a quick polish with Brasso and stuck it in his satchel while Mum's back was turned. What was I thinking of? Half an hour later I'm handing it over to Miss and basking in her smile. She did question if my mother knew, and I lied through my teeth.

By the time I got home in the afternoon the whole thing seemed less and less of a good idea. As soon as I walked in I knew I'd made a terrible ricket. The questions started straight away and I had to hold my hands up before she called the police, which was bloody difficult while I was trying to cover my arse. It was one of those scenes that Tom O'Connor captured so well in his early act. She punctuated every word with a stinging slap to my head, bum and the backs of my legs, and called me every little bastard under the sun. Yes, Mum thought she was on a different plane to everyone else, but when it came down to it she had a very rich vocabulary. Never ever used the eff- or c-words, but what was left was enough to curl my ears.

Next morning, first thing, and much to my embarrassment, she went round the school. Though I never found out what was said, amazingly she let Miss Sail keep the cruet set.

The shame of all that knocked our one-sided love affair on the head, and I made up my mind to stick with girls of my own age – for the time being anyway.

For a man who has very few regrets, as I'm lighting another cigarette it reminds me that the habit itself is one of my biggest, and that my very first puff of a fag had repercussions that should have made me think. Obviously it didn't.

Mum was a heavy smoker and extremely careful of waste. So if she was going to wash her hair or cook the dinner, she wouldn't grind out half a cigarette; she'd pinch the end off for later. I've nicked one of these 'stoopers', as they were known, shot over the road into the cemetery and had a good lungful.

Believe it or not, some few weeks earlier I'd had the offer of another trip to Scotland. Same scenario as before – utter joy and unbelievable excitement. This time the offer had come from Anne and Cyril Nesbitt, who were friends of Mum and Dad, and who knew someone in Scotland who had a farm. A farm – a real farm, with cows, horses and pigs. I'd known about the place for a long time, and over months must have driven the Nesbitts mad with questions. How big was it? What animals did they have? Were there haystacks to climb on? In the end, Anne said one night, 'Michael, would you like to spend the summer holidays in Scotland with Harry?' That was their boy, who was my age. I had the same reaction as when Dad asked me – I was dizzy with the thought of it. Then Mum chipped in, all smiles for our visitors, but nevertheless still said, 'Oh, I don't know, dear.' 'Dear' – that was her favourite word, especially just before a knock-back. Eventually she capitulated and said I could go.

That was until I stole that poxy little dog-end, and Mum knocked my trip on the head. She must have had a heart of stone to withstand my tears, and I cried for days; not just put on an act – I was heartbroken, sobbing because I was so devastated. She stuck to her guns, though, and I missed out on what at that age would've been the holiday of a lifetime.

Anyway, going back to my interest in girls, I can remember playing truant one day and sneaking into the picture house at Bruce Grove with my mate, Jimmy Hockley. Didn't pay, just crawled under the cashier's window. Remember, those were not permissive times, and the film was *Where No Vultures Fly* with Ava Gardner. If memory serves, there was a scene where, after this desert trek, she got under a waterfall wearing a white blouse – no bra. Well, her nipples stood out like organ stops – that'd never been seen on screen before, and me and Jimmy just went 'Ffffffuckinhell', as both our tongues fell in our laps.

In those days they ran the film continuously, so we sat there all day waiting for that thirty-second scene to come round again. Once it had, we stood up – and so did the rest of the cinema. Everybody had stayed, like us, to watch it over again.

Nowadays kids wouldn't look twice, but then the only rude pictures we could get hold of were those pink corset adverts in *Woman's Own*.

This Jimmy was about a year older than me, and ordered me about like he was ten years older and I swallowed it. I was making a few shillings catching and selling grass snakes and those king newts, plus breeding white mice, while Jim had a job in Berry's, the off-licence. This gave him the opportunity to nick fags that he'd sell at school. God, he was a tight bastard. I mean, regular every day he had a packet of Gallagher's Blue cigarettes.

One day we were behind the wall in the cemetery and he opened up a twenty. I said, 'Giss one of them.' He goes 'What?' I said, 'Where's mine?' 'Oh, no,' he said, 'I've only got nineteen left.' I thought you bastard, I won't forget that, and I never have.

He had a few quid and so did I; the upshot being that we put our money together and bought a fly tent. Tiny little thing, about three foot across and two foot high, but we were so proud of it. The idea was that we'd use it together or each have it for alternate weeks.

Our first trip was to a place called Dobb's Weir at Ware, in Hertfordshire. Like I've already said, Mum didn't turn a hair, even though it was a very long cycle ride. She was probably glad to see the back of me. This place was where Dad used to take me as a small boy, so I knew it well. The attraction, apart from the scenery, was that this weir took the outflow of a power station, and consequently the water was always as hot as a bath, and kids from all over congregated there.

A lot of these were girls, and by tradition a corner of one field was where they all changed into their swimming gear. Dave Butler and another couple of mates were with us, and being red-blooded boys, we decided to have a peek at the mysteries of womanhood. We crawled Indian-fashion through the bushes and long grass until we were right up by the fence. We lay there giggling and nudging each other until a group of girls turned up and started to get their kit off. First the tops, giving us an eyeful of budding boobs, then the knickers – leaving nothing to the imagination. Then, costumes on, they ran down to the river.

Jesus Christ. I lay there sweating and feeling decidedly uncomfortable. Moving back into the trees, it was our turn to get into our cossies, and as I dropped my shorts without embarrassment because I was with mates, Jimmy Hockley pointed at me and shouted at the others: 'Eeeugh – look at Reidy's dick.' I've gone, 'What? What?' and he said, 'It's huge. Your willy's massive.' By this time, I'm brick red and covering the old chap with my hands, screaming, 'No it ain't. No it ain't.'

Do you know, those lads never let me forget it and took the piss for years. That was until I was about fourteen, and by then I'd learned what a fella's assets were all about. When one or the other brought up the old story to wind me up, I suddenly came out with, 'Yeah, he's right, but it's even bigger than he's telling you.' That shut them up, and I never looked back.

When I first put my name down for that tent, I never realized how educational it would be, or how popular it would make me with the girls.

When it was my week, I'd put it up in the garden and practically live in it the whole time with my dog Lucky, Lisa and Alison. It must have brought out their maternal instincts or something, because they'd bring round a tea service they'd got for Christmas and we'd have lemonade and biscuits off it. Once that was out of the way, we'd play doctors and nurses or mothers and fathers, and I don't think I have to describe that.

But it was all innocent stuff. We were kids and full of curiosity. Mum wouldn't have looked on it like that, but she never came near. Either she guessed what children get up to, or more likely her imagination didn't stretch that far.

Certainly the girls found it entertaining, because when it was Jimmy's week they were always asking me, 'When's it your turn? When's the tent coming back?'

Anyway, it was my week and Jimmy came round and said, 'I want the tent.' I've gone, 'Why's that?' and he said, ''Cos I'm going camping.' 'Not without me,' I said. 'Well, I'm taking it because it's mine and I need it,' and he started to pull up the ropes. Up until then I'd always been subservient to him, but suddenly – and this was the first time in my life – I felt real anger. It welled up inside me out of nowhere. The blood pumped through my head and without warning, bosh, I've punched him full in the face and he's gone down.

I was big for my age, but he was bigger and he jumped to his feet, got me round the neck and threw me full force onto my back, knocking every breath out of me. Then he jumped on me and twisted my arm up my back, so with my free hand I stuck my fingers up his nose, and it was stalemate. We couldn't move until Dad came out and broke us apart. Neither of us won, but I kept the tent.

It was that anger I remember most. It was so powerful it frightened me. The same thing happened at other stages in my life, but I could always control it to my advantage. Even today, it's still there if I'm provoked by circumstances, but it very rarely surfaces.

For a number of years, me and my closest friend Bill have had a saying between us, and that's 'Lucky old boys'. We rarely speak without that cropping up sometime or other. What we mean, and we don't take it lightly, is that we're both very comfortable and life has been good to us. On the other hand, Bill lives in Spain all the year round and doesn't find the need to work, while Reidy grafts his plums off on *EastEnders* every day and does the rounds of cabaret clubs in the evenings. So when he throws 'Lucky old boys' at me, I sometimes can't help replying: 'Yeah, but some are a lot luckier than others.' What I'm saying is I've had a lot of luck, if that's the right word, not only in my career, but also with incidents where I could have lost my life.

I've mentioned the lorry accident. Well, the next one was when I'd been out with the girls and a couple of mates and we were coming back across Bruce Castle Park. I was a fanatical birds'-egg collector, and weeks before I'd clocked a crow building a nest up in an elm tree.

I knew it was a crow because they're always on their own, unlike rooks. So this particular day, as high as the nest was, I knew she was sitting, and I'm up the tree like a monkey.

The girls are shouting, 'Don't do it', and the boys are shouting, 'Go on, Mike. Go on.' Elms are one of the tallest trees, and I don't exaggerate when I say I was sixty feet off the ground when I've reached the nest, stretched up to grab a thick branch and it tugged out of its socket like a cork out of a bottle. For a second I just hung there; then I was on my way down.

They told me afterwards that I screamed all the way as I crashed through the branches. Then I hit the ground completely flat and the lights went out. Next thing I was aware of was Mum flying towards me across the park yelling like a banshee. One of the others had run off to tell her. I sat up as Mum got to me, laughed and said, 'I'm all right', then passed out again. But before I did, I noticed that inches from where I'd landed a rock stuck out of the ground as big as a melon and shaped to a point. A little bit nearer and it would have severed my spine. I was black and blue for weeks, but never broke a bone. What does that tell you?

Even before I left Lancasterian School and went up into Rowland Hill in Lordship Lane, I'd led quite a full life, but basically an uneventful one. Granted, I'd got up to more than the average kid of my age. I was self-sufficient, reasonably streetwise and a proper ducker and diver.

Ducking and diving can cover a multitude of enterprises, and they don't all have to be a bit iffy or against the law. What had started off as kid's stuff, messing about with mice, grass snakes and newts, trading them in for sweets and a few coppers, gradually grew into a good earner.

It kicked off when I bought a rusty old motorbike. I was down the scrap place where I used to sell the lead I nicked, and there was this bike leaning against a wall. It was hanging in pieces, didn't have an exhaust and turned over like a piece of shit. But it did turn over, so I gave the scrappy half a note for it, then spent hours over Hackney Marshes tearing about at ten miles an hour.

A couple of pikeys stopped me one day, took a fancy to this old pop-pop and offered me a palomino pony in trade for it. Cor, not much! To me it was beautiful – to anyone else it was a broken-backed old nag that was hairier than a Welsh cob. But it was mine. After that, I had to find some money to hire a stable, which was no big deal because there were old sheds all round the Marshes.

I spent hours looking after this pony, brushing it down and generally looking after it until it looked a treat, then I traded it in for another one plus two goats. Though it meant getting up at five in the morning and cycling over to Hackney, I felt it was worth it. I loved the animals, and they earned me a few quid.

At one stage, and remember I wasn't even ten years old, I had five ponies, seven goats and I don't know how many chickens. In all, it was just a wonderful way of life for a little kid.

Well, young, but not so little. I was big for my age, not too bulky but tall and, I'm told, not bad-looking, so often I was taken as being older than my years. This must have been the case when I pulled a seventeen-year-old girl – a great landmark in any boy's life – and, to coin a phrase, I potted the raspberry.

I know I was ten, because I hadn't yet made the move to Rowland Hill. I forget the actual build-up, but I do remember standing on the corner of Beaufoy Road with a bunch of lads who were a good deal older than myself, as was often the case, when this attractive girl turned up. A load of banter went on between her and the others, much of which went over my head, though the eff-word seemed to play a strong part. All of this was out of my league, as I still wasn't too far past the doctors and nurses stage.

Memory fails me, though I can't imagine I instigated what happened, but next minute I've invited her into the bungalow knowing that Mum and Dad are out visiting Uncle Fred round the corner in Birkbeck Street. Actually, it wasn't a bungalow as such, but one of those prefabs they slung up after the war, so it was all on one level. Brian and me shared one of the two bedrooms and we had a divan apiece, and for some reason I chose his to do the business on.

Thank God for instinct, because to be honest I didn't really have a clue. We both started taking our clothes off and I said, as cocky as hell, 'Have you ever been undressed with a man before?' Me. Ten years old and I reckon I'm a man! She just said, 'Yeah – 'course,' then out came these massive tits and I was dumbstruck. I can see them now. Down came the knickers, and with Brian's blankets rolled back she laid out full-length on the bed. I've had a good look for maybe fifteen seconds, then gone onto autopilot. No foreplay, just straight on and in, and in no time my little arse is a blur with her saying over and over, 'Not in me, don't do it in me,' so I pulled out with a second to spare. With her still spreadeagled I got off, sat on the end of the bed thinking, 'That's it, I'm a man now', and the bedroom door burst open and there was my mother in full sail.

She went apeshit – absolutely berserk. She's given me a clout across the side of the head that knocked me onto the floor. Then, grabbing the girl by the hair, she dragged her to the front door, slung her out and slammed the door behind her. I was on my feet by the time she flew back in, knocked me down again, grabbed the girl's clothes and slung them after her.

Dad stood in the hallway all this time and never said a word – he just stood there, with a grin on his face. And no wonder! He was about forty, and he'd just had a buxom, naked teenager parading in front of him.

I still hadn't had a chance to get dressed by the time Mum charged back in for the third, time and did she take advantage of that. The only part of my body that didn't get a kick or a slap was the guilty party that had my hands firmly clenched over it. I'm a man one minute and the next, a crying, screaming little boy. God, did she pay me – that was the stropping of my life. I think she would have kept it up all night but Dad opened the door. He didn't say anything, but it stopped her and she crashed off through to the kitchen.

As I got dressed I couldn't stop sobbing. I was hurt inside and out. I didn't really understand what I'd done that was so terrible. But that wasn't the end of it.

Something I forgot to say earlier was that I had a nice little business going minding cars up at White Hart Lane station – nothing to it, really, and I didn't mind them anyway. All I had to do was be there when the owners arrived to drum up the business, then show up at night when they got off the train to collect my sixpence. Good earner, but what with all this going on, by the time I escaped from the prefab without Mum noticing, ninety-nine per cent of my customers had gone. So I limped up to the station, collected one shilling and sixpence, then called into the off-licence on the way back to comfort myself with a box of Maltesers.

I'm trying to kill a bit of time, so I was talking to Davey Gurling outside my house, when Mum crept down the path and claimed me from behind. Then it was off again. She kicked me indoors, and I've gone arse over head. She shoved me into my bedroom, all the time hitting me in the face, crash, crash, crash. I'm more concerned in case my chocolates got crushed, so when she put me on the floor again I stuck them under the bed. Then she calmed down, leaving me to crawl under the blankets, still breaking my heart.

My stomach turned over when the door opened again, but she was only putting Brian to bed and she left me alone. As my brother was getting in he piped up, 'Mike.' I said 'What?' He said 'You've weed in my bed.'

Now Mum hadn't had two kids not to know that that wasn't wee on Brian's top sheet, and she laid into me again. Christ, how many good hidings was losing my cherry worth? I was trying to hold the blankets over my head, but she pulled them back and said, 'Look at me; look at me.' When I did she put her face right up to mine and said, 'You little bastard! You're too mature for your age.' Then, with a last bosh – hold that – it was all over.

I lay there in the dark thinking nothing worse could ever happen to me, then I heard *crunch, crunch, crunch,* and I looked under the bed and the bleeding dog had eaten my Maltesers.

In a way, going to Rowland Hill School opened up a new way of life for me. Until then, I'd lived and gone to school in the comparative oasis of a decent neighbourhood. Surrounding us was a much tougher environment, so once I was shoved into that I found myself mixing with a different class of contemporaries. It was toughen up or go under. And that was what I thought would happen in those first few days at my new school.

At the end of the first day I was grabbed by the Laranka Street boys and dragged off for my initiation. Now these kids came out of a street just off White Hart Lane, and it was nothing but a breeding ground to keep our borstals and prisons filled up. Coppers only walked down it in pairs and every brother, father and uncle was a would-be villain. So I was caught by this mob that didn't give a toss.

Round the back of the school there was this six-foot-high chestnut fence. The palings were all strung together with wire, so these kids pulled a few out and made me stand in the gap with the main wire about three inches above my head. Stand to attention! Don't move! I was paralysed, petrified and pissing myself with fear, and I could feel the tears pricking at the backs of my eyes, but I just stood there holding them back. Then *whack!* one of them belted the wire with one of these palings and it bounced down on top of my head. It really hurt, but fortunately wasn't cutting in. He did this over and over, then got a bit too clever, misjudged his aim and smashed me full on the crown with the pointed end of the stick, and the claret just poured down my face.

With that they've all run off, allowing me to burst into tears, run across Creighton Road, into the cemetery and head for home without being seen. I told Mum I'd fallen over and she bandaged me up without too much fuss. Next morning I had everything from belly-ache to the onset of polio, but nothing got past Mum, and I was on my way to school at the usual time.

Now whether those tough kids thought I might have grassed them up overnight, I don't know. But I was no sooner through the gates than they got hold of me again and this time practically carried me to the toilets. Didn't matter that my biscuit was wrapped up like a baby – bomp. Without a word of warning my head was stuck down the filthy stinking toilet pan and the chain pulled. Not, once but three times. Honestly, I'm not being dramatic when I say I thought I was going to die. Then, like before, they ran off, and I was violently sick.

Day three I was almost too frightened to walk through the gates, but I forced myself because I'd no other choice. Straight away this mob surround me, then, as the biggest one said, 'Wotcher, string bean – want yer hair washing again?' that anger flared up in me and I kicked him straight in the nuts with all my force and he went down like a bag of shit. He must have been two or three years older than me – now he's on the floor crying his eyes out. And do you know what? Not one, not one of the others made a move towards me.

I shoved my way through the lot of them, and to be honest, never had another day's aggro in that respect for the rest of my schooldays.

In fact, once word got round and it all got enlarged, I gained a bit of a reputation as a hard man.

To be honest, I don't really know why I ended up in this school because, as I've said, in Lancasterian I was a very bright spark, always top of the class. I was shit-hot at geography and history because I loved both these subjects, but as far as spelling, writing and maths went I was hopeless, though none of this has held me back in life.

I can spot a dodgy percentage in a contract from half a mile away, though I'm still not very keen to put pen to paper, even if it's only signing a form. Drives my missus mad. She'll say, 'Have you done that form yet? It's been three days', and I'll say, 'Later, sweetheart, later'. Then, a week later, she does her nut and I pick the pen up.

Perhaps I failed some exam; the eleven-plus if it was around then. I really don't remember. Shame really, because I think I might have trod another path in my early years if I'd gone to grammar school instead of being slung in amongst aggravation merchants and toughies. Still, the die was cast, and it wasn't long before I was indistinguishable from all the other 'Rowland Rogues'.

As I got older, and naturally bigger and stronger, my academic interest went down the pan. To be honest, I played truant and messed about so much you could say I frittered away my chances of a proper education. Not that the teachers cared too much. They saw us in Class C as the dregs of the system, and I did nothing to change their minds. I can't remember one single occasion when the truant officer made contact with my mother. Not even in my last year, when I hardly turned up at all.

When I was at school I was an absolute nuisance. One time I set the science class alight. The teacher, Mr Evans, got out five bottles of phosphorus for some experiment and put them on his desk in a bowl of water – something to do with keeping them cool or they'd ignite, or something. I got my mate Ray Taylor to go into the storeroom with Mr Evans on some pretext, then shot up to his desk and tipped these bottles out. Nothing happened until he came back into the class, then, like it was on a timer, this stuff went *whoosh* and burst into flames. No good chucking water on it because that makes it worse, so by the time we'd run for buckets of sand it had burned right through the desk and halfway through the floor.

Evans was a bit of a nerdy sort of guy, so he called up the heavy mob in the shape of Nobby Martin. His real name was Dennis, and he was equally as big as his brother Ruby, who had been Mr Universe at some time. Tough as we thought we were, just the sight of him made us shit ourselves. A powerful man, quietly spoken, who had our total respect through fear. I can remember seeing him throw this big lad right across the room when he gave him some lip, smashing him up against the wall on the other side and knocking the wind out of him for five minutes.

So in he came and started growling at us all, and that started a load of backchat all round the room. Now setting a thief to catch a thief, I'd been made class captain, so before he exploded I shouted to the others: 'Shut up, let the big man speak.' Now I'd done it. He walked slowly over to my desk, got me by the neck and lifted me out of my seat, saying, 'Big man, huh? So I'm the big man? See me in my office.'

Never mind the fire, that was forgotten, all part of Class C's day, but now I was in for a good hiding – and could he give one. I did the old trick of book down the trousers and turned up at his room. He just sat on the edge of his desk looking at me for a minute, then he said, 'Reid, you act the fool but you are an intelligent young man. Stop running with the crowd and do your own thing. You've got the potential to do something with your life, but only if you forget being Jack the Lad to all the other no-hopers.' With that little speech he said, 'You can go now, and for your own sake think about what I've said. And, by the way, take the book out of your pants.'

I won't say what he said changed the course of my life, but the fact that he didn't hit me and treated me like a young man certainly changed my attitude within the school.

After that, I made a conscious effort not to get involved in stupid pranks. As for pulling my weight as class captain, if things started to get out of hand with some of the lesser lads I'd say, 'All right fellas, leave it out', and they did, making me feel good about myself and quite grown-up.

Pity I didn't carry that new-found maturity into my life outside school, but I was making myself busy earning a shilling and having a good time. I didn't stop to think that I could be heading for trouble.

It's been suggested that I was a criminal from an early age, and when I've heard that I've gone, 'Whoa – hold up, that's a bit strong for a few larks.' But in hindsight, that's exactly what I was. It wasn't to my mind at that time, but as I'd been stealing cars by age eleven, robbing this, nicking that, what other name is there for what I was doing?

I pick up a paper today and all I see is, 'Joyrider this and joyrider that', and I think they all want locking up, but in truth I don't suppose they are any different to the way I was.

I could handle a car by the time I was seven, and what with Dad driving for a living I expect he was proud to teach his boy the business. It wasn't legal, but he'd often let me take the wheel when we were out in the sticks in the car he'd made, and we wouldn't see another vehicle for miles and miles. So I was no stranger to motors, and with the way my mind worked it was inevitable that I'd start nicking them. I did it on and off for years and never got a tug – it was all a bit of a laugh, and I was always careful not to damage them, unlike today, when trashing them is part of the fun.

Anyway, me and a mate hot-wired a beautiful Vauxhall and drove round in it all day, fags in mouth, elbows out of the windows. We were 'the dogs'. That same night, when it got dark, I forgot my principle of taking care of the motor and backed it into the glass front of a jeweller's in Turnpike Lane. We grabbed a load of gear and then were back in the car and away.

I drove over to Hackney where I knew I could fence the jewellery, then ended up in Epping Forest to kip in the car, ready for the next day with money on the hip. Five o'clock in the morning, just as we were coming into Edmonton, a police car clocked us, did a quick U-turn and turned on the bell. I stuck my foot down to give us some time, more than expecting to get away. I told my mate to chuck the poxy money or we'd be in the shit. Eighty quid was an enormous amount of money in those days. He got the notes out of his pocket, then said, 'No, I can't do it', as we've gone round a bend and out of sight. I leaned over, snatched the roll and flung it out of the window. Fifty yards up the road I lost control and smashed into a temporary bus stop. Game over. We both got a good hiding at the side of the road, and next thing we were in Brixton Prison as young offenders. Losing the money meant we weren't tied in with the jewellers, so with no previous we were out in a few days with a fine to pay.

I was five foot six and ten stone, and Mum knocked the bollocks out of me and I could do nothing but stand and take it. Dad never said too much, even though he'd had to fork out that fine, but I could tell he was disappointed in me. He possibly thought it was a one-off because he didn't have a clue what I got up to. Buried his head in the sand.

What he did was suggest I join the army cadets. That was his way of dealing with it. Give the boy an interest, and he'll be too busy to get into trouble. To please him – and I did want him to think the best of me – I signed on with the Tottenham Young Army Cadets. To be honest, it wasn't much more than a glorified youth club, but it was all taken very seriously. Private this, Private that, and in no time I was made up to Sergeant. Me? Sergeant Reid? Laughable. It didn't have the desired effect Dad was after, because outside the hall I was as bad as ever. But while I was there I made the effort to join in and quite enjoyed the ceremony of it all.

Apart from the marching and army drill, they placed great emphasis on boxing, and I put myself up for that because I'd already done a fair bit in past years at school. I had the weight and the skill but lacked aggression, and without that I was wasting my time. Still, I had got up to the semi-finals in the ABA championships in the first year. Trouble was, I wasn't too keen on the digs in the eye, digs on the earhole and bangs on the chin, though it was those clouts slipping through my guard that helped me win most of the time. I needed the motivation of a good belt on the nose to bring out my fighting spirit.

Then, in the area finals, I came up on this geezer who had such a punch he's knocking all his opponents out, unheard of in amateur boxing. I'm beaten before I start with the psychology of it all. I've thought, 'Oh, bloody hell, this bloke's going to nail me.' Turned out he was a shit boxer, but he had this powerful punch. Funny, this reputation thing, and half the time it's not deserved.

I get it myself even today. People are very wary of me. I know what

I look like and I certainly don't look like a silly boy, so people think that Mike Reid's a bit of a handful and all that. But they are totally wrong. If anything, I'm a bit too placid most of the time. Nobody has anything to fear from me unless they really get out of order. And by that, I mean ridiculing me or taking the piss, not asking for an auto- graph or stopping to shake my hand in the street. But then again, loads of stories have gone round, most of them old bollocks, so as I say, people keep their distance.

So this guy's reputation finished me before I started, and he hammered me. He didn't put me down because my pride wouldn't let me go off my feet, but he gave me a bloody nose, eye out here, and after the bout I decided, 'Stuff this for a game of soldiers, I'm going to quit.'

As usual, if I can't do something well I knock it on the head. I gave the whole business up with a great deal of joy, but in the TAs boxing wasn't quite as competitive, and I began to enjoy it again.

Nothing lasts, though, and it came to a full stop when Alan Stoughton took over running the cadets. He was about twenty-five, a bit full of himself, and to us he was an old man. This night he got us in the hall and was going to teach us how to defend ourselves in the ring. He picked me out because I was the biggest and he said, 'OK Reid, hit me.' I went, 'I can't do that.' He said, 'Go on, hard as you like.' I've gone, 'No way.' But he kept on: how could he show us the moves if I wouldn't co-operate? He's grinning away and I've gone straight through his guard – bang, and his lips just burst open. What a mess. He was stitched up and had a face like a pudding for weeks. Give him his due, he didn't hold a grudge, but I felt I'd outworn my welcome and jacked that in as well. I had other things to do.

Funny really, my mum's double standards. If I heard 'thieving bastard' once from her, I heard it a thousand times. 'God help me', she used to say, 'you were born to end up on the gallows.' Not long after that first tug and the fuss she kicked up over it, I was doing my car-minding job up Park Lane by the football ground. The set-up was, I had this end of the road and Dave Gurling had the other, and there'd be a ruck if either of us poached off the other. So up my end there was a little old five-hundredweight van parked up. It had *Something Dairies* painted on the side, and as I'd never seen the geezer, I knew he wasn't one of my punters. I've had a good look round, then given it a toss. It was full of cheese, eggs, butter and every dairy product you could think of. I thought, I'm having some of that! So I rolled – I literally rolled – these great cheeses down Church Road and into Beaufoy, where I parked them in Dad's little shed. Then back again for slabs of butter about fifteen inches square and dozens and dozens of eggs. I could have knocked the lot out for a nice few quid, but no: this was a present for Mum.

When she came home and saw this lot her face lit up like a light bulb. 'Ooh, you are a naughty boy – give me a hand to take it indoors.' It must have broken her heart, but even she realized we couldn't eat this amount of stuff before it went on the turn – no such thing as fridges then. So all the family and a couple of neighbours had a share.

Was I the flavour of the week! 'My Michael got this for me', as though I'd bought it, and I can imagine they raised their eyebrows thinking, 'Yeah, we know all about your Michael.'

Another time I came across a little gold mine. Same road, similar situation. Only this time it was more long-term. Were people more trusting in those days? Nine times out of ten, vans and cars were left wide open, just begging to be turned over. This was a Saturday, and up came one of those tall-bodied Morris vans – a clothes van – known all over. Usual stunt: 'Mind the van, guv'nor?' 'Yeah, go on', and off he'd go to watch the Spurs for a couple of hours.

Two minutes, and I'm inside and it was packed with ladies' dresses. Now, instinct was to fill my arms, but I said, 'No, Reidy, use your loaf. Two won't be missed, a dozen will.' So it was two dresses, very occasionally three, but I did that every week, apart from when I was away, for years. Was I popular? It got to a stage where I was being asked to sort out colours and sizes. When it suited me and I wanted to do a bit of brown-nosing with some girlfriend's mother, I'd give them away, but mostly I fenced them to an old geezer up the market.

I never broke into any of the cars I was minding, but like I said, most of them were left unlocked. I remember one time getting into a big black sedan – this was up by the station – and collaring a leather Gladstone bag. I've nipped home, stuck it in the shed, and it wasn't until I opened it up that night that I found it was a waste of time. Apart from printed forms and a couple of pens, all that was in it were hundreds of tiny little glass phials, full of yellow liquid. Each one had a little label saying *Morphine* – whatever that was.

Over our tea I said to the font of all knowledge, 'Dad, what's morphine? I heard them talking about it on the wireless.' 'Well, son,' he said, 'that's a very dangerous drug used to stop pain, but when the wrong people get hold of it they turn into drug addicts and end up dying.' What have I got hold of here? I couldn't get out of that house quick enough. I stuck them all in a brown-paper carrier bag, went over the cemetery and crushed them with my feet until the bag disintegrated. Then I kicked the remains down a rabbit hole. Whew! Fortunes, worth bloody fortunes even in those days, and I slung them away.

Strange thing for me to say when you think of what I got up to, but I've always had this strong feeling of self-preservation. Or, put another way, too much imagination, and that was always enough to hold me back from becoming a fully paid-up professional villain. I came close, but the thought of doing time invariably made me pull back from the brink. Normally, though, when I rifled through those motors, all I came up with was a packet of fags, leather gloves or a torch. Cars then rarely had radios, but a couple of times I managed to collar a portable. These were like small suitcases, and uncommon enough to fetch good money. In the main, though, this was petty pilfering and not worth a light, let alone a nicking. But I still did it, and strange as it may seem, not once did I get accused by my punters of being the one who'd robbed them.

So I'd kicked my school education into touch, but there was another area where I was eager to learn as much as I could.

After my first sexual initiation and the beating it got me, I practised safe sex: I made sure Mum was well out of the way. Though to be truthful, I left it alone for a long time. Of course, I fiddled about with girls of my own age and enjoyed it immensely, but it wasn't until I got involved with Mrs Smith, as I'd better call her, that a whole new world opened up for me.

She wasn't a very pretty woman, and if memory serves, very plain, with buck teeth. But below the neck she had everything it takes. I'd known her for years because she was the mother of one of my mates, and I suppose then she was about thirty, and I'd be thirteen or so.

I went round to Coniston Road where this pal lived to see if he was coming out to play. 'Sorry love,' his mum said, 'He's gone out for a bit but he won't be long. Come in and wait.' OK, it wasn't the first time. It wasn't until hours later that I remembered he'd told me he was going to Southend with his dad, so she knew damn well he wasn't going to show for the rest of the day.

I'm sitting there drinking a glass of lemonade and she came and sat on the settee beside me and said, 'You're a big boy,' and touched me on the leg. My drink's gone down the wrong hole and sprayed out of my nose. Bet Casanova never did that! Now the blood's not only rushed to the back of my neck but somewhere else as well, and she wasn't slow in noticing it. I couldn't believe it; she said: 'Do you play with yourself?' Now I'm brick red. 'No, no, 'course I don't.' Lying bastard. I was thirteen and been throwing it over the thumb for years, but I wasn't going to tell her that. 'You'd better come through here,' she said. 'I'll show you how to get rid of that,' looking down at my trousers.

Into the bedroom we went. This was a bungalow and the curtains were already drawn, which nobody did during the day, so I had half an idea that what she had in mind had been thought of in advance. She laid me on the bed, took my kit off and got her head down to me. It was absolute heaven. Never mind an older woman abusing a young kid. Her old man's probably giving her one twice a month; now she's got this young stud with a permanent hard-on. To finish off, she sat on me and showed me what to do, as if I didn't know already. Afterwards, she washed me, told me to get dressed and then fed me up with sweets and biscuits.

Before I left she said, 'Come round whenever you like, as long as my husband and son are out.' Not much! I was there every day after that, left, right and centre.

I don't know whether it came from her, or word had got round that Reidy had this 'huge dick' from the swimming episode. Either way, I was round another mate's house and this geezer was a fanatical athlete. I'd just got there and he said he was going for an hours training down the local park, so would I wait for him. No problem.

I sat myself down in this well-worn old chair – they never had any money – and his mother sat opposite me sewing. We sat like that for about five minutes, and I'm flicking through his *Dandy* or *Beano*. All of a sudden she held up this brassiere she was stitching and asked me if I knew what it was. I've gone, 'Yeah, it's what ladies put their breasts in.' No such word as boobs in those days. 'Well,' she said, 'would you like to see mine?' I went all light-headed, and up came the old chap like he had a life of his own. I didn't need to answer, I just got up, went over and undid her blouse. Jesus. She put her hand on the front of my trousers and said, 'I think you know what you're doing.' I denied it but she said, 'I think you do.' I did, and she got the service of her life in an upstairs bedroom.

A long while after, I was round her house and a friend of hers turned up. Now this must have been virtually on top of Christmas, because I can remember bottles of wine and spirit lined up on the sideboard, and that was the only time of year people from our society kept booze in the house.

A load of giggling and larking about went on, and one of them asked me if I wanted a drink. 'Oh, yeah, not 'arf.' So I was given a large glass of red wine – two bob for ten gallons and a gnat's cock from being vinegar – but I thought it was great. Never had a proper drink before. Three of these and I was well happy. Then they started getting a bit saucy, coming out with, 'Show us your dick, Mike', and all that. Supposedly joking, but at the same time deadly serious. One thing led to another and eventually they've both got me up to the bedroom. Once again, my mate was out with his training, so it was no problem. They did everything to me, those two. They had their fun and I loved every second of it. My eyes didn't go back in their sockets for days after.

Now Mrs Smith had a lodger, like so many people did in those days, and she was a girl of about seventeen. So, based on the premise that the more you get the more you want, it was inevitable that I'd get my leg over her as well. I was so full of my discovery of the joys of sex I would have screwed the crack of dawn. So without her landlady knowing, I was giving this girl one at every opportunity. Then suddenly she's pregnant, and my mum got to hear about it.

Funny how you don't give your mother any credit for knowing what life's about. They cook, clean and tell you off, and that's as far as it goes. Sex – they haven't a clue. But my mum wasn't silly by a long way, and though my name hadn't been put in the frame, she put two and two together and went storming round to Mrs Smith's.

She'd had her suspicions for a long time that it wasn't natural for a young boy to spend every waking hour at this woman's house, even if her son was my mate. So she's round there shouting the odds. 'It's my Mike that's done this. It's him, the dirty little sod.' Even though Mrs Smith must have been surprised to find out I was striping her lodger, she stuck up for me and tried to be protective. 'No, it can't be young Mike, he's a decent lad', and all that. Nearly convinced Mum, until this Mary came out with that I was the last man she'd been with. That was it. 'You'll have to get married,' says my mum. 'Married?' I've gone, 'What do you mean, married – I'm not even fifteen.' Mrs Smith's answer was an abortion, and now Mum really went berserk. Nothing to do with the morality of termination – it was the thought of laying out good money. Fortunately at the end of the second month Mary had a period, so the whole business was washed out the window.

Did all that panic frighten the life out of me and put me on the straight and narrow? Did it buggery. Weeks later, I'm at it again with a friend of my cousin, Linda Harris. She was beautiful, the same age as me and I'd had my eye on her for a long time, because she often came to my house with one of my girl cousins.

First time I did it, or nearly did it as it turned out, was in the crematorium grounds down Cemetery Road. I was all over her like a little puppy. Feeling this, feeling that, up against the boiler shed. Then she lay on the grass, and I've chucked myself on top of her. Now I was excited and ready to go, but obviously she wasn't, and as I've gone to put it in, she's pushed my dick down so it was between her and the ground. I was so carried away I wasn't aware of that it the time, because I'm going at it like a steam train. Then she just got up and walked away, and I realized I'd been ploughing up the earth instead of her.

Bad start, but after that we did it everywhere. Then I didn't see her for a week or so, and was beginning to wonder what had happened to her when I bumped into my cousin Jean and she said, 'You'd better go and see that Linda Harris.' I've said, 'I'm desperate to see her anyway.' So I met her outside Risely Avenue School that afternoon,

and the first thing she said was, 'I'm pregnant.' Jesus Christ, here we
go again. 'You're joking, ain't you?' 'No,' she said, 'I'm having a
baby and it's yours.' I didn't offer to marry her. I just said, 'Leave it
out,' and walked away.

She had a boyfriend and he was in the army and two nights later,
with nothing resolved, we were walking down her road, eating sweets
I think, when out stepped three squaddies in uniform. This is me set
up for a right seeing to – but it's part of my character then and now
that I never run away from trouble. Doesn't matter how frightened I
am, I force myself to front it up. So when this boyfriend starts digging
Linda out, I stepped in and told him she was with me now, so bugger
off. The three of them weighed me up and the boyfriend said to her,
'You bitch, I don't want you anyway', and they walked off. Perhaps
I looked tougher than I really was.

I had a few weeks of sleepless nights about this baby, until she told
me the red flag was up and it had all been a false alarm.

When I was a bit older, but not too much, I used to go up the
Tottenham Royal to dance to the big bands. Marion Ryan, whose sons
had some number-one hits in the seventies, was only young then, and
she was resident singer with Ted Heath and his band. Then there was
Stan Kenton and occasionally Joe Loss. Sounds a bit old-fashioned
now, but to us then music couldn't have been more exciting.

Anyway, I met this stunning bird, and everybody was after her, but
I was the lucky one to take her home. That first night she pulled me
into the alley at the back of her house and crash – down came the
knickers, give us your hand, put it there, this is what you do. Bloody
hell! This lovely young woman couldn't get enough of me.

A couple of nights later I was in her house and all over her like a
rash, kissing, cuddling and putting lovebites all round her neck like
kids did, and still do. When her mum and dad came in, we're both all
straightened up and sitting innocently on the settee. Then her dad
suddenly said, 'Dear oh dear, what's that on your neck?' Then he
turned her head and said, 'Oh, my God, it's spreading,' and he only
went and dug out a tin of Germolene for her to rub on these lovebites.
Probably never seen them in his life before.

Trouble with this bird was that I fell in love with her. So much so
that sex went out the window. I was so overwhelmed by this beauty,

all I wanted to do was kiss and cuddle and just make her happy. This was the first time in my life that I'd had feelings of this nature, and I didn't understand them. That I was willing to forgo the pleasure of sex for the pleasure of just being in her company said a lot to me.

I remember she was into a particular singer at that time, Mel Torme, known as the 'velvet fog', so when I drew my car-minding money and sold some hooky gear – wherever I got the money from – I shot round the local music shop and bought this record for her.

When her parents were at work we ended up in her bedroom and she laid on the bed and said, 'Come on, then.' Instead of getting on I held the record out like it was a bunch of roses. She didn't even look at it, just said, 'Are you going to or what? You're wasting time.' I've gone, 'But darling', and she cut in and told me to sod off. I couldn't believe what she was saying. I'm stammering, 'Wha— wha— what do you mean?' and she's saying, 'Just bugger off – go away. I don't want to see you again.' She cut me to the quick and I ran home sobbing, literally sobbing. I just couldn't stop. I thought it was love, and all she wanted was a seeing-to.

With hindsight, I don't suppose it was real love or anything like it. All I know was that I had been totally engrossed in her presence, and preened when she was available. That hurt me very badly, because I had always treated girls and women with respect, and now here was one treating me like a piece of shit.

I know I've made myself sound a bit promiscuous, and without doubt I was. But – and this is a big statement – not one woman in the world could ever come out of the woodwork and say Mike Reid made an improper suggestion to me, took advantage or sexually abused me. Almost without exception, certainly in my younger days, females gladly took advantage of me, not the other way round.

I can remember, even as young as ten, listening to other fellas saying about some girl, 'Look at that slag coming down the road', and I'd say, 'Hold on, what do you mean, slag?' 'Well, you know, she'd shag anything.' 'And so would you,' I'd say, 'doesn't that make you a slag as well?' They'd look at me as though I was mad. But I meant it. That sort of talk never failed to annoy me.

I suppose you could say I'm a ladies' man. Not one of those wavy-haired, smooth ponces, but I do genuinely love the company of women and have always treated them with the greatest respect. I brought my boys up to be the same, and even today, doesn't matter where we are, if a woman gets up we all stand. She might be just going to the loo, but we're up out of politeness. Old-fashioned it might be, but there's nothing wrong with that.

Notice how Frank Butcher is over-the-top courteous with the ladies. That's not acting, that's me putting myself into the part.

Before I leave the endless story of my youthful sex life, I'm reminded of an incident one Christmas. In fact, it was the Christmas just before I left school at fifteen. I was at a party round Uncle Fred's, when this young teacher turned up. Not one of mine; I think she taught at Risley Avenue, and she was a friend of the family. Twenty-two years old and gorgeous. This was one of the first times I did the running. I'd gained a lot of experience, and this time I did know what I was doing.

The beer was flowing, Dad was on the piano and everyone was singing. So I took the opportunity to slip her upstairs into my cousin's bedroom. I've filled my boots and I'm just on the short strokes when somebody grabbed my earhole and Uncle Fred said, 'Come out of it, you randy little sod.' Still gripping my ear, he said to the teacher sprawled on the bed, 'You should be ashamed of yourself.' I'm going, 'No, Uncle Fred, no, no, no', and he said, 'Never mind no Uncle Fred. Your mum catches you at that and she'll murder you.' With that, he's dragged me out of the room. He never said a word to anyone, but he looked at me in a different light after that.

Considering how many years I'd looked forward to the day, leaving school was a non-event. One Friday I was in class – which was an event in itself – and on the Monday I was at work. Schoolboy to working man in a weekend.

CHAPTER TWO

T HE VERY FIRST WAGES I TOOK WAS WORKING FOR A SMALL
builder, helping him put up a brick wall round some factory by
the River Lea. I cycled there every day and shovelled cement and
loaded bricks like a man. I was knackered every night, but at the end
of the week I picked up ten pounds – good money at that time.

I'd already got it worked out in my head what I was going to do
with my first week's wages, so on the way home I called in the baker's
and bought Mum this enormous fruit cake. It was beautifully iced,
and wouldn't have looked out of place at a wedding. But that wasn't
enough. In the china cabinet that I'd robbed the cruet set from, she
had a very dainty Chinese patterned teaset. Trouble was, if memory
serves, I had smashed six of the cups. I could remember her pointing
out identical replacements in a shop down Bruce Grove, but of course
she couldn't afford them. To cut a long story short, I presented her
with the cake and cups and she was genuinely pleased. She said I
shouldn't have wasted all my money, but thank you dear, you're a
good boy to your mum. I felt ten foot tall to have been able to do it.
So you can see that, even though we had the strained relationship I keep
coming back to, I obviously did love her and wanted to make her happy.

Over that first weekend I studied the blisters that were practically
up to my elbows, and made up my mind to do something else.

Over the following month, perhaps forty days at the most, I must
have had thirty jobs. I'd start one job in the morning, like running

46

barrows in the market, then by the afternoon I'd have moved on to cleaning windows or delivering bread. I just couldn't stick at anything. The longest job I held down was for two weeks, and that was only down to the fact that I enjoyed a side benefit more than the actual work. It was in a big old warehouse packed with dried fruit. Lorry-loads would come in, and lorry-loads would go out full of apricots, grapes, bananas – you name it. Right now I can't even remember what I was employed at, probably sweeping up, but the thing was, that place was absolutely alive with rats.

Everybody was scared shitless of these things, even the biggest blokes. That first day I killed about twenty-five, because without blowing my own trumpet, I'd been handling livestock since I was five years old. When you're confident enough to pick up a poisonous adder, a rat's a piece of piss. Those I didn't kill with a stick I grabbed out of a corner or from under a packing case, then with a quick bite across the back of the neck – chomp – it was all over.

In these enlightened times that might seem cruel or disgusting, but that's what I'd been shown as a kid, and I didn't know any better. Same as docking puppies' tails – again not done today – feel the second vertebra with your teeth, a firm bite and the job was done. Much safer than using a knife.

Anyway, next day I took in my dog, Lucky, as I did for the next fortnight, and we cleaned the place out. Once the fun went out of the job, I jacked it in. This was one of the few times a guv'nor actually begged me to stay on, because he knew as well as I did he'd be overrun again the next week – those were the times we lived in.

I thought I'd give working for someone a miss for a while, and rely on my own ducking and diving skills. I didn't say nothing to Mum, because she had this idea that having a job wasn't just about money: it was a way of life, something all men had to do. So I just went out at my usual time, then told her a few porkies about how great the warehouse was. As long as she got part of my wages, she never questioned anything else, and to raise her share I decided to go back to school. To be exact, my old junior school, Lancasterian.

All I needed was my old hunting knife and a decent pair of plimsolls. Oh yeah, and I had to wait until it got dark because I was going to nick the lead off the flat roofs.

Getting to the roof was nothing to me because I'd been climbing trees all my life. Up the stack pipe, bit of a struggle getting over the gutter, then with a quick kick of the legs I could pull myself onto the flat. All I had to do then was score through the lead with my knife, roll it up like a carpet and drop it over the edge. Lead, being soft like it is, goes down with hardly a sound. Walking, not riding, I could carry three pieces a night, weighing in at nearly a hundredweight. A nice little earner, considering it went on night after night for weeks.

This was a glorious summer. What happened when the rain came I've no idea, because by then I was locked up in Wales.

What with the lead and other bits and pieces, I was managing to tick over, but something was missing. It must have showed, because I was sitting in the front room with my dad one night and he said, 'What's up, son, you don't look too happy.' We were on our own, so I told him how I was feeling. How I thought life would be exciting once I left school, and how I didn't seem to have any sense of direction. Probably didn't quite put it in those words, but that's the gist of it. He sat and thought, then gave that lovely big grin of his. 'What about the Navy? Good money, and you'll see a bit of that world you're always on about. We'll look into it.' Then he sat back, pushed his wig to one side and scratched his head like he was Solomon who'd just solved some great problem.

That horrible wig. Dad, God bless him, looked ridiculous in it then, and right up to the day he died. Like me, he suffered considerable receding of the hairline and hated it. I'm not exactly in love with it myself, but the thought of sticking a syrup on my biscuit doesn't exactly thrill me. Not after looking at his year after year. I can't say I haven't been tempted at different times, though. Sometimes when I'm on set and the make-up people are fitting other actors up with wigs, I'll say, go on, stick one on me for a laugh. The transformation is unbelievable. In the time it takes to put the wig on I look ten years younger.

I remember when I was just a dot, him and Mum had gone to the pub to meet a friend and his missus. As he walked into the Eagle at Tottenham he overheard the geezer say, 'Here comes the monk.' It broke his heart. He went on about it for days, and after that took to wearing my school cap or my cub hat. He looked like a Jew with this tiny cap perched on his head, but that's how much it affected him.

Later on, someone must have paid him two bob to take away this piece of ginger rug. With it lying on his nut like a freshly cut divot, he was a new man. He wore this thing for the rest of his life, even when his own hair had turned white round the edges. I said he looked ridiculous, but of course he didn't to the family because we grew up with it. Here we go again: for a bloke who has no regrets I wish, I honestly wish that when I became affluent I'd taken him to Wigmore Street and got him kitted out with an expensive barnet. But, as I said, we didn't notice it until he was gone and we started looking through our photographs.

A week after this conversation, Dad dropped me off at Liverpool Street station and I was on my way to a merchant navy training ship at Rochester.

I was eyeing up this blonde who had her back to me, when she turned round and it was a bloke about my age. I'd never seen anything like it. Talk about forty years before his time. The only people you'd see with shoulder-length hair in those days were poofs, and most of them wouldn't have wanted to advertise it so blatantly. I felt my cheeks clenching up when he came over and asked me if I was going to Rochester, but it turned out he was just an ordinary guy with a very radical haircut – or lack of it.

I was expecting a billet on a boat, but it turned out that this training centre was miles from any water, and the whole place was like an army barracks. I found out later that these places could be on top of a mountain and they'd still be called 'ship'. Now I was no pushover, but the majority of the other trainees frightened the shit out of me. Most of them seemed to be from places like Liverpool, Manchester and even Glasgow, and they were very tough boys.

The first four days were so busy, nobody had a chance to step too far out of line, but on the fifth, and I suppose it was inevitable, the piss-taking and ridicule Dennis had taken over his hair came to a head. One of the toughies started shoving him around and finished by nutting him in the face. I was scared, but it wasn't in my nature to stand back, so I've rattled the scouser's plums with my boot, then done him again as he was lying on the ground. Fortunately for us, two of the officers, or masters, broke it up and everyone was supervised until it was time to turn in to our separate huts.

After lights out, it went quiet for about ten minutes, then all hell broke loose. First of all there was a lot of shouting from outside, then, as I peered out of the window, a brick came through it and I was showered with broken glass. Then they started on the others, breaking them with sticks and shoving tree branches through them to get at us.

All I can think is that the masters had gone down the pub, because this riot would have woken the dead. They're kicking the doors and ripping boards off the outside of the hut and pushing them through the windows. I was virtually crying because I was scared shitless. Then the ringleader, the one I'd kicked, shouted above all this racket, that if the other boys in the hut came out and that us two put up our hands to the damage, they'd call it a day. Thank Christ for that. Thirty seconds, and the place was empty except for me and Dennis – then the place went up in flames. Those bastards had poured paraffin all round the hut and set light to it. I can't describe the terror we felt as the place filled up with smoke and the flames leaped up all around. Incredible to think that those kids outside – and that's what they were – deliberately set out to murder us.

In the nick of time the masters turned up and pulled us out, and we were both frogmarched to a room in the main building. Before the door was locked, we were told that we would be up in front of the ship's captain on a charge of riotous assembly and criminal damage. I thought sod this, shoved Dennis through the window and followed him pretty smartish.

Middle of the night we walked into Rochester, found the station and climbed onto a coal wagon, pulling tarpaulins over us. We haven't got a penny, and all our gear was burned to a crisp. When the coal wagon started to move at about five o'clock the next morning, I didn't care where it was going as long as it got us as far away as possible. As it was, we ended up at London Bridge. I borrowed tuppence off a woman, phoned Dad and he came and got me.

After giving Dennis his fare back to Doncaster, we went home to face Mum's 'I told you so'. For days I expected the law to turn up and arrest me, but I never heard another word.

It's a great pity that didn't work out, through no fault of my own, as it would have saved me a lot of grief, and Mum more grey hairs.

Within days I was back to ducking and diving. Now whether my mind wasn't really on it or I was getting a bit reckless I don't know, but it seemed Old Bill was forever knocking on our door for various petty offences, and, to put it mildly, Mum was getting fed up with it. Lucky for me, I managed to talk my way out of any nicking.

I was picked up carrying a load of brand-new torches and my excuse, used before, was that I'd found them on some waste ground. I was caught inside a factory compound and told the law I was having a piss. Not long after I was pulled over in a stolen car and got away with it by saying the driver was giving me a lift and I didn't know him. The truth was, I nicked the motor, then picked up Tommy Philips. He begged me to let him drive, and that's when the police stopped us. Give him his due, he kept shtoom, got four months' borstal and I walked away.

Then it was my turn to take a fall. Four of us went out to Wormley Woods down Cheshunt way to turn over a big mansion. We were after the lead on the roof, not the house contents, because I had a moral code that wouldn't let me rob the personal property of individuals. OK, their car, their roof, their factory, but I was no housebreaker.

I stole a van for the job and we hid it in the bushes, while two of us went up top with our knives. We'd hardly started when a police car came steaming up the long drive. The two in the van have taken off at about a hundred miles an hour. The kid with me went down the pipe like a snake. I was a bit slow and got grabbed as my feet touched the ground. The 'I was having a pee' wasn't going to work this time, so I put my hands up.

I was a juvenile, and this was a schoolboy prank. Or so the judge seemed to think when I appeared in court with my mum some time later. I didn't have a record, apart from that week in Brixton, so as far as he was concerned I'd just stepped over the line a bit and he was going to treat me accordingly.

That was until Mum jumped up and said, 'Please, Your Honour, I can't handle him – he's out of control.' Jesus Christ! What was she saying? He went into a huddle with a couple of others and came up with two years' approved school in Wales.

On the long bus journey I had plenty of time to consider what I thought of as betrayal by my mother. I knew she couldn't wait to see the back of me – but this. On the other hand, it was getting me away from home and into an environment I was very comfortable with – the countryside.

Although I'd been told this place was a farm as well as a kid's prison, I really did expect to be banged up every day like I had in Brixton, so I was pleasantly surprised to find that it was as I'd been told, a working farm. The whole point was to get us wayward kids away from unhelpful influences and to educate us about farming. Though what help that would be back in deprived inner cities, I can't imagine.

We were supervised at all times by these hard-nosed Welsh boys, none of them over twenty-five, and each one of these fellas a teacher as well as a screw. So they taught us building, path-laying and, of course, how to handle cows, chickens, pigs and what have you.

On top of that, at weekends we were taken in groups to places like Abergavenny or Cwmbran and shown castles. History had always been my favourite subject, so I just soaked up all the information.

Apart from being away from girls, my mates and familiar surroundings, in a funny sort of way it was like an extended holiday. How I'd feel after one year, let alone two, remained to be seen.

The downside was that I was the only Londoner. All the other kids were taffies or jocks, and at first I had to fight every day until they realized that I might be a cockney, but I could hit twice as hard as they could, and the aggravation got less and less.

The running of the place was down to a husband and wife, and they were both Salvationists. Now with the wife, where I came from had the opposite effect. She loved me. What it was with her was that during the Blitz, she'd been stationed in the East End and she'd seen Londoners bombed one minute, then singing and laughing the next while they cleared up the mess. She was totally amazed at the courage and bond these people had amongst themselves and with strangers, so I could do no wrong.

I'll give you an instance. Me and this jock were out in the fields. He was driving a tractor and I was walking in front chucking rocks out of the way. All of a sudden something went wrong and he fell off, trapping his leg under the wheel. By the time I jumped up and turned the engine off he'd been dragged about thirty foot and his leg had been stripped to the bone. He was out like a light, so I shouted for help, then put my jumper under his leg. There wasn't a bit of blood, just this horrible white bone. He started to come to, and I cradled his head in my arms and talked to him so he wouldn't panic.

By the time he was carted off in an old jeep the blood was running out of him and I felt a bit sick. The governor's missus had turned up, and she gave me a cuddle and said, 'Good boy. You are a lovely lad – all that East End spirit.' I don't know about that, but I went even higher in her estimation from then on.

She was a nice woman, yet her husband was a perverted old bastard who never let one day go by without interfering with one of his charges. I've got a notion that he guessed I was too close to his wife, so he never once made advances towards me, but I doubt whether a single one of the other kids escaped being talked into the chicken shed and the door bolted behind them.

That whole experience was a turning point in my life. I knew exactly what went on, because some boys laughed about it and others cried when they spoke of it. He was a man of God. His life revolved round the Sally Army, and every morning at assembly he lectured and preached about God and the Ten Commandments – suffer little children – and it was all bollocks.

I made up my mind then, and nothing that's happened in my life has made me change it, that there is no such thing as God. How could there be?

If He does exist, all I can say is He's got a strange sense of humour. Little babies dying before they've hardly drawn breath – and that strikes very close to home when I say it. Thousands of people wiped out in some terrible famine, or old people racked with pain for years until they get their release. No: don't talk to me about God.

But I do believe there is something. Perhaps I've borrowed this from another culture, but I honestly believe that there is some sort of plan for all of us. Your life is set out from day one, and whatever happens after that is preordained. That said, I've pushed my luck on this fate thing on more than a dozen occasions.

Apart from what that dirty bastard was getting up to, talking to other boys in the dormitory at night I learned things I could never have imagined. Abuse by fathers, mothers, uncles – it just went on and on. I thought of my own family, and even the constant friction with my mum paled into insignificance.

Like I said, I loved the open air, the animals and occasionally visiting interesting places, but that darker side took the dairy off it for me and I started counting the days, but they went by very slowly. Dad came down a couple of times, but it was a long way to travel and I think we both found it upsetting, so it was better he didn't come at all.

Another contradiction: I swore to myself that there was no God, then before I went to sleep I prayed to go home.

Five months to the day, I was selected to tear down this old brick chimney that stood in the grounds. With the constant grafting and stodgy food, I'd filled out, so I was a strong old boy – that's why they picked me. Showing off, being Jack the Lad in front of the other boys, I've shinned up the ladder leaning against the tall chimney, stood right on the top and started swinging a pickaxe, laughing and shouting abuse to them below. I'll never, ever forget the feeling of the bricks moving under my feet, knowing that in one second I was on my way down. Then I felt myself falling, and it went through my mind that I was going to die, and I don't remember anything else.

I'm told I was completely buried in the rubble, and it took twenty minutes to get me out. I was cut, bruised and bleeding, and my leg was smashed to pieces – history repeating itself. When I woke up I was in hospital somewhere in the Rhondda Valley.

The first week went past in a blur of pain, but I was young and fit and started to mend at a fair rate. Not the seven compound fractures in my leg, but the rest of me soon started taking notice of my surroundings. And, I suppose like every young man who's ever been in hospital, I fell in love with my nurse – my night nurse, that is. Her name was Maureen and she had dark hair, dark eyes and was lovely.

The first time I noticed her was when she brought me a bedpan. I was absolutely breaking my neck to use the toilet – I mean, I was desperate. She put the pan in the bed, said, 'I'll leave you to it', and walked out of my cubicle. I didn't make it. God knows what happened, but I've tipped this thing and it's gone everywhere. Terrible mess, and I was mortified – more than that, traumatized.

Now I'm surprising myself even telling this story, because all my life I've been very shy about anything to do with toilets. I never mention the subject. I don't do toilet gags, ever. I've been with my wife Shirl for thirty-eight years and I'll swear she's only heard me break wind twice in all that time, and it was an accident both times. If we're in bed and I feel one coming on, and it's a perfectly natural function, I get up and go out of the room. Funny as most people find it, I don't do it in front of guys and I don't want them to do it in front of me. So as you can imagine, I was affected more than your average bloke.

What could I do? I couldn't move my leg. I just had to wait until she came back. What made it even worse was her saying, 'Oh, Michael, I never expected this of you.' I was sixteen and a big lad, but when it was all over I laid in the dark and cried myself to sleep with shame.

After that I pretended to be asleep whenever she was around, until one night she came in unexpected about two in the morning. I looked at her with one eye and pushed my head back in the pillow. But she was having none of that. She pulled a chair up, took hold of my hand and asked me why I was avoiding her. Well, it was like a dam bursting and I poured my heart out. I'd been through a long emotional period and bottled everything up inside me, so all it took was someone to show an interest in me and it all poured out.

She got my life story and more, because to finish up I told her I thought she was beautiful and that I was in love with her. Four o'clock in the morning, against all the rules of nursing professionalism, she leaned down and gave me a passionate kiss that made my hair stand on end. If I need to make any excuses, she was only a kid herself, and got carried away with the moment.

A week later I was on my way home swinging between two crutches.

Whatever entity watches over us, my prayers had been answered. Before I left the hospital, Mum and Dad had received a letter saying that as my injury could take longer to heal than the time remaining on my sentence, they were releasing me forthwith. Looking back, I would like to think the authorities were more concerned about being sued for negligence and wanted to sweep it under the carpet. They needn't have worried. In those days ordinary people were in awe of their betters, and wouldn't have dreamed of causing a fuss.

Everything had changed. Obviously it was me that had grown up or grown away, but I didn't realize that. The prefab seemed smaller, Mum was sort of distant and I didn't seem to know little Brian any more, though at eleven he wasn't so little. The only consistent thing was Dad, but he was a one-off and never changed his ways until the day he died.

What I was keen to do was get back into Lisa's knickers. With a libido bigger than it should have been at that age, it had been a long time and I was a randy little sod.

Mum and Dad both liked young Lisa, so there was never any problem with us being left alone together. So, first opportunity I've got her into my bedroom, I said to her, 'Have you been with anybody else while I've been away?' and she said, 'Of course not. When I wrote to you in Wales I told you I'd wait, and I have.' Male ego being what it is, I was well pleased. We got on the bed. I should explain that whenever we made love she always laid on her side with her back to me. We'd always performed like that and I don't suppose she knew any different. So we're kissing and cuddling and I manoeuvre her into position, when all of a sudden she pushes herself onto her back, throws her legs right up in the air shouting, 'No, no, no – like this.'

At that stage of the game I never said a word, but it made me think afterwards that somebody had taught her a thing or two.

With the apparent changes at home, it wasn't long before my thoughts turned once again to joining the Navy, but this time, forget the training.

By the time I showed myself at the Merchant Seaman's school round the back of Whitechapel, my plaster was off and I only had the slightest limp.

I've talked my mates Davey and Kevin into giving it a go with me, so we all presented ourselves at the desk out the front. We're standing there nervously, muttering to each other and shuffling our feet, when some geezer at the end of the room shouts over: 'What do those likely lads want?' 'Want to go to sea, boss.' 'Send them to fucking New Zealand then,' and that was that.

Two days later we're on our way. I was hoping to go as a seaman, because it carried a bit of status, but when I had a quick medical the following day it turned out my eyes were a bit trumpy, so it was catering side as a steward or nothing. Davey and Kevin got through, but as we were all in this together, they decided to stick with me.

Unbeknown to us was the fact that Davey's brother Charlie was on the same ship. Of course, we knew he was in the merchant, but as he was on turnaround he hadn't been home for months, so even Davey didn't have a clue. I thought it was handy us having someone to show us the ropes, though with him being topside we could go for days without seeing him. Yet it was that bastard that set me up for something I still cringe about today.

It was a different world to anything I'd ever known, an education in every sense. My first lesson was, don't give lip to the old hands. Young and full of myself, I couldn't keep my tongue in my head. A wrong word to one of those hairy arses and bosh – hold that. I'd think to myself, I'll keep away from him, then the gob opens again and bang – get some of this.

It was like this every day until I realized they were all the same – straightened me out, though.

In those days it used to take four weeks to cross the Pacific, then you had the Atlantic and then the Suez and Panama Canals to go through, so a trip would be in the nature of about two and a half months.

Being nothing but glorified skivvies, we weren't allowed near first class, we were stuck in tourist. But Charlie, who was a few years older than us, was up top, and he came to us one day and said, 'There's a bit of a do going on tonight with the officers and all the nobs. There's going to be loads of booze flying about, so if you lot come up and keep out of sight, I'll see you all right.' Yeah, we were up for some of that.

Later on, we sneaked up all the decks and tucked ourselves away. Every now and then Charlie would show and slip us a drink. When it had quietened down he joined us, and we were standing talking when this bird with long black hair came walking along. Now I am a complete sucker for dark tresses – they turn me on like nothing else. My missus would tell you the same. A girl with black hair might be walking away from me so that I can't see her face, yet immediately I'm in love with her. So I'm eyeing this lovely piece and Charlie says,

'Go on, Mike, give her a tug.' Normally I would have hesitated, but being full of piss I dive in and start talking a load of shit, finishing off with, 'Do you want to see my berth?'

Talk about Jack the Lad in front of my mates. I've cracked it and they're sick. I practically dragged her to my cabin, but once the door was closed she took over. I didn't have a chance to lay my hands on her before she's all over me, kissing and rubbing me everywhere. She pushed me onto the bunk and started tugging at my belt. Off came my strides and she's got her head down to me – Oh, Jesus – I've died and gone to heaven. I'm just about to burst when I hear a load of screaming and laughing. I've opened my eyes and there's Davey, Charlie, Kevin and another couple of fellas in the doorway shouting, 'Reidy's a shirt-lifter – brown-hatter', and all that.

The bird's run out of the cabin leaving me going, 'Wh – what's up with you lot?' Turned out my raven-haired beauty was a bloke – the geezer who bought in and looked after all the fruit supplies for the ship. Fruit was his job and fruit was his nature, because he liked nothing better than dressing up in women's clothes when he was off duty.

I'm as broad-minded as the next, but this 'thing' had stuck its tongue halfway down my throat. I spat for a week afterwards, and they never let me forget it.

Before I signed on I'd done a few little deals, so that meant I was holding a bit of folding and I carried my wedge in one of those Royal Navy money belts. By today's standards, I don't suppose it was too much, but it allowed me to do a bit of investment.

The ship's unofficial moneylender was a Jewish fella, Benjamin, and he took a shine to me. Taught me how to combine travelling and making money. His lending rates were absolutely phenomenal, but I never got into that; I didn't need to. Once we got to New Zealand, my money had grown by nine hundred per cent.

What Benjamin got me into was buying jeans in Curaçao for ten shillings, then knocking them out for five or six quid at the other end. People would be queuing at the dock gates wherever we pulled in for refuelling. I've never seen anything like it.

The highlights for me were all those times when I could explore what were, to this green kid, exciting and exotic places. Sometimes we'd be in port for just a day – other times three or four, depending on what was going on.

Naturally I did my share of pissing it up the wall, same as the other fellas, but time permitting, I always made a point of investigating or learning about these different cultures. Then – and I'm going back almost forty-five years – places like Auckland, Wellington and Sydney weren't the massive cities they are today. Once you reached the city limits, bosh, that was it – you were out in the wilderness. It wasn't a gradual thing. There'd be houses, then step over a line, and nothing. I was in awe of the magnitude of the countryside. I had thought Wales was a bit remote, but it had nothing on this.

A couple of days from that first trip still stick in my memory. We were laid up in a place called Port Chalmers, which is on the North Island of New Zealand, and the other lads and me thought we'd take in some hunting. We hired four old nags, then went to the local police station and hired .303 rifles. It was easy then. Sign here, away you go.

We were after wild boar, because the place was overrun with them and they were classed as a pest. If you ever want a smack in the mouth, go into a bar and call one of the locals a 'pig islander'. They go apeshit.

We had beer, food and bedrolls in our knapsacks, so were well kitted for a couple of days. The other fellas treated it as a lark, but I took the whole thing very seriously. I could ride a horse after a fashion, and I was quite used to a gun, though nothing so powerful as a .303.

The first day I shot a boar, and by the second I'd bagged four. This was many years before I realized that every living thing on this planet of ours has a right to live. So these magnificent animals were left to rot without a second's thought.

By the time my first experience of world travel was over and we docked at Tilbury, I felt I'd found my vocation in life. Everything I'd ever dreamed of was condensed in that trip. Amazingly, I came home with jack shit. I'd been fed, clothed and paid a fair wage. On top of that I'd earned fortunes with the jeans, and flogging anything I could nick off board, but all I came back with was enough to weigh Mum out with a couple of shillings.

I'd drank and smoked away the lot – though some of it had gone on presents for my family. A fancy carved pipe for Dad, which I don't suppose he ever put in his mouth. A bush knife for Brian, and God knows what tacky tourist stuff I'd bought for Mum. But she loved whatever it was because whenever anyone came in she could say, 'My Michael brought me that from his world travels', like I was some jet-setting executive.

That first day back my brother seemed a bit cheesed off, so, I asked him what was up. He said that his dog Lucky needed an operation. He'd taken over my Lucky as his own when I wasn't around to look after it. Whatever it was, the cost was going to be about four pounds fifteen shillings, so I dug down my hip and pulled out my last fiver – not that he knew that – and handed it over.

Now I was b'rassic, with three weeks before I signed on again.

I haven't said too much about my Brian and our lives together, for the simple reason that we were, and always have been, worlds apart. From day one he had this really special relationship with our mother. Not that this set him and me apart – the age difference did that. Five years is a lifetime when you're kids, and we never did get close because of that.

I've said that things seemed to change while I was away at approved school, but this applied to others, too, not just my very close family.

Until then I'd spent a lot of time with my cousins, who happened to be mostly girls, but we had some good times. All that came to a sudden stop once I found there was another life away from home.

That fiver to Brian was the last bit of close contact we were to have. We never ever fell out – we just went in different directions.

Now, and for many years past, he's been in the same game as me, and in his own way he's been very successful. OK, he's not a household name, but that's never stopped him being very popular and worth a considerable amount of money. Dad taught him to play the piano, same as he did me, but being the person he is, Brian stuck at it until he reached a very high standard.

When he was nineteen, before I'd made a name for myself, he was in a group called the Londonaires, and they made a record. I can remember thinking, that boy really has got something. Later on he moved to Spain, and found his niche in the entertainment game, though what must have given him the arsehole too many times was people going on about how successful I was.

I've never told him this, and perhaps I should have done, but I am very, very proud of him. What he's achieved has come through talent and hard graft. Not once has he asked me to put in a word for him, or give him a leg-up. He's his own man, and though it might be years between visits, he knows I'm only ever a phone call away.

Funny how it is when you pull yourself out of the frame and spend a long while away from the neighbourhood. It's like everyone closes up to fill the gap you've left. That's what I found.

All my girlfriends were webbed up with steady blokes, and my mates were off doing their own thing, so I was at a loose end until my ship sailed. I put myself about chasing up a few deals for a while, then took off to South Mimms to see if I could pick up a few brace of pheasants or some rabbits.

Now this wasn't in the same league as hunting boar, but it was something I'd done all my life and I was very skilled at it. This time I borrowed Dad's car, but when I was as young as seven I would've cycled there and farther. Not much older, and I'd cycle as far as Thetford in Norfolk with an old game bag slung over my shoulder.

As usual, whether on a bike or in a motor, I parked up about a mile away from where I wanted to be, because what I was up to was illegal. It still is, but then it was almost a hanging offence.

I remember one time when I was eleven creeping through some woods, and I fell arse over head over a tripwire. Bang! It set off a cartridge. These were set up to scare off deer, but it worked with poachers as well. I ran on a bit, then dived into a ditch and waited. Now Old Bill and the gamekeepers must have been on watch anyway, because minutes later I could see torches flashing through the trees. I took off and could hear them shouting behind me. I must have run about a mile to where my bike was hidden under a bridge over a river. They weren't far behind, so I got right into the water with just my head sticking out. This was September and it was freezing. I was just thinking, 'It's no good, I'll have to give myself up before I get pneumonia', when I heard a voice say, 'Got him, sir', and another voice saying, 'Apprehend him then, constable, apprehend him'. There was a different class of copper in those days.

They'd only got hold of some other geezer up to the same game as me. As usual, Reidy was a 'lucky old boy'.

Pheasants have always been a good earner, though at first I only got the odd one for our dinner. It wasn't until a young mate of mine asked me to get a brace for his mum and dad's anniversary that I realized I was onto something. His old man loved them, and when I delivered he slipped me five shillings. He must have told a mate, and so on, because from then it escalated and the price went up to ten shillings a brace.

If you look at it that Dad wasn't earning much more for a day's work, it was bloody good money.

Up until then I'd been knocking the odd one out of a tree while they were roosting, but now I found I had to boost the numbers, so I started coning them. Simple, but very effective. First of all I'd throw corn in the area that I wanted to work, then after a couple of days go back armed with a stick, paper and birdlime.

The lime had been banned years before I was using it, and it was the stickiest stuff man ever invented. Being difficult to get hold of, I found the recipe and ended up making my own.

First of all, I'd open up a small hole in the ground with the pointed stick, then I'd fold the paper into the same shape and size as an ice-cream cone, dab birdlime around the top edge and place it in the hole, pour in a small amount of grain, and that was it.

The very first time, being a bit enthusiastic, I did loads and loads of the things. When I came back later in the day, there was about forty of these birds just sitting beside the holes with these cones on their heads. As far as they were concerned, night had come down in a flash and they were going nowhere.

No way could I get this many home, so I necked about two dozen of them and then rounded up the rest, took off the cones and washed their necks with the white spirit that I carried with me. I did that for two reasons – one, it would've been cruel to leave birdlime on their feathers and two, if I hadn't got it off, some gamekeeper might have spotted the lime, got wise to what was going on and then kept an eye open. I only had my bicycle, so there was no chance of getting them home under my own steam. I hid them up, then got Uncle Fred to collect them in his motor, as he often did for me over the years.

He was a lovely man, Fred, and he was badly missed when he died at the comparatively young age of fifty. His house was like a second home to me, and I was always round there. He loved a hand-rolled smoke, and I'll never forget that a couple of days before he died I went to see him, sat by his bed and gave him half an ounce of Nosegay tobacco. He was dying of lung cancer brought on by the fags, and in total ignorance I was giving him a little present of baccy to cheer him up.

My auntie Marge had died in childbirth years before, leaving Uncle Fred the job of raising four young girls the best way he could. When he died Jean took over, and she wasn't too old herself. She was mother and father to my cousins, and made an incredible job of it. But eventually the strain was too much and that sensible, vivacious girl had a complete mental breakdown. It doesn't matter how – suffice to say, it was a tragedy for the whole family and she was ill for many years after.

Going back to my poaching, I have to say it wasn't all about killing. There was a great market then for songbirds of all species. Same with birds' eggs, and I had one of the best collections for miles around. Dad taught me only ever to take one egg from a nest, and always to replace it with a pebble roughly the same size, and I never did otherwise. I know, I know, today it's frowned on, as well as being illegal, and I wouldn't encourage it. But I don't think the past can be criticized just because, and rightly so, we're more enlightened now.

In the main I was after goldfinches, because I could knock them out anywhere for at least five quid. Paste a bit of birdlime on some teasels and bomp, they're in the bag. Sometimes I'd tie a live decoy or call-bird among a clump of these teasels and it might bring as many as a dozen flocking down. I might catch fifty or so, then only keep one of them because I was after healthy cock finches. Use one of these for covering a canary, and the resulting brood would sing and sing all day long. These could fetch as much as seventy notes each. Best thing was these birds were always infertile and known as mules, so no-one could breed from them. Once they were gone, and their lives were not that long, it was back to the supplier again.

Sounds a cruel old game, but as much as I liked my pound notes, I never let that harden me at the expense of the birds or animals. I'm not making out I'm Mr Wonderful, but whether I was killing something or selling it live, I always treated it with respect.

I saw something one day that made me despair of human nature. I was out at Cheshunt and I came across a couple of pikeys boiling up a tin of tea over a fire. I was no traveller, but in many ways followed their lifestyle, so I got talking to one of them. As we're chatting, a fluttering and squeaking made me look over to his mate by the fire, just in time to see him blind a linnet with a red-hot needle. I knew it went on, but seeing it horrified and disgusted me. From that moment on that bird would just sing its heart out – that's why they did it. I was just a little old boy, and they were grown men, so all I could do was wipe my mouth and walk away, but it haunted me for years.

When I got a bit older I traded a pair of worthless billy goats for a twelve-bore, single-barrel shotgun. Black-powder guns they were called, and there's something in the back of my mind that says that for some reason the cartridges for these were illegal, but as just owning a gun at my age was against the law, it was a bit academic. This thing was pitted and rusty, but I spent hours and hours rubbing it down, polishing the stock and re-bluing the barrel until it was a piece. Even now I can't cut a slice of bread that doesn't look like a wedge, but with anything mechanical I took after my father and was shit-hot. So much so that at twelve years old I made a silencer for it from the exhaust of a 125 cc James motorcycle, and it worked. It made the gun a bit of a lump, but I only used it when it wasn't prudent to make a noise, or for short-range killing, like popping roosting pheasants out of trees.

I'd no licence for a firearm at that age, so I used to carry the gun in an old fishing-rod bag with a rod sticking out of it, and never got a pull.

Quite often I'd stay out all weekend. I'd set off on a Friday afternoon and cycle for hours to get to where I was going. It might be winter and snowing heavily, but that never deterred me. In fact, I looked forward to days like that because it meant I could do the business without being seen. You'd think it would be the opposite, but what I would do was park up a mile or so away as usual, then trudge off to the intended spot and dig myself an igloo.

After baiting out with bread or corn I'd sit inside this little snow cave with my dog and flasks of soup and wait. Down would come the pheasants – bang, send the dog out – over and over again.

Any farmer or gamekeeper scanning the field would see nothing. It must have driven them mad.

The time I spent at South Mimms before sailing, I don't think I even had a gun then, so the method I used was grain soaked overnight in cheap whisky. It was so easy it was laughable. All I had to do was spread the corn, then wait for the birds to get so pissed they couldn't walk or fly. They must have a low tolerance to alcohol, because five minutes and they'd be lying all over the place. All in all I had a good week; I took almost sixty brace and knocked them out through the back door of any butcher's shop that had a licence to sell game.

Now I had a bit of folding to keep me going until I started earning again on the ship.

That last night at home before I sailed, I took myself up to The Royal for a drink and to see what was going on. I got paralysed; completely rat-arsed. All that I could remember, up to the point where all my brain cells died, was that I had met an attractive girl by the name of Sheila. We'd had a kiss and a cuddle, nothing more, swapped addresses, then it went blank.

If I'd known where this was going to lead I'd have signed on for ten years. As it was, Reidy had his heart on his sleeve, and planned to take it further once the trip was over.

I don't know how I got home from the dance hall, but I woke up with my face glued to the front-room carpet and Dad saying, 'What have I told you, son? Moderation – everything in moderation.' He was used to this. I'd been a piss artist since the age of fourteen, yet he never bollocked me. Just tried to make me see sense, because that was his way. All his life he only ever had two fags a day and perhaps a glass of Benedictine. He'd seen his own father ruined by drink and the fags, so obviously wasn't going to go down the same path. Me? I was too far removed from Grandad Reid for it to mean anything.

This trip was going to be different, I knew it. Two and a half months at sea, and I thought I was the ancient mariner.

That business with the gay fruit-buyer last time round had played on my mind, or more to the point, the piss-taking that came after it. I mean, it was striking at the heart of my manliness. I'd mentioned it to Dad, because we were close enough to talk about anything (not Mum though), and he'd said, 'Just play along with it, Mike, and they'll get fed up with it.'

Sure enough, two minutes after meeting up with the same crowd, Dave, Charlie and Kevin, they kicked off. 'What's in the bag? Pot of Vaseline?' Or, 'What's the rush? Heading for the galley?' And I've gone, 'Too right, it was marvellous. If you haven't tried it, don't knock it.' They shut up like clams. I'll bet it was going through their heads, 'Is he serious, or what?' Whatever, that was the end of that joke.

After that business it made me wary of making advances aboard ship. I didn't do a strip search, but I checked first for tell-tale bulges or razor rash before making a move.

We were stewards or, like I said, waiters, and the passengers we looked after were known as 'bloods'. Don't ask me why. A very strict rule was that absolutely no fraternization was allowed. We weren't allowed to steal cutlery or joints of meat and flog them on the docks either, but we all did, so stuff 'em.

Two weeks out, and I've got my eye on this girl of my own age. A few days before I'd been sniffing round another bird, but that had gone a bit pear-shaped.

To be honest, I'd clocked her walking up the loading ramp, but with her being first class, I didn't get many opportunities to get close to her. She was the most gorgeous creature you've ever seen. I spent every moment staring at her from a distance. Imagine Joanna Lumley or Cindy Crawford – that was the class she was in. If you think that puts me out of the running, remember, I haven't always had the lived-in face I've got today. I was young, fit and was told many times that I was a good-looking young man.

I've waited my chance, and one morning managed to catch her looking out to sea. I caught her eye and she smiled at me. I melted. I've got a tongue as big as a saveloy, but I managed to blurt out, 'Did you enjoy your breakfast?' 'Eeh, thanks, chook, it were loovly,' she said. 'Ah've had aggs and baaacon.' The broad Brummie accent nearly knocked me over, and that one sentence turned her into a frog.

Times have changed and today, regional accents are everywhere.

In fact, we don't even notice them. But then, I was completely deflated.

So back to the young girl. When I was serving meals I'd say things like, 'You're sweet, madam', as I gave her a pudding, or suggestively ask if she'd like 'an extra portion'. She got the picture and invited me to her cabin. She wasn't all that naive, because she'd got rid of her sisters who were in the same berth.

Large portion? Not much! I made love to her for hours. This was against all regulations, and somehow the skipper got wind of it. As I'm trying to sneak back to my deck, he's got officers blocking off every companionway. I was caught red-handed and hauled in front of the captain. Jesus, did he roast me. Now a reprimand is bad enough on your record, but I was charged with one crime below piracy. 'Tampering with cargo', and given a double dishonourable reprimand and a fine in lieu of being put off the ship.

I would imagine the skipper got a bollocking for allowing it to happen, and he got his own back some time later, with a vengeance.

As usual when we anchored up in all these different ports, I'd hire a bicycle and go all over the place soaking up every bit of local culture that I could. No wonder tourists to this country say our policemen are the best in the world. I got lost one time, so I asked an Australian copper for directions. He was a big bastard, and he stared at me, twirling a two-foot baton, then said, 'What do you think I am, a fuckin' information bureau? Piss off.' I think that was the first Aussie I ever spoke to – some introduction.

Imagine what it was like for a seventeen-year-old out of north London. Fiji, Hawaii, the Pitcairn Islands. Wonderful, wonderful places straight out of my books of knowledge. Nowadays I suppose they're all hotels, apartments and golf courses, but then everything was unspoiled and uncommercialized.

We'd stop off at all these places to replenish the stores with fruit, and as we'd get off the barges (there weren't even proper runways or harbours then), these beautiful Polynesian women would place wreaths of flowers round our necks. Just like they must have done for Captain Cook years and years before, when he discovered the place.

I remember my first trip to Hawaii. Before we embarked, we were told with big red notices and over the tannoy not to drink the local brew and not to go with local women. Some chance of taking any notice of that – we were going to fill our boots.

Their rum was about ninety-nine per cent pure alcohol and the women ninety-nine per cent animal – at least the one I picked up was. She clawed my back to pieces. Beautiful, and smelling sweetly of natural perfumes and flowers – she was a dream, but left me in total agony.

I went to the ship's doctor the next day, and when I took my shirt off he just gasped. 'You prick. How could you let a woman do this to you? I presume it was a woman?' My whole back was a festering mess. I was one of the lucky ones: three of the crew nearly died of alcohol poisoning, and eighty members reported to the MO with VD. For weeks after, if I got the slightest itch down there I'd shoot to the heads, whip out the old chap and give him a thorough examination. Nothing, thank God.

Another time I went to Charles Bar in Wellington, where all the women went to pick up merchant seamen. They knew we could get hold of fags, jeans and nylons, and were willing to sell themselves for any of these bits and pieces. Now you didn't have to make a play for them because they were all over you like flies as soon as you walked in.

I was a young pup and for the first time, and possibly the last, I actually had two birds physically fighting over me. One was part Maori, tall, elegant and with wonderful bone structure. The other was Spanish-looking, with this gorgeous raven hair – and they both wanted to take me home.

I would've taken them both on, but no, each one wanted me for herself, and to settle it they kicked, punched and scratched the shit out of each other. The Maori won, and I went off with her. Oh, to be seventeen again! I had a lovely couple of hours with her, went back to the bar, found the Spanish-looking girl and gave her a right seeing-to.

Drink was always a problem. Dad's advice had fallen on deaf ears, and at every opportunity me and the other lads got out of our brains.

We docked in Panama, and me and Kevin and Davey decided we'd take in the sights of Panama City. It was well known as a den of iniquity, and also as the capital of vice. Horny as ever, we wanted to experience everything, so we got in one of the cabs that always queued at the dock gates. We weren't due to sail until noon the following day, so that gave us all night, then a few hours to recover before we started work.

We bartered with the Colombian taxi driver and he settled for six dollars to drive us round all the hot spots, wait for us, then bring us back to the ship.

What an eye-opener. Unless you've seen what goes on in these dives, you couldn't imagine the low entertainment that was on offer. I'll tell you something, I've never looked at a donkey since without my mind going back to that place.

Bar after bar, seedy club after seedy club, and the three of us were not only completely pissed but were getting a bit lairy with it. So when Abdul, as we called him, started with, 'Six dollars me – you ship now', we all told him to piss off. He kept on, 'No piss – six dollar, six dollar', so I gave him a dry slap. That was all, nothing serious, and he took himself off. So what, we'd find another cab.

I was just suggesting to the lads that we move on to another bar, when the swing doors burst open and I was lifted up in the air by a gun stuck under my jawbone. The pain was terrible, and I was frightened to move. Kevin and Davey both had guns to their heads. I went from pissed to sober in the time it took that copper to push a hole in my neck. Once he got me stretched up on tiptoes, he stepped back and smashed the gun into my kidneys and I went down like a bag of shit. Being the biggest of us three, I was taken as the ringleader and potentially dangerous. Dangerous? It took all my effort not to burst into tears.

From the bar we were kicked and punched into a police van and driven off at speed. Next thing, we were slung into jail. Not in a cell, but a large holding area filled with the most evil cut-throats and villains you could imagine.

So far we hadn't understood a word that had been said, and once we were locked up nothing changed. The other prisoners were jabbering away, then came the shoving and poking, and within twenty minutes we were robbed of everything we had: watches, money, fags, and although I hung onto my clothes, Kevin lost his shoes and Davey his jacket.

All day we sat huddled in a corner, too scared to raise our eyes. We'd no food and nothing to drink, and around our feet wandered big rats, as casually as your cats might at home. The stink and the noise was like something out of hell.

At two o'clock in the morning we were ordered out at gunpoint and pushed into an all-night court, and we were all thinking the worst was over. No-one spoke English, and whatever was said took about two minutes before we were back in the van again and off to who knows where.

If we'd spoken to the British consul he could have got in touch with the ship, but it was never offered, and by this time, as far as we knew, it could be halfway across the Pacific and we'd been marked down as AWOL.

By the time the van stopped it was getting light, and we were forced out and made to sit on the ground for an hour with our hands behind our heads. A lorry pulled up with about twenty prisoners standing in the back. Before we joined them we were given a tin of water, half a loaf of black bread and had a twenty-pound ball chained to our legs.

Next stop was a part of the Panama Canal that ran through the thickest jungle you've ever seen, where we were set to breaking rocks.

For some reason we were segregated from the rest, and thank God, because that first day the three of us couldn't stop crying. Forget Jack the Lads, we were three terrified boys. Remember, we didn't know what was going on – we could be doing this for years.

At night we slept in a hut. No locks, no fences; they didn't need them because there was absolutely nowhere to go. The canal was filled with crocodiles, piranhas and God knows what else. If we could have swum across – and there was no chance of that – it was the same impenetrable jungle on the other side. There were snakes and spiders in the roof, and scorpions, fleas and lizards on the floor. All night long all we could hear were cougars coughing, the whoop-whoop of howler monkeys and cicadas rattling like castanets. My love of nature temporarily went out the window, because I honestly believe I never got a wink of sleep the whole time I was there.

The chain rubbed the skin off my ankle and it bled most of the time. And one time, when the heavy ball dragged me down a bank and into a drainage gully filled with water, by the time they pulled me out I was covered in leeches. A geezer with a machine gun over his shoulder took his cigar and burned them off, laughing like a drain.

Only once did my bolshy London spirit show itself, and that was when one of the guards gave me a kick to make me get a move on. With a bit of universal sign language I told him to go and fuck himself, and he put me on my back with the butt of his gun, then held the muzzle to my head. After that I behaved myself.

For twelve days we suffered this nightmare, then as quickly as we were nicked we were suddenly released to one of the Castle Line officials and flown on to meet the ship.

We found out after it was all over that somehow the skipper had got wind of what had happened to us, and had contacted one of the company's people with instructions to let us sweat for a day then get us out. To be fair, I doubt whether he knew the shit we were really in, and probably thought we were tucked up in a nice clean cell considering the error of our ways.

Trouble was, the geezer who could have saved us from that misery got himself injured in a traffic accident on the way over, and any thoughts of us went straight out of his head. The ship went through the Canal, and it's funny to think of it, but they must have passed us. It waited at the other end for us to show, and when we didn't, the skipper said, 'Leave 'em to it,' and sailed off.

Nearly a fortnight went by before telegraphs started flying backwards and forwards. And it was only then that they found out that, down to that minor fracas, we'd been fined forty dollars or forty days' hard labour.

To cut a long story short, the money was telegraphed to the agent in Panama and we were released and flown to Auckland to meet the ship. The fine and fares were taken out of our wages; we got the bollocking of our lives and a dishonourable reprimand. But we were so relieved to be out of that hell-hole, we would have gladly scrubbed the decks with toothbrushes.

Jumping forward a number of years, this wasn't the only time I came up against foreign law, or had the shit frightened out of me when I was far from home. On this occasion, we were docked in Caracas, and though they pulled it down a few years ago, you used to be able to get a cable car right over the mountains and into Venezuela. And this is what me and about ten other fellas from the ship did.

What an experience for young lads. We got pissed on this side of the mountains, had a load of beer in the cable car, then got legless once we got into the city. We were young blokes and fresh away from ship's discipline, so we were hollering and hooting, singing and making arseholes of ourselves. Not breaking windows, just drunk and noisy.

We were in the middle of the main street when we were surrounded by the local *carabinieri*, all on horseback, guns on their backs, three-foot battens in one hand and a net in the other. They started spinning these nets over their heads, then threw them over us. We'd no chance. I got meshed up with this guy and we both struggled like mad. He's kicked me, I've kicked him, then these uniformed bandits – because that's what they looked like – jumped down and laid into us with their sticks. We were battered senseless. The nets were tied to their saddles, and we were literally dragged down the street.

By the time we were locked up, every one of us was dripping blood. We only got out when we pooled all the cash we had between us and paid a bribe, or fine, as they called it.

Places like these really opened my eyes to the violence that, in this country, we never come into contact with. Another time, on the same trip but further down the coast in Lima, we had a very close shave. Back then, this was a totally lawless city, and we had been warned not to leave the dock area. Usual thing: notices, tannoy, lectures. So what do us flash young bastards do? Ignore the advice completely, and decide to take a bus ride up to some village.

It was great for about five minutes, and I was just wondering why the officers thought this was such a dodgy country when war broke out as we entered the jungle. The bus was being shot up from both sides of the road. The windows went out, people were screaming – me included I expect – and all we could hear was thump, thump, thump as bullets dug into the side. The bus nearly stalled, but the driver managed to keep it going and stuck his foot to the floor. That stands out as one of the most frightening experiences I've ever been through.

When we arrived at the village and climbed out of the bus, it really came home to me how lucky we'd been because the sides were riddled with hundreds of bullet holes. Strangely, there was only one casualty, and that was a woman whose leg was practically cut in half by a bullet. We were taken back to the docks in an army lorry, and I'm not ashamed to say I lay on the floor all the way.

Needless to say, when we docked back in England I'd made up my mind to give the sea a miss for a while. I'd seen the other side, dipped my bread and taken on board a tremendous amount of knowledge – a bit too much in some areas. But I'd got the wanderlust out of my system, for a while anyway, and was ready to settle back into the ducking and diving.

Back home, Mum couldn't wait to tell me some bird had been knocking regularly to see if I was home yet. 'Seems a really nice girl, Michael.' This was Sheila who I'd met just before I sailed, and yes, she was a bit tasty.

I got myself round to her house where she lived with her parents, and after that we dated regularly. In all honesty I don't think I was in love with her. Not to the extent where, as I mentioned earlier, sex goes out the window, because we were at it like knives a few days after we got reacquainted.

Two months later she told me that she was pregnant. I can recall saying to her, 'You're having a laugh with me, you must have got your dates all mixed up.' Remember, I'd been down this road twice before and worried myself for nothing. Two months after this, she told my mother and the shit hit the fan. 'You've done it this time, Michael. Now you'll have to get married. Think of the family's name.'

Married! Bleedinwell married! Family name! What bullshit are you giving me? Not that I swore in front of my mum, but I ask you. I didn't think something like putting a bird in the club was going to make the name any different. Well, not mine, anyway because I was known all over Tottenham as a bit of a tearaway?

No. What it was, Mum wanted me out of the house. She wouldn't chuck me out, but if there was a legal way, like this, she wasn't going to let go of it.

Sheila was growing by the week, and in the end I got fed up with the earache from both our mums, thought, 'Oh, bollocks – at least I'll get my leg over every night', and agreed to go along with it.

No romance, no sense of responsibility to that unborn child. Just, 'Yeah, go on then, let's get it over with.'

I was too naive to consider it then, but in hindsight I often wondered if Sheila, who was four years older than me and light years ahead mentally, had allowed herself to get into this condition to snap up a husband. Either way, three days past my eighteenth birthday we tied the knot.

I might have been the reluctant groom, but I did it in style. The style of the time, that is. Looking back, I must have looked a total dickhead. I was a 'Teddy boy' then, and went right over the top. I wore a lime-green suit that had a velvet collar, cuffs and turn-ups. On my feet I had a pair of pale blue suede 'brothel creepers' that had three-inch crêpe soles. Considering I was six foot two then, I stuck up beside her like a pole.

I say then, because over the years, with my back problem, I seem to have lost two inches.

We moved in with her elderly mum and dad – a disaster in itself – and waited for our baby. While Sheila waited she knitted bootees, little jumpers and all that. Me? Life didn't change. I was out every night with the boys.

In May 1958, our baby was born in the North Middlesex Hospital. Five days later he was dead. We were told it was some sort of mouth infection that had spread through his system. He was born, and then he was gone.

I can't believe I'm saying this because it doesn't do me any favours, but I don't remember being too upset, and if I don't tell it how it was I'm wasting my time. Put it down to the callowness of youth or my immaturity, but my life went on as though he never happened. It must have touched me, though, if only in a small way, because I remember being up town with the boys and coming across a preacher giving it to a small crowd. I wasn't being flash or showing off in front of the chaps, because I think I surprised myself when I shouted to him, 'Your God, if He cares so much, why did he let my little baby die?' He came over to me and got all pious. 'My son, who can question His motives? He moves in mysterious ways.' Which meant jack shit to me, and only reinforced my feelings for religion and the cloth.

With that bond broken between me and Sheila, we drifted even further apart. Her family didn't help matters. Mum, Dad and sister Maureen absolutely hated me. It got to a stage when I'd creep indoors during the small hours, slide quietly into bed, then just as I'd be dozing off her mother would be standing over me screaming, 'How dare you come in at this hour?' And I mean screaming.

Eventually I got fed up with mother-in-law having a dig every time she set eyes on me. And though I hardly spent any time with Sheila any more, and didn't intend to change that in the foreseeable future, I splashed out and got us a flat in Sussex Gardens, Islington.

After that things got a bit easier – for me, anyway.

CHAPTER THREE

ABOUT THIS TIME, I MET UP WITH A FELLA WHO WOULD HAVE A great influence on me for years after. Now, by virtue of the area I lived in and what I was getting up to, as a matter of course I was mixing with and coming up against some likely lads.

What I'd done or what slight, real or imagined, I'd caused escapes me now, but whatever the reason, Frankie Donovan, one of the toughest geezers on the manor, had me marked down for a serious talking-to.

I was six foot two tall, fourteen stone and had done my share of the weights. So who knows, perhaps I could have given him a good hiding. I'd never know, because the psychology of his reputation made me keep my head down and well out of his way. That was until a couple of mates and me were driving down Caledonian Road, when a big old Standard Vanguard cut us up and forced us into the side of the road.

Out jumped this Frankie and, running up to the driver's door, he just got his hand on it when Old Bill drove up mob-handed and grabbed him. As he's shouting, 'I'm only talking to my mates', one of the coppers asked if we were all right. I've no licence and no papers, and all I want to do is get well out of it, so I told them, 'No problem, we're great pals.' Frankie got a load of 'sorrys', and that was that.

As I've driven off he's just given a nod. I didn't know if that squared things or not, but I still kept a low profile just in case.

Some time after that incident I got myself a cash-in-hand job at Haringey Arena where I was moving pens, horseboxes and railings around during the Horse of the Year Show. They had me on all kinds of shifts, but it didn't matter what time of day I went into this local café, there were always the same young fellas sitting drinking tea. I say young, because they were, but all of them were a few years older than me. And that was something about my younger years – I always seemed to gravitate towards, and mix with, people who could give me three or four years. I wouldn't say I was more mature than my contemporaries, but I was certainly more streetwise.

I never got too close to this little firm, but I'd say hello and pass the time of day. I didn't even know their names.

One afternoon trouble flared. Five geezers walked in and set about the mob I used to talk to. None of my business, until one of this lot decided to spank me across the head with a sauce bottle. Red rag to a bull? I went apeshit, stuck my pennorth in and we ended up knocking the shit out of these guys and throwing them out. Tables were knocked over and cups were smashed, but we helped the guv'nor straighten up and that was that.

The following evening I'm in the café having a bacon sandwich, and in walks Frankie Donovan. My arse'ole dropped out, but instead of kicking off he just said to me, 'You again?' I nodded and he stuck his hand out saying, 'Thanks for helping my people yesterday – you're all right.'

The following Saturday I was in the Manning Hotel at the top of the hill at Highbury. The place was heaving with taffies down to support the away team at an Arsenal match. One thing led to another, there was a ruck and before I could get out, one of these blokes called me a cockney prick. Crack, I've put him on his back. Worst move I could've made. The rest just steamed into me. I managed to get out and started running backwards down the hill with that mob chasing me, every one of them armed with bottles.

This was a new world to me. I tripped and went down, and they're all on top of me. Frankie turned up out of nowhere. He's carrying a bicycle chain and swinging it into these Welshmen like a raving lunatic. By the time we got away we were both covered in blood and laughing like a couple of drains, but our friendship was cemented.

He was a good bit older than I was, but I was proud to be his mate and proud to be associated with his firm. It did wonders for my ego that I was thought of as a bit of a celebrity in the area. 'Did you hear about Reidy? He got Big Frankie out of a bit of bother – tough old geezer.' Got a bit blown out of proportion, but that's what getting a rep's all about.

While we were still living with Sheila's parents, I'd managed to put together a few bob. Not much, but I bought an S-type Bedford lorry, ex-army and still in its dark green. I'd done a bit of coal work as young as fifteen, when I worked for Harvey's at Canonbury. Later on I did a spell for Charrington's at Alexandra Palace. But with my own transport, I could treble what I'd been getting. Hard graft, but I've never been afraid of that. In the summer when it slowed down I'd go out picking up a bit of scrap.

Now this was a game that a lot of fellas were at, and it was always a struggle to find a decent bit of gear on a regular basis. But I struck gold one time when I took a look up the side of the Thames. I came across empty warehouse after empty warehouse, so many, in fact, that it was like walking into a ghost town. Every one of them was untouched, undiscovered by all the other pikeys and dealers. It was like Christmas every day. Every floor in these places was massive and just full of lead, zinc and copper, and I systematically cleared the lot over a period of time.

I'd just tipped a big old oil tank out of a loading bay and straight into the back of the lorry, when I had a brainwave. It was something like a five-hundred-gallon tank and fitted perfectly across the front of the lorry. So I got a mate who was a bit handy with a saw to box this tank in with four-by-two timbers and cover the lot with old floorboards. Once that was done, I cut a filler hole in the top, and on the bottom welded a wide-mouthed tap. I was all set.

When you pull into a scrap merchant's yard, you have to sit on a weighbridge. You do the same on the way out after offloading, and the weight difference is what they pay out on. What I was up to wouldn't work with copper or brass, because I would've been tumbled immediately, but with non-ferrous metals like cast iron or light metal, it was a steal.

What I'd do was fill the tank up with water, then chuck on all this old shit, pipes, conduits and whatever, and drive over the weighbridge. Once I was down the bottom of the yard, I'd open up the tap while I was unloading and get rid of the water. Time after time Lofty, the guv'nor, six foot six and as thin as a tanner rabbit, would come down scratching his bald head and stand looking at this wet patch. 'You know what, Mike? I think we've got ourselves an underground stream or a burst pipe, 'cos it's always effing boggy down 'ere.' What the silly old sod didn't realize was that the muddy patch on the ground was costing him twelve to fourteen pounds every time I showed, because my little scam with the water was adding a ton weight to every load I took in. He never did get wise to what I was up to.

When Frankie first clapped eyes on this lorry, his brain went into overtime and came up with a nice little job for it: turning aluminium scaffold poles and clips into scrap. What a waste, but what an earner.

I think it's safe to say that Frankie and me were the instigators of this particular brand of villainy. Eventually everyone jumped on the bandwagon, and then there was a big clampdown, but by then we'd slung the job out the window and moved on.

I've always had a lot of front; that's why I'm in the business I'm in. Cool as you like, we used to drive onto a big building site or yard. Never touched the small ones. I'd jump down, collar some foreman and ask him where the scaffolding was. 'Over the back by the fence. Why's that then?' 'Got to pick up a load for the other job.' 'Go on, then.' Never queried who, where or what. Occasionally we'd get the offer of a couple of labourers, and that speeded things up and lessened the risk. It was so easy we laughed our nuts off while we loaded up literally thousands of feet of poles and hundreds of clips. Christ knows how much this stuff cost new, but we were knocking it out at two bob a foot and the clips, which I do know cost half a crown, went out at a shilling.

We earned fortunes while firms were losing thousands of pounds overnight. Must have been a bit of an actor then, because I got into the part by carrying a selection of coats and clipboards in the cab – anything to make myself look legal.

In all the time we did this job there was only one nicking, and considering we drove all over Canning Town, Croydon, Woolwich, wherever, we were lucky it was only once.

We got a whisper from someone's uncle who worked on the railways that there was a siding at Wormley where they stored thousands of tons of rails. It takes four blokes to lift one of these, so we went mob-handed. Five of us; four to lift and one to keep lookout.

The first day we loaded the lorry until it was on its springs, then spent all night cutting up the rails for weighing in the next morning.

On the way to Wormley next day, we offloaded the scrap, drew our wedge and went back for more. Some lookout! He's no sooner given a whistle, than Old Bill's all over the siding. I was the only one up on the lorry, and as I jumped down to follow the others over the wall, a jagged piece of metal hooked me straight up the jacks and left me swinging like a puppet – and I was collared.

My defence in court was that these pikeys had hired me and my lorry for the day. I didn't know their names, and I thought the scrap was theirs. I copped a one-hundred-pound fine. When the magistrate asked me if I had anything to say, I said, 'This is police persecution.' Well, it sounded reasonable at the time, even if a giggle did go round the courtroom.

Frankie turned up and paid my fine out of our bundle, and it hardly made a dent.

We called it a day after that. Not that my arsehole went or anything. Far from it; but I've always had this thing about self-preservation. If something gets a bit iffy, kick it into touch.

A lot of people, Mum and Dad included, thought I was led by Frankie Donovan. That was only true up to a point. He had the name and ran our little firm, but he did listen to me. Again, with this self-preservation thing, if I said, 'Hold up, no way is this going to work', he'd take it on board and we'd slide sideways and move on to something else.

This time we moved into hijacking loads from lorries. I don't mean holding up the driver and nicking his vehicle; Frankie was too cute for that. What we did was get inside information that such-and-such would be parked in a certain place, then it was up to us – for a drink, that is. Eventually we had people from all over saying, 'I'm a driver' or 'I've got this mate' and so on. 'See me all right for a monkey (five hundred pounds) and here's the key.' Piece of piss. We'd clean out the lorry into my Bedford, then smash the lock off to put the driver in the clear.

All this was going on over a long period but it wasn't every day of the week. Between times I did my own thing. There was the scrap metal, the coal round and, of course, my erstwhile missus Sheila. God, she didn't deserve me. She was a nice girl then, and still is, and I think that was the trouble – too easygoing.

I mean, I'd go out on a Friday night, and she might not see me again until the following Thursday. Did she kick up a fuss? No. All she'd say was, 'Oh, darling, I was worried about you. I nearly rang the police.' Police? For Christ's sake! They certainly had more idea of where I was and what I was up to than she did. If she'd given me more stick I think I might have straightened out, but it wasn't in her nature and I just took the piss. Not deliberately, but my youthful ignorance led me to believe that a woman was never happier than when she was cleaning the house. Blokes did their own thing.

I'll tell you what, my idea that marriage was worth it for regular leg-overs went by the board in about five minutes.

I started to get too well known to the law, what with running around with the firm. Nothing too serious, and a lot of it to do with unpaid motoring fines. Then – and I've got to say the same is true today – I'm a very fast driver. I'd get a pull and tear up the ticket perhaps half a dozen times before they caught up with me. I'd spend a night in Brixton nick, pay up and start all over again.

Not always, but sometimes, I could get myself out of something a little bit more serious with a few gags. The reason escapes me, but there has always been a strange rapport between the police and regular villains; or would-be villain in my case.

If the ordinary bloke in the street only did half of what I did, he'd have been put away. I've never been vicious, either mentally or physically, but I was a bit saucy and the coppers went along with it. 'Reidy, you rascal – we'll get you one of these days', and we'd have a laugh. It didn't always work if one of them didn't like the look of you.

Me, Frankie, Frank Wheeler and Snake Hips Thomson went up to Thetford for something or other. On the way back Frankie said, 'Cor, look at all those pheasants!' Nothing new to me, but being a city boy he thought they lived and died on a butcher's rail. To impress them, I got him to pull over and dug out the shotgun we always carried.

I brought one bird down as it left the ground, reloaded and got another before it was forty foot in the air. I'd only just slung them in the motor when up came a Land Rover and the farmer's doing his nut. 'Get off my land. I'm calling the police.' He was lucky he didn't get a slap. Instead, we gave him plenty of 'Bollocks, you old prat,' and drove off.

We're not stupid; he's going to take down the number. We went straight back to Frankie's place, because it was his motor, took out the brace of birds, then cleaned and polished inside and out. When we had finished, there wasn't even a spot of fag ash to be seen.

Sure enough, the law traced the motor and turned it inside out. They've got nothing on us, so we just lean against the wall making smart-arse remarks. Then one of the coppers leaned in the car and picked up a tiny feather. 'And what's this then?' He looked at us, we looked at him. We were sure the feather had to have come out of his pocket book, but of course we couldn't prove it.

He got a result, and we wiped our mouths to the tune of sixty notes apiece. It was all a game.

To be honest, I don't think I've ever heard of any person being fitted up unless they deserved it. What goes around comes around. You might have a long run of good luck and cover every angle, but you're not only aggravation to the law, you're taking the piss. So what do they do? There'd be a gun in the boot, snide fivers tucked in the glovebox or a pull on suspicion. The plant all depended on whether they wanted you put away or warned.

Funnily enough, my very first encounter with drugs was when a mate got stitched up. He'd made himself a pain in the arse. Old Bill got the hump with him, and out of the blue they stopped his car and found bags of cannabis behind every hubcap, and that wasn't even his game. Still, it took him off the streets for a good stretch. Perhaps if he'd played the game and paid his dues he'd have been left alone.

That was something Frankie taught me right from the beginning. I'd stepped over the line many, many times and had my collar felt more than once, but I always had a grudging respect for the police.

A necessary evil, my mum used to say. So it came as a bit of a shock the first time I saw a copper taking a bung.

There was a car full of us and we were up to something. We'd either done it or were on the way to do it. If memory serves, that first time the boot was stuffed with safe-breaking gear. Anyway, we got a tug and Frankie jumped straight out of the motor and went into a huddle with these two constables. His hand went down his hip pocket, a few notes were passed over and we were on our way. Frankie never said a word, just gave me a wink. Talk about education – the law might have closed their eyes, but it certainly opened mine.

After a while, this sort of lark was just part of our business and I'd be throwing out fives and fifties to Old Bill like it was the most normal thing in the world. As you can imagine, having the local law on the payroll made life less risky. I'll rephrase that, because saying 'on the payroll' is nonsense in a way, though that was the flash way we talked then.

We were a tasty little firm, but we were hardly the Krays. Truth is, we'd drink tea in different cafés and if a copper stopped off on his way round the beat, so what? He might sit at our table eating his dripping on toast and have a chat, all perfectly innocent. What the other punters didn't know was that he was giving us the SP on what was on offer: when a certain shopkeeper was away, a factory that didn't have security or what time patrols were going out. Vital information to us young thieves. Sometimes a fifty would slide under the table; other times they'd want a cut of the profit, and this caused us more trouble than it was worth, half the time.

We'd get word that a certain clothes factory would be out of the bounds of the law over a period of two or three hours. One-third share of the profits for our sleeping partner in uniform. Lenny would do the business on the alarm system, and we'd get away with a grand's worth of suits or ladies' dresses.

Now in truth, we've done the factory owner a favour, because this geezer then bumps the price up for insurance purposes and says he's lost three grand's worth. Back would come our informers with all the paperwork, demanding their share; one thousand pounds and no excuses, because the amount we nicked is on the form in black and white. All the power was on their side, so they're not going to suffer any shit from us, so we hand over the lot. We've put ourselves on offer for nothing, not even expenses.

It didn't happen too often, but when it did I used to think Old Bill might as well cut us out and rob the place themselves, because they were worse than us.

This Lenny, Lenny Hornby, was a real asset to our mob. He was only a kid but he could hot-wire cars in two seconds. That's not too difficult, but when it came to alarm systems he was tremendous. Learned it from his uncle, who was into electronics. So what with this specialist and a few other things, muscle included, we were the firm and we strutted round Wood Green with our chests out, the absolute dog's bollocks.

I've got to say, we never got into what I'd call big villainy. We didn't go out to hurt people or run in and out of banks with shooters, and half the time we carried out jobs more like the Lavender Hill Mob than with any sense of professionalism. When it came to safe-breaking, we weren't very bright at it. All we knew was brute force and ignorance. None of that carefully tripping combinations. No; get in there, son, and smash the back off with a sledgehammer. Many times we would absolutely wreck a safe, knock lumps off it, dent in the sides and still the bastard wouldn't open. Hours we'd spend on it, then have to walk away. We'd have earned more digging holes.

Same as with the lorry game, we'd get people slipping into us with information about a safe at the place they worked. 'Piece of piss; this peter's about five hundred years old and wouldn't keep a mouse out, plus it's bang full of cash – thousands.' Nice one. They'd get a tenner for the info. And then it would turn out that it was all bollocks and we'd end up with a fiver and the company accounts.

What used to worry me, and I was a worrier, was that these sorts of jobs nearly always required us to be about six-handed, because it took that number of bodies to manhandle these things about.

One time we shoved, dragged and rolled a peter to a second-floor window with the idea of taking it away in the lorry. We've managed to get it up on the sill, then dropped it twenty feet onto the grass. This bastard thing buried itself about two feet in the ground. It might have had a fortune inside, but we just had to walk away.

Same as the one we chopped out of a wall. It was about five foot up the wall, and again on a second floor. By the time we got it free, we were totally shagged and covered in dust. One last pull and out it came, and fell straight through the floor. We left it buried in the wreckage underneath.

What with shit information and the numbers of us in for a cut, we rarely made a lot out of the safe jobs.

A good mate of ours, Wally the Terrible, worked in a twenty-four-hour garage in Maida Vale. This was a phenomenon in those days, almost unheard of. Wally told us the set-up: the manager he worked alongside always went for a sleep in the house next door at two a.m. – never failed. So there'd only be him out the front and the safe was right out the back.

When we turned up, the safe was well cemented into a wall, and all you could see was the door and a little slot they would drop the money through during the day. This geezer wasn't taking any chances because he'd been robbed at gunpoint too many times. We set to with hammers and bolsters, chip, chip, chip, and the noise! Jesus, it could've raised the dead.

At half past four we gave up, rooted round the garage and came up with a bundle of welding rods. We flattened the ends in a vice, then sat there for an hour fishing little packets out of the safe using the rods like chopsticks.

Next morning they've nicked Wally, saying, 'You must have heard something, or you was in on it.' He sat all day in the station making out he was deaf. He stuck to his guns and never broke, so in the end the law had to let him walk away. The manager got the sack, and Wally got a nice little bundle.

For want of a better word, this branch of our activities just petered out. To be honest, I was getting a bit edgy – we never got nicked, but I began to think our luck was going to run out. This was mainly because of the number of guys involved. Two or three's OK, but sixes and sevens made me nervous. I trusted our own, but sometimes Frankie pulled in a couple of geezers from another firm, and I was never sure how they would react if it came on top.

My ideal would have been for me to be lookout man. Any trouble, give a whistle and disappear smartish. But being the right-hand man, I was always up the front. I mean, I wasn't forced into it, but sometimes I wondered what I was getting myself into, and knew that I could end up with years behind bars.

This period of maybe three or four years that I'm writing about was in some ways pretty full for me. I kept myself busy with all sorts of ducking and diving, and the firm was only part of it. Sometimes we'd go for a couple of weeks without getting a result from any criminal venture.

I'm very proud of the fact that not once in my life have I ever signed on the dole or taken any sort of handout. Perhaps I was too proud, because on many occasions I didn't have a pot to piss in, but something would always turn up before I went down the pan. Or, more to the point, I went out of my way to make something turn up. Remember, I had a wife to support and rent to pay. Which was a joke, really, because I spent hardly any time with Sheila, and rarely saw the inside of the flat.

Coal, scrap, poaching, thieving: it all helped to keep things together, and on top of that I turned a coin by doing a turn in the local pub. And, in a sense, that simple beginning gradually evolved into a lifelong career, though to be honest, I never saw it like that, nor had I great expectations that one day I would be able to command more wages in one evening than I could earn in two years back then.

Having said that, I always had this feeling that I would become rich and famous. Any of my childhood friends could back that up. I was always going on about how I was going to be 'A Someone' when I grew up. Perhaps most kids and young people have these dreams, based more on hope than reality, then as life goes on forget them and accept whatever hand's been dealt. But I was serious.

No doubt whoever was in the limelight at the time was going to be my role model. I never aimed to be a train driver or a fireman. My imagination conjured up being Douglas Fairbanks, or Jimmy Cagney, Frank Sinatra, Roy Rogers – and riding off into the sunset with a bird like his missus, Dale Evans. I was never one of those nerdy kids that ended up a bank manager or a politician. I can see their stereotype now. Anoraks, pebble glasses and pale complexions. No; I was robust and confident, and had more front than Blackpool. And that's why entertaining people has never caused me a moment's nervousness.

I've mentioned the parties and pianos when I was just a sprout, and basically that's when it all started.

Going back to Dad taking me and Brian into the countryside and never failing to answer my endless questions, I'd say, 'What's that singing?' and he'd tell me, 'Oh, that's a chaffinch', or 'That's a blue tit.' He was very knowledgeable, and, in the end, so was I.

I'd be about four, and all us kids were having a party in our neighbour's prefab – Sid and Doris Grey. It got to a stage when Doris said everyone had to do a turn. That started it. First one kid would hide under the table, then the next. One would burst into tears and another want to go home. They were all crippled with shyness at that age. Not Reidy. I'm up there on a chair, doing bird impressions for all I was worth. Went on for ever, and they all sounded the same, but I was presented with a whole orange. This was such a wonderful thing I could hardly bear to eat it.

After that, I didn't have any fear and took every opportunity to get up and show people what I could do, whether it was impressions, singing or telling jokes. I could always tell a good gag, even at school. Other kids would say, 'Go on, Feet.' That was my nickname – even then I had plates like boats – 'Go on, Feet, tell them that joke I told you. You can do it better than me.' I was never one of those people that act the clown to get a laugh – I never pulled faces or talked in a funny voice. I just told the gag in my own way, and obviously I had some sort of delivery, because I always got a laugh. Timing is what it's all about, and don't ask me where it came from, but even as a kid mine was bang on.

The singing I loved, and that came from Dad. I went to no end of parties with him, because he got every invite that was going down to his talent on the piano. He couldn't make his mind up whether he was Frank Sinatra or Bing Crosby, so he dodged between the different styles. Me, I was always Sinatra. He'd do a bit, then he'd say, 'Come on, son, your turn', and it didn't matter how many people were there, up I'd get and sing my heart out.

Because of my bass voice – and even when I was young it was pitched quite low – my party piece was 'The Fishermen of England', an old-fashioned sort of song, but the old people loved it.

Miss Sail, the teacher I was in love with, was also the music teacher, so as you can imagine my voice carried over everyone else's just so she'd notice me. And she did, making me head and soloist of the school choir. As you can see, I had an early grounding at the very edges of show business.

That's where I might have stayed if I hadn't discovered that you could actually get paid for something you enjoy doing. Sweets, drinks and crisps as I grew up were one thing. But actual cash! I'll have some of that.

I was well into my teens and working on the coal, as I've already said. I was with a few other guys when we worked for Harvey's, and on a Friday night we'd drop into Manning's behind the Finsbury Park Hotel and share out the tips. We'd have a few drinks and watch whatever entertainment was on. It's all different now, but then there was always something going on in pubs. Every now and again the lads would gee me on to get up and do a bit. Nothing formal; I'd sing a song or tell some gags. Just messing about really, for a few laughs.

One night when I was sharing out our bit of cash, I upset one of the blokes. Proper coalman; he was built like a brick shithouse, and that night, pissed out of his brains. Perhaps I short-changed him, I can't remember. Well, this geezer chased me all the way back to the yard. He might have been pissed but he could still hoof it, and was a few feet behind me all the way. In the yard he got hold of a starting handle, and honest to God would've caved my skull in if I hadn't managed to get away.

Next morning I was shit scared to go to work, but I did anyway, and there was this guy. 'Morning Mike,' he said. 'Must have been a blinding night – can't remember anything about it.'

Anyway, one of the nights at the Manning Hotel, the guv'nor came over and asked me if I'd stand in for the compère, who was leaving. I thought, 'Why not? I don't mind doing him a favour', but at the end of the night he stuck twelve shillings and sixpence in my hand and I nearly fell over. I loved every minute of being up on stage in the limelight. I was no stranger to being up there doing a turn, but this was different, because in a way I was in control of the audience, most of who I knew anyway, so I wasn't in the least bit nervous. I enjoyed myself, and got a bit of wedge for doing it, and that opened my eyes to the possibilities of the game.

After a while, when I got the hang of what it was all about, I got myself other jobs in this line. Nothing flash, but I was learning; learning all the time. Now this compère lark wasn't like you see on polished TV shows. This was the front line, and half the time the punters were noisy, pissed and out of control. So often I was less compère, and more of a referee. And this is where what I think of as my distinctive style developed.

If you only know me as Frank Butcher you won't have a clue, but if you've seen the videos or caught my act live, you'll know I can be very aggressive. I do a gag, and while the audience are having a laugh I'm giving it, 'Shut up, shut up, leave it out, for fuck's sake', as though they're annoying me by laughing, so I get a double round of applause.

In those early days, my having a go was for real, because I had to quieten down the yobbos and loudmouths before I could introduce the next act. I was a big fella, bit of a Jack the Lad, so I never really got any comeback from these verbal attacks on the crowd. But there was one time when I told this geezer to fuck off. Full of piss, he was getting a bit lairy, heckling and abusive, so I told him where to go. It might only have been, 'Shut up', but it gave him the hump. I knew him; his name was Charlie Vincent and I often used to see him round the manor. He was a total and utter nutcase. Used to wear glasses like bottle bottoms.

I'm trying to let you see what types of people were walking about at the time.

I had a mate called George Grainey, and he was a very big man. I was giving him a lift in my car one day and he asked me to pull over. I did, and he jumped out and hammered into this guy who was walking past. He battered this geezer so badly I really thought he meant to kill him. All done, he got back in the motor and I said, 'What's all that about?' He said, 'He told me to fuck off last month.' Last month – I ask you! Those two words had eaten into him like a cancer, and it was probably just a throwaway remark.

Same with this Vincent. He's taken what I said on board, and it's festered in his head for two weeks before he comes down to the café with the sole intention of caving my head in with an axe. There was a car sitting outside, not even mine, and Charlie ran up to it and stuck his axe right in the bonnet. Then the headlights got the treatment; and all the windows.

Overcoming the fear that was inside me, I went out and fronted him. He's raving, 'Nobody tells me to fuck off', and waving this axe about. He cornered me in the doorway next to the café, and if Frankie hadn't turned up he would have chopped me. Frankie was either respected or feared all over, so all it took was a word and Vincent was all burned out.

Imagine if this mental case had got his hands on a shotgun. It was when people like him did, that things often went boss-eyed. In fact, I got myself into a situation where one slip of the trigger finger could have got me hung or put away for life.

Our little firm had set up a job, and it was going to be a real earner. Lorry-load of, can you believe it, sausage skins? There must have been about twenty miles of these intestines all packed in wooden barrels, and for each one we'd already arranged to get five hundred pounds. So you can imagine, the whole load was worth thousands. Everything was sorted: we'd got the keys, the driver had been paid off and we were told exactly where it would be parked up. The idea was to drive it away, unload the barrels into our own lorry somewhere quiet, then fire it.

It all went wrong. When we got to the place the lorry wasn't even there. Naturally we went after the driver, and he suffered a few digs before we accepted that he was telling the truth, that some other bastards have had it away. Nothing – and I mean nothing – is ever completely secret when you're working on the other side of the fence. One guy in a firm has a piss, two minutes later some other guy in another firm knows all about it. And not only that, but which wall he did it up.

We get a very good whisper on who'd tucked us up, and went after the only name we had. We always carried a shotgun in the car, but broken up. Stock under the seat, barrels in the boot, so if we did get a pull we could say to the law that it was just some crap gun we'd forgotten about. Lousy defence, but better than carrying one all set up.

We've turned up at this geezer's house and I've put the gun together and stuck two cartridges in it. We bang on the door, he's opened it and as I've said, 'This is it, pal', Frankie's pulled him outside by the throat and banged him up the wall. I cocked the piece and stuck it in his chest. This would-be gangster dropped straight to his knees and burst into tears, which is exactly what I would have done in his position. But at that moment we were the tough guys, so I just said, 'What a state to get in.' We just looked at each other, Frankie gave him a dig and we walked away in disgust. There was never any intention of shooting the guy – it was all down to bravado and putting the frighteners on.

I've said before that I had too much imagination to be a paid-up villain, but on that occasion it must have deserted me. And the best of it was that this twenty-eight-inch Greener I was carrying had a hair trigger; one slip and *boom*, the geezer would have been out of the frame and me and Frankie on the end of a rope, because hanging didn't go out until four or five years later.

The café I mentioned where Vincent came to do me with an axe was actually owned by me and the boys. In a way, I suppose we were taking a leaf out of the book of bigger villains like the Twins and a few others. They had their clubs or drinkers, and us being second league, had our café up by the railway cutting. Whatever, it was our place to hang out in.

I don't think we imagined it was an investment, and just as well because it never made a copper coin. The firm was a bit mob-handed then, and every one of them, me included, filled up on tea and fry-ups daily, and no-one put anything in the till. The only thing that kept the place going was that it was handy for the railway workers. We stuck in about eight pin tables that were all rigged, so what with one thing and another, we broke even.

Going back to Sheila, I can safely say that at that time our marriage was well and truly over. Whenever I did see her I'd slip her a couple of pounds and something else as well, but we both knew it was going nowhere.

At that age, approaching my twenty-first, I think I might have been unconsciously looking for a proper relationship with someone, but at the same time couldn't be bothered to put any effort into the one I was already legally in. So when I did meet a beautiful and very sexy young lady, I was ready to fall in love – and did; head over heels, totally smitten. Yet like a lot of things that happen to you in life, it came as a complete surprise out of a very unlikely situation.

Lenny Hornby, our wiring specialist, got a nicking with Frankie and me over something or other. We were banged up for a bit, given a fine. Nothing serious, and all part of the business. He was younger than us, and I suppose he thought, 'Stuff this. I'll keep away from the firm while the Old Bill's got our number.' So he's gone off to do a bit of work independently.

OK with us – we didn't own him. Next thing we heard, from one of our coppers on the bung, was that Lenny had been nicked for robbery. And worse: that he'd been picked up after someone had grassed him.

A few quid changed hands and we got a name, and surprisingly it was a woman, the wife of a minor villain in the area, Jimmy Collins.

I wasn't too happy that one of our own was banged up on somebody's word, but Frankie was absolutely livid. He really took it personally, and I knew it was genuine because as we drove around looking for her, he never opened his mouth. Just sat all hunched up beside me with a mean look on his face.

With a word here and a word there, we tracked her down to the Railway Tavern. Frankie's burst in, gone straight up to her and given her a mouthful. 'You done this, done that, you bitch, you grassed our mate up.' I mean, Frankie could put the shits up anybody on the manor, but this tiny, and I mean tiny, little scrap of a girl fronted him up and denied any knowledge of what he was talking about, cool as you like.

He was having none of it, and carried on shouting. In the end she got off her chair and said, 'I'm not frightened of you, you fat prick,' and spat in his face. He went white, reached behind him, picked up a glass and was going to put it straight in her face. I jumped forward, pushed her out of the way and held his arm. I'd never seen him go for a woman, ever, and I think he surprised himself at what had nearly happened, so allowed me to ease him out of the pub.

I think the shock of being sworn at – something nobody ever did – made him overreact, because by then, same as me, he could tell by the way she was acting that she wasn't lying. Perhaps her name had been put up as a way of getting back at her husband, or some wires got crossed. Either way, we never found out who stitched up Lenny.

Some weeks later, I walked into our café and there was this Shirley Collins sitting by the window with her mate Diane. Now even when that row was going on some weeks previous, I'd registered that she was a very tasty piece, so I went out of my way to let her know I was there. I swaggered up to the counter and ordered a tea in a loud voice. 'Giss a tea, Dave. How's my business today?' so she'd get the message I was the guv'nor. She never even looked up. I walked over to the jukebox, stuck a coin in and said to her, 'Fancy a dance, darling?' She looked me up and down and said, 'Piss off, you prick.' Her mate giggled, and I felt about two inches tall.

I don't think I'd had a knock-back since I was a kid. I was completely deflated. Being a self-confessed Jack the Lad, my ego was as big as my head at the time, and I couldn't believe that this little thing, who barely came up to my chest, could dismiss me with a few well-chosen words. Especially those words. I had my own pride, so I thought, 'Well, you can piss off as well.' Didn't say it, though.

Over the next five or six weeks I didn't see too much of Frankie and the chaps. It might have been winter, and I was up to my neck in the coal round, or scrap prices were up and I was making the most of it.

What brought it about I don't know, and Shirley and me have never spoken of it, but her and Frankie made up their differences. He may have gone round and apologized for the mistake he'd made, what with being a bit out of order. Or it might have been that Shirley swallowed what he'd said to her when she needed a bit of help.

Her husband, though he was a highly intelligent man and an immaculate dresser, was in my book no man at all, because behind the door he was a violent bully. Not only to Shirley, but to their young son Jimmy. I learned later that she was convinced that one day he would hurt her very badly or even kill her. I won't say any more than that, because he's dead and gone now and I can't see any mileage in raking up a past that's best forgotten.

It was probably after one of these violent incidents that Shirl had called on Frankie to help her out and he'd warned her old man off. I won't say that he was the reason that her husband left, but the threat of what might happen to him must have been a contributing factor.

After that, Frankie kept an eye on her place. So when I wanted to get hold of him, that was one of the most likely places I'd find him.

I went round there one day and asked this Shirley if she'd seen Frankie. She looked me up and down, said, 'No I haven't', and I turned to walk away before she told me to piss off again, but she said he'd probably be showing later on if I wanted to wait. I went in and sat down, and there was this lovely smell of cooking. Remember, I practically lived in the café eating fry-ups, so a bit of home cooking went right to my head.

After a bit with my usual front, I asked her if any of that stew was going spare. She called me a cheeky sod, dug out a plate and I never left.

That was thirty-eight years ago, and it's been her and me ever since. She was no Sheila, and I found that out the next morning. I got out of bed, had a shower then reached for my customary glass of Scotch. Forget the tea – a nice drop of whisky got my day kick-started. I got back into bed and she said, 'You prick.' I thought hello; this is where we came in. 'You prick,' she said, 'what are you doing with that at this time in the morning?' I was so taken aback that believe it or not, I poured the Scotch back into the bottle.

I wasn't setting myself up for being under her thumb, but suddenly here was a woman I could respect. I wasn't just in awe of how she looked, I admired her. She had balls, but in a very feminine way. Because or in spite of that old man of hers, she was tough, independent and didn't care two monkey's what anyone thought.

Within weeks I'd made up my mind that this woman was for me – for life. I was twenty-one and she was four years older and miles ahead of me in maturity. Either she didn't know any other way to be, or she saw something in me that needed keeping under control. She never let me have my head, not even half a head. And she was right. With my sort of track record, I needed a woman who'd say, 'C'mon, hang about a minute', when I got out of order. Obviously I'm the sort of man who, if someone wanted to keep me, they had to be very strong. And that's where my first wife, and indeed every girlfriend I'd ever had, went wrong. They were too soft, and our relationships just dwindled away in a very short time.

Don't think it was easy for me, and don't think I didn't kick back time after time after time, but after a blazing row, and I mean BLAZING, I'd get back on a shorter leash – again, not because I was intimidated by her, but simply because I loved her.

Rows? Don't ask. We've had some over the years. Even today, neighbours for miles around must prick up their ears and say, 'The Reids are at it again'. But – and a very big but – when I'm not working away, I kiss her every morning, I kiss her last thing at night, and a good twenty times between. Hands up how many people can say that after nearly forty years together?

That's now, but in those early days things were not easy, for various reasons. No matter how hard I grafted or bobbed and weaved, my income was up and down like a bride's nightie. One week we'd be living off the hog, the next jack shit. Regardless of the fact that I thought myself a man in every sense, in some areas I was still only a kid. Overnight I'd taken on responsibility for Shirley and her two children. Jimmy was eight, going on nine, and Angie was two years old. I took this very seriously, but at the same time didn't want to give up my life as a single man. I was drinking, out with the boys, in fact doing everything a young man gets up to, so there was always a conflict.

Angie, being just a baby, was a little darling, and I was her dad from day one. With Jimmy it was a different kettle of fish, and things were a bit strained between us then and for years after. I'm not criticizing him, he's a man now and will understand what I'm saying. But what's that they say? 'Give me the child and I'll give you the man.' Well, that's how it was. At nine he had been mentally formed by his own father, and had his own ways and opinions. He must have thought, 'Who's this geezer moving in here and trying to tell me what to do?' Remember, I was only a dozen years older than he was, so it was difficult to play the heavy father and try to guide him when a lot of the time I couldn't guide myself.

Once me and Shirley had lived together for a while and moved on from that early lustful stage, I began to realize just what a catch she was. I've got to admit that the first thing that appealed to me about her was her knockout looks – she was an absolute darling. Blonde hair, beautiful blue eyes and so tiny, the top of her head just about reached the middle of my chest. And at six and a half stone, so light it seemed I could pick her up and put her in my pocket, which is just what I felt like doing almost the first time I clapped eyes on her.

But as we all know, looks aren't everything and like I said, it was only after we'd spent a lot of time together that I found out exactly what was under the surface, and realized for sure she was all I'd ever want. She was outgoing, broad-minded and could look after herself, and I loved all these things in a woman. But there was a much softer side that she didn't let too many people see. Tears would spring up over the silliest things, like weddings on the telly or stories about sick children in the paper. And she put everybody but everybody before herself. She was totally unselfish, kind and caring and I loved her to bits. Sounds like a reference or a testimonial, but in all honesty I can't speak highly enough of her. The best part is that over the years, she hasn't changed one bit. She's grown older, yeah, but then I'm not a young man myself any more. Inside, though, she's remained exactly the same, and I bless the day I went looking for Frankie and found myself a little treasure.

That first flat where we lived was in a big block – Nichol House in Finsbury Park. But either I wanted to make a fresh start away from the association of Shirley's first husband, or we couldn't pay the rent – the latter, more likely – so we moved into a place over Hornsea Rise.

Shirl was fiercely independent. She wanted me but she didn't need me. She was more than capable of looking after the kids herself, and she had a job that brought in a few quid every night, and she hung on to that no matter how much I said knock it on the head as I was there for her. This job was as a waitress in a restaurant in Old Compton Street in the West End, at a time when going up West was an exciting night out. All the clubs and eating places were open until the small hours. Prostitutes were on every corner, and it was alive and bubbly. Then they took the toms off the street and the place died overnight. It was killed stone dead.

The place my old woman worked at was run by a Greek, and one night she had a bit of a ruck with him. It wasn't even her argument in the first place, but she does love to poke her nose in. So when he's had a go at her friend Romy, Shirl's jumped in, given him a slap and been pulled off by this geezer's henchmen that were all

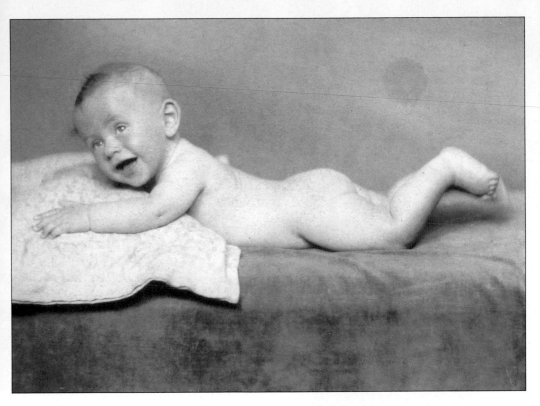

Mike Reid – exposed. I said I'd bare all for my book, but I didn't expect to go this far!

Me and my mum. Little did she know the grey hairs I would give her.

Spot the future Frank Butcher.

My mum and dad.

A happy-family day on the beach.

Me and Frankie Wheeler – one
of 'The Firm'.

Me, David and Kevin – off to see the world.

Jack the Lad.

My Shirl – not long after we fell in love.

Look out, ladies, Reidy's on the pull. On board the *Amerikanis*.

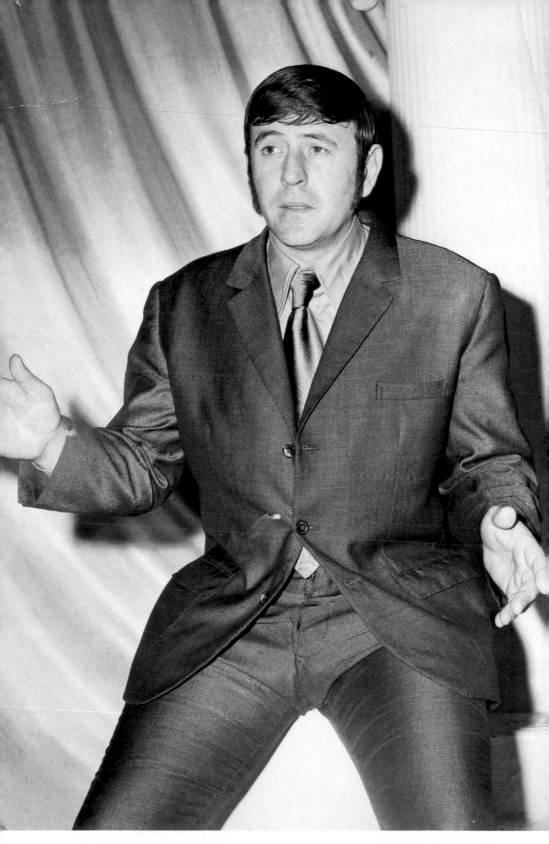

Nervously waiting in the wings at the London Palladium.

My first acting break as Benny in *Yus My Dear*, with Helen Keating and Arthur Mullard.

Shirl, me and my one-time manager – the formidable Eve Taylor.

Me, Bernard Manning and Johnny Hamp.

'T'rific.'
Greengates Studio

I just *love* to sing.

round the place. That all died down, but when I picked her up at the end of her shift, as I did every night, I noticed she had a red mark on the side of her face. She said it was nothing, and it wasn't until we'd got home and seen off the babysitter, that she told me the Greek had landed her one, because by this time the mark was a lump.

I went completely mad. I got her to tell me where he lived, which was in a very exclusive part of Muswell Hill, jumped in the car and flew over there. I didn't care if he was out of a family of top dogs; nobody was going to lay a finger on my girl.

I got there about half five in the morning, knocked on the door and after five minutes a housekeeper opened up. I pushed my way in, demanding to know where he was. She was so frightened all she could do was point above her head. I dived up the stairs and burst into the first bedroom I came to. He might have been a tough guy ten-handed, but as I came through the door he pulled the blankets over his head. I was thrown for a second because I'd never seen such luxury in all my life; everything was beautiful, carpet, curtains, and furniture. I leaped on the bed, pinned him down with my knees and pulled the covers off his face. And Jesus, what a mess. His face was like a pizza, it was covered with holes, digs and lumps out of it and the one under his eye, a fraction closer would have blinded him. Shirley had used her favourite trick – slipped off her shoe and hammered him with a stiletto heel.

This geezer's shaking like a leaf, but as far as I could see he'd been well paid, so all I did was warn him about following this up, gave him a dig as a matter of principle and walked out. Shirley had proved her point and I'd proved mine – that nobody's too big to get away with interfering with my family.

For a while I half expected the flat to get shot up one night, but it never happened. Given what she'd done it was academic really, but I said, 'Princess, you ain't going back. Trust me to look after you and the kids', and she accepted it.

One of my ways of putting bread on the table was getting into the second-hand car game. Almost like a rehearsal for my eventual part in *EastEnders,* I had a short but very lucrative spell on my own car lot. I was picking up old bangers, tidying them up and knocking them out from home for less than two hundred quid. I couldn't seriously call it a living, but it was a bit extra to everything else I got up to.

Then I got talking to someone and ended up renting a site off him at Rainham near the roundabout, just past Ford's of Dagenham. I was standing there one day with about three of these old wrecks behind me priced at nothing, and I couldn't help noticing the amount of flash-looking Yank motors going past, and it gave me an idea. Next day I drove up to the American base not too far away, talked myself past the gates and eventually got to see the sergeant in charge of the motor pool. I told him I was interested in buying cars, and what I found out was that while the army was quite happy to ship over the GIs' personal motors, when they'd finished their stint it was up to them to pay for shipment back home. Invariably they just wanted shot of them, and I was the man to take these cars off their hands for peanuts.

While it lasted it was marvellous, but in those days enough was never enough for me, and I always had to look for some fiddle to make life interesting. And that came about when I bought a couple of bottles of Jack Daniel's from out the back door of the stores. That was all right until two became a dozen, then I was picking up crates, until in the end I'd be filling my motor to the roof with not only booze, but catering cans of hot dogs and ham.

It couldn't last. I'd made a pick-up at the base, unloaded the lot into a back room on the car lot, when I spotted military police jeeps pulling in the gates, followed by our own Old Bill. I kissed everything goodbye, climbed over the back wall, legged it and never went back. Nothing was in my name – not even my own motor that I left out the front, so I was never traced.

The next time I showed my face on a car lot was in the studio, but that was a long way off back then.

Never one to stand still, out of one thing and into another, it wasn't long before I got myself involved in the West End and for a while money was no problem. I was still doing my bit of compèring and turns in the pub, and though I'd no experience in actually running a club, it was down to this that a mate of mine, Dave Conway, and I got ourselves into the club scene.

If you weren't around in those days, the word 'club' could conjure up some flash place with glass chandeliers, thick pile carpets and wall-to-wall dress suits, and on one level that would be correct. But the sort of place we got into was basically a drinker, nothing more, nothing less. The Club de France in Wardour Street was below a take-away named 'Sam Widges' and right in the centre of the dirty bookshop game with their porn books, films and what have you. So a lot of our customers were these boys, and of course their girls, who, because of the business they were in were a bit 'how's yer father', so Shirley hated me being there.

I think half the time she thought I was giving them one, but hand on heart I never did. If I put any money into this venture then I don't know where it came from. It was a long time ago, and a lot of water's gone under the bridge, but I should think Dave stuck up the funds and my percentage came from me fronting the place. Either way, we were soon turning over a few quid, and I thought I'd cracked it at last. Now I was up there with the big boys, people I'd held in the greatest of awe as I grew up, like the Krays, the Nashes and people like Freddie Foreman and Ronnie Knight. The fact is, though, I never was or could be in their league.

One side of me would have loved the notoricty of being one of the Kray firm, but the other side was very grateful that I was never asked to get involved. I often bumped into the Twins when I went for a drink in the Regency, the club that the Barry brothers owned. And it would be safe to say we were on more than nodding terms, but not to the extent where they might have said, 'No, Mike, you can't walk away – we need you to do this or that.' It never happened; and when I look at people like the Lambrianous, who got life sentences just for being in a certain place when they were just kids and younger than I was, I thank the God I don't believe in.

I say I was never asked, but there was an incident where I put myself forward. I was in the Nag's Head over Finsbury Park, having a quick drink before I went home. Reggie, Ronnie and I think it was Connie Whitehead came in and sat in a corner. Reg raised his hand to me, Ronnie just stared. Christ, that look of his went right through you. I was just thinking about leaving when half a dozen geezers burst in, looked round and went straight for the Twins. Then it was off: bosh, the table's gone over as they got stuck into the boys. Connie wasn't a big fella, so the odds were a bit uneven, and I waded in and started throwing a few rights. My bit of help may not have been needed, because Reg and Ron could have a fight, but I was always a mug for getting involved.

It was all over in five minutes and the mob were seen off. We dusted ourselves down, Reg bought me a drink and that was the end of it. I wasn't invited to join the firm and it was never mentioned again, but I don't think it was forgotten.

It would have been handy to have stuck their name over the door of the Club de France because once me and Dave started to make money, in came various gangs looking for protection money. Some of these people were heavy; a lot were chancers, but I saw them all off.

One lot of cheeky bastards came swaggering in and said they were acting for the Krays. I said, 'Oh yeah, well you lot stand there while I give Ronnie a bell and ask him what it's all about,' and I picked up the phone. They were out of it in two seconds.

A black mob wasn't so easy to get rid of, and while I was telling them there was nothing in the till, one of them nutted me. Then they dragged me outside and kicked me up and down Wardour Street. By the time the Maltese mob came looking for a pension, I'd really had the arse'ole with the whole thing.

I'd taken to keeping my shotgun behind the bar, so as soon as they went into the old spiel I bent down, pulled it out and rested it on the counter. All I said was, 'If you want money, come and get it, but just think – I might get myself nicked, but one or two of you'll be dead.' They left it. Sounds like I was a real tough guy but the truth, as always, was that I was petrified; literally shitting myself.

In the end, the only mob that made any serious money out of Dave and me was the biggest firm of the lot – Old Bill. They robbed us blind. We were virtually on top of Trenchard House, so it was convenient for the law to pop in and out for a drink and have a laugh with the bookshop boys. We even had the vice squad in quite regular after they'd turned over these places, nicking their dirty mags and films.

The police knew we didn't pay any tax, didn't pay protection and didn't have a music licence for the jukebox. But worse, they knew they weren't getting a piece of the action themselves, and that gave them the right hump.

The first night they decided to rectify this state of affairs sticks in my mind, because earlier my Shirl had been in. I told you she hated the place, but that didn't stop her coming in for a drink when she got bored being stuck at home. This was OK, but once she'd had a few she'd want to give me the earhole about those birds I mentioned. So this night she came along and I told her I wasn't letting her in. With her usual ladylike tenacity she said, 'We'll effing-well see about that.' I told her there was no way she was getting a drink, so she might as well go home. She disappeared, and I didn't give it another thought. Unbeknown to me she'd snuck into the ladies, and every time a woman came in for a wee, she'd ask them to get her a gin and orange. This went on for hours.

The first I knew of it was when I heard a scream and a crash from the toilets, and when some girls investigated there was my old woman stretched out on the floor, completely paralytic – totally gone. They've called me in, I picked her up, slung her over my shoulder, took her out to my Alvis that was parked at the front and put her in the back seat. I was bloody annoyed to say the least.

I drove home, got to the flat and laid her on the bathroom floor while I filled the bath with cold water, then dropped her in it, fully clothed. While she's giving it, 'What's going on?' I picked up her little dog, stuck him in the middle of her chest and said, 'I bloody well warned you about coming up the club,' walked out, slammed the door and went back to work.

The place was empty. My partner had been nicked by the law, along with two grand's worth of stock. Afterwards they gave us all this bollocks about no music licence, but we all knew it was about them not getting a drink – so they'd taken their own, and a bloody good one at that. Dave paid a nominal fine and the booze was confiscated.

It wasn't easy, but we managed to scrape up about eight hundred quid for some new stock, and made up the balance on sale or return.

We were back in business, and it wasn't long before the gangsters in blue had their hands out. I told them, 'You greedy bastards have had more than your share.' Crash – a month later they cleared us out again. Everything went, even the cash out of the tills, and I was so gutted I walked away.

I hadn't saved a penny. What was the point? There was always plenty more at the end of the week. Now there wasn't, and I was back to square one – completely potless.

CHAPTER FOUR

PROBLEMS NEVER COME IN ONES. I'D BEEN OUT COLLECTING A BIT of scrap metal, and the engine of my crap old lorry had blown up on me. It wasn't worth two bob anyway, so I had it towed away and weighed in for scrap with what was already on the back. So I was well pissed off when I walked indoors and into some news I could have done without. Straight away, Shirley told me that my mum had been round with a message that Sheila wanted me to go and see her urgently.

Nothing more was said until I was going out of the door and Shirl threw after me, 'If what your mum says about the size of her belly is anything to go by, you'd better stay with her.' Oh, Jesus! All the way over to her place I'm thinking, 'Nah, my Shirl's having a dig at Sheila for putting a bit of weight on', because understandably they'd never hit it off. She was right, though, and my very ex-missus was nearly eight months pregnant. I couldn't believe it. Three years, I'd been with her. More off than on I know, but apart from the baby that died, she never even came close to falling pregnant. And now, down to one last attempt at reconciliation before I met Shirley, this had to happen.

To be honest, at the time I wouldn't accept that it was anything to do with me, because for a long time it had been an open secret that she was more than a neighbour to the bloke in the upstairs flat. I'd buggered off and his wife had left him, so the two of them cried on each other's shoulders, and as far as I suspected, a bit more than that.

In a way I wanted to believe that, because if my Shirl got her sums wrong and thought I was giving Sheila one while I was with her, I'd be out on my earhole.

I half-heartedly denied responsibility for that baby right up to and even beyond the birth of little Jane in December of 1961. That was until her likeness to me was so marked that I couldn't and didn't want to deny that she was definitely mine. And no sooner had I recognized the fact, than I agreed never to see her again – something I came to regret more and more as the years went by.

Sheila wanted to make a fresh start, and obviously didn't want me dropping in and out. So she made me promise that I'd keep well out of it.

I was back to ducking and diving and I was in love with Shirley. Plus, at that time I'd no concept of paternal feelings, so it suited me to agree. Which, as time went by, I came to realize was one of the most stupid things I'd ever done.

I had this burning desire to see my daughter, but because I felt I'd given Sheila a tough time that she didn't deserve, I swallowed my own needs for her sake. Eventually I was allowed two concessions, and they were that I could see her at Christmas and on her birthday. The condition was that I had to pretend I was her rich uncle who lived abroad. It broke my heart. What no-one knew was that I watched her grow up from a street corner. Not every week, but as often as I could I'd park near her school and catch a glimpse of her coming out. I can't tell you how many times I stopped myself from approaching her. This went on for fourteen years, and it was strange how it was resolved.

Jane always had a dark complexion, and because of this the cruel little bastards at school (and I was one in my day) called her a Paki. When it got too much for her, she told her mother who said, 'You tell them at school you can't be a Paki because your dad is Mike Reid, the comedian on television.' Can you imagine how a fourteen-year-old girl felt when not only did she find out who her father was, but that he was comparatively famous.

We met for the first time as father and daughter, and have never looked back since that day. A wonderful bonus is that my Shirley has loved her like her own since they first met.

Without a lorry I couldn't earn, and without picking up a bit of dough I couldn't get myself another lorry – catch-22. Going against my decision to knock the criminal side of my life on the head, I got myself into a bit of work with the firm. Me, Frankie and another couple of the lads turned over a jeweller's shop down in Croydon. It was one of the few jobs that went the right way, and we came away holding a bundle.

If you're wondering why I didn't do a bit of robbing every night and get myself out of the financial difficulties I always seemed to be in, I've got to say I was trying to move away from anything heavy. With my luck holding for so long, I felt that the law of averages just had to catch up with me eventually and the thought of going away for years filled me with dread. But I told myself that this was a one-off, for a real emergency.

The jewellery blag pulled me right out of the shit. I mean, we didn't cream off fortunes, but it did allow me to pick up another lorry, even though it was a bit of a banger. Once I'd replaced the clutch (I took after Dad in that department), it was sound as a pound and more than good enough to get me back into a bit of totting and collecting scrap.

Not only that, there was plenty left over for me to put down some up-front money, then meet the exorbitant weekly rent on 28 Lordship Lane. So in effect, over the years I'd moved around in a big circle, to arrive back a stone's throw from Mum and Dad in Beaufoy Road.

I couldn't believe how the area had changed. When I'd been at Rowland Hill School there was one black kid in the whole place, and he was a novelty. Now as I looked round there were three coloured people to every one white. Not that I saw it as a problem, because I haven't got a racist bone in my body. I'm just saying how it was.

I rented this flat off a geezer by the name of Joe Gurber, and could he charge. The place was a tip, but in about a month Shirley had it looking beautiful. She was the decorator; always has been. The reason for that is that I am completely useless at the art of DIY, though at first I didn't realize it.

There was so much to do, it was knocking her out. While she could even tackle papering ceilings, I knew she wasn't looking forward to doing our bedroom because it was in a state, all up and down, cracked and peeling. So Reidy decided he would help her out and give this ceiling a facelift when she was out of the way.

I think I got the idea out of one of the new weekly magazines that were popping up around that time all about DIY. Prior to that, there was no such thing. You either paid someone to do a bit of work or you did nothing.

On the quiet I got hold of a load of egg trays, the cardboard ones, then painted them bright pink round a mate's lock-up. It took hours and hours. When the missus went out for the day, I brought this pile of trays home and set to sticking them all over the ceiling with drawing pins. To me, the finished job looked like the Sistine Chapel, but I don't think Shirl had the same opinion, though she did have the grace to smile and say it was lovely.

That night, we were in bed and I was getting a bit romantic when something touched my bare arse. I've leaped in the air like a scalded cat and got another tap on my head. I looked up, and one by one these trays are falling off and floating down. We ended up in hysterics, screaming our heads off.

Three times in my life I've had a go at home improvements. Three times in nearly sixty years. That was one. The next was when the 'Department of Works' was desperate for a serving hatch between the lounge and kitchen in the first house we ever bought. I told her I'd do it and she said, 'No, just leave it.' I said, 'It's only a hole in the wall – piece of piss.' Her words as she went out for the day were, 'I mean it, don't touch it.'

By the time she got back I'd hammered, bolstered and smashed my way through nine inches of brickwork. It looked a bit rough, so I'd cut up strips of Formica and stuck this all round the inside onto jagged bricks. The top piece I had to nail up because it kept falling down. The finishing touch was fluted architrave on every edge to cover up the holes.

To me it was a lovely job, but when Shirl came in and said, 'What have you done?' I could tell by the scream that I'd made a ricket. To prove a point, before she called my dad in to put it right, she put a plate on one end of the hatch and we both watched it slowly slide down to the other. What could I say?

After that, I never touched another thing beyond the front door of any house we ever lived in, but some years later I got some ducks and I needed a pen for them. Little old shed outside. What could go wrong?

By this time I was on the telly and earning serious wedge, so not only did we have this lovely house but grounds to match. And in them was this great big pond crying out for a bit of wildlife.

Old habits die hard, and even though I was well off, I couldn't resist going to Chelmsford market and buying these old ducks at about tuppence each.

Unfortunately, this pond backed on to the road, so I had to think to myself, how am I going to contain them. I didn't want to clip their wings because it seemed cruel, so until they got used to the place I decided to shut them up in a duck pen. The ducks cost a few coppers' and the timber I bought cost about a hundred quid.

I sawed and hammered all weekend, then had the blinding idea that this duck house would be a real feature if it was floating on the pond. A dozen two-gallon plastic containers and a tin of UHU glue later, it was ready to float.

I shut the ducks inside, then using a series of pulleys, skimmed it over the surface and anchored it in the middle with a twenty-eight-pound theatre weight. Who said I was useless at this game?

I went off for a game of golf and when I got back, the family was in uproar. They dragged me outside just in time to see my creation touch bottom, and sticking out of the ventilation gap in the top were a dozen beaks straining upwards. The gardener had to swim in and rescue them, so after that I was banned from picking up a tool. Even today I've only got to look at a hammer and the family go, 'Oh, no, you don't.'

Back in Lordship Lane, we were getting on well and I was getting myself into trouble. From an early age, as I've described already, I couldn't keep my hands off other people's motors. I had this passion for speed that a clapped-out lorry was never going to satisfy. On the other hand, the way my finances were I could never see my way to actually buying any of these tasty machines that caught my eye.

I knew I wasn't a kid any more, but what with moving back to my old stamping ground, when I needed a couple of quid I took up the car-minding again. Though in this case, it happened to be a motor-bike. What a piece! I'd see it Saturday after Saturday when the geezer parked it up to go and watch Spurs. I don't think I'd ever spoken to the bloke that owned it; he'd sling a bit of silver at me for minding his bike, and that would be it.

As far as I was concerned, I never stole his poxy bike and never had any intention of stealing it. I took it for a short test run, and I would have got away with it, except the prat gave up on the game before the final whistle, came out of the ground and his bike's gone.

As I pulled up thinking I had plenty of time to spare, he's come running over with a couple of coppers. They've caught hold of me and as I'm trying to say to the geezer I'd only been giving it a quick try-out, he's screaming over and over, 'Nick the bastard. Nick the bastard.' They were going to anyway, but he had to chuck in his ha'p'orth.

I was banged up locally, and quite honestly I couldn't have been lifted in a worse place, because the sergeant of the manor hated me with a passion. He was one of those who'd never fallen for my 'like-able rascal' act, and he wanted me badly.

Shirley came up to see me before my court appearance, and I told her to prepare herself for me going down. With my MO and that bastard after me, there was no way out.

I'm standing in the courtroom and this Sergeant Davison got up and started reading off my previous convictions. Even I was surprised at how long the list was. He went on and on – nicked for this, nicked for that – all the dates, everything. In the end the magistrate stopped him mid-flow and said, 'Is there anything really significant on your list?' Davison told him it was all much the same, so the judge waved his hand saying, 'Well, stop there, stop there.' Then he turned to me and said, 'Mr Reid, you're obviously a pest – come on now, you really are a pest. I'm going to send you away for a few months to straighten you out.'

Now, unbeknown to me, my Shirl had come to court to speak up for me. Fortunately she's got a very good head on her shoulders, and knowing what a predicament I was in had decided on drastic action – namely a large cushion stuck up her dress.

When she arrived at the court first thing Monday morning, she'd spoken to Davison and he'd told her to wait down the corridor and he would call her before sentencing, with absolutely no bloody inten-tion of doing anything of the sort. She kept pestering the usher on the door as to what was going on with my case, and when she found out things were moving to a finish, she slipped past the geezer on the door and burst into the court.

This was the first I knew she was even there. I couldn't believe it, she's eight months pregnant and looks like Orphan Annie. She just stood at the door saying, 'Please, sir, please sir, may I speak?' The magistrate beckoned her down to his desk and she went off in an act that would have brought tears to your eyes: 'Kids at home with no shoes; landlord going to kick us out; I'm pregnant and he's a really good husband.' Then she burst into tears and ran out without hearing what he had to say.

I reckon she choked the old geezer up because he had to give his nose a good blow before he gave me one last chance: a twenty-pound fine – you may leave the court.

When I got home, she told me she'd felt like Sarah Bernhardt in one of her black and white movies and did it all over again. 'Please, sir, don't send my husband away', and we both pissed ourselves laughing.

Before that, while I was still downstairs in the cells, Davison came down, slammed the bolt back, crashed the door open and got hold of the front of my jacket. He was livid, spitting feathers. He said, 'You and your missus think you're fucking clever. Well, let me tell you, if it's the last thing I ever do I'm going to send you down for a very long time.' Then he slammed the peephole in the door shut and whispered, 'I'm going to get you for something heavy, just to make sure.' I could see he meant it, and my arse'ole was opening and closing like a clown's hat.

Funny really, what with Shirl pretending to be pregnant in court, because not long after that's exactly what she was. Trouble was, as she got bigger and bigger, my income got smaller and smaller. When I'd taken the flat on I was holding a good bit of folding, and not being one for looking too far ahead at that age, I'd never given a thought to the fact that the scrap game was up and down. And once my wages dropped, I found I was going to work every day to pay the rent. With that place bleeding us dry, I could barely feed the four of us, never mind an extra mouth.

With this, plus the fact that Davison was out to get me, we made up our minds to move out – or, to put it another way, our minds were made up for us.

Finding somewhere else to live turned out to be much harder than we'd expected. Even the roughest one-roomed places didn't want to know as soon as we said we had two young kids, and in desperation we sent Jimmy and Angie away to Shirl's mum and dad in Norfolk. They loved it, what with going to the countryside and being spoiled rotten by their grandparents, but it broke my old woman's heart.

Once it was just the two of us, it made finding a flat much easier. I dug this place out of the local paper, and without taking Shirl or mentioning her condition, I went to view it and put a month's rent down on this couple of rooms up four flights of stairs in a big old house.

Moving into that place was a mistake from day one. As soon as our landlady and her Polish husband saw that my Shirl was well pregnant, they wanted us out. On the other hand, they had our bit of rent and they were going to hang onto it. So as a compromise, until the money ran out they made life unbearable for Shirley. I say her and not us, because most of the time I was out of it.

They didn't know what to do next to wind her up. They banged doors, they played their radio full blast, they wouldn't let her hang her bit of washing in the garden, and gave my missus lip every time she passed them. Shirley swallowed it. Once the month was up and a bit more, half a dozen times a day the old man would be banging on the door shouting, 'You go. You go.' And well out of character, she never said a word.

Until one day, she just lost it completely. With only one week to go before our baby was due, she was exhausted, swollen up, depressed and desperately missing the kids.

I don't even know what kicked it off, very little I expect, but it was the final straw. I was out at work so I didn't see her in action, but I have done, and God help anyone who comes up against her in full swing. She's gone down the stairs four at a time, screaming her head off. The old man saw her coming, ran into his room and slammed the door in her face. She punched her fist straight through the glass, cutting her arm. That brought the old woman out, and as big as she was, Shirl gave her a full arm punch in the mouth. Next thing, these two have got the law in.

In front of the copper, this woman is giving it plenty of old trap. 'Go on you cow,' she's shouting at Shirl. 'Go on, hit me now in front of a witness.' So Shirl obliged her and gave her another couple in the face. Then she's screeching. 'Arrest her, arrest her.'

I suppose the copper's looked at this waif-like, very pregnant little thing, then this massive cow, and he said to the landlady, 'I'm sorry, but you gave this young lady total provocation.' Then he took Shirl to one side, told her he wouldn't take it any further, but advised her to find another place as soon as possible.

And that's what we did. With no chance of getting somewhere on the hurry-up, Shirl went to stay with her brother Verdi over at Hornsea and I went home to Mum's in Tottenham. Though not before my missus made sure that our landlords wouldn't forget us in a hurry. She went down the market at the end of the day when everything's cheap and bought a load of fish for pennies, then called in to the butcher's and got two big slabs of lard. Back in the flat, she hammered tacks through the fish into and under every surface she could find. Stuck some behind the boiler, and what was left went through any holes in the floor. The fat she melted in the chip pan, then poured it down the plughole of the basin, bath and kitchen sink. Then we moved out.

This was one of the few places where we did walk out of the front door. Usually it was out of a back window at night, leaving behind as many weeks' unpaid rent as we could have conned out of the land-lords.

As time had gone on and it had sunk in that I was going to be a father, I could actually see this baby in my head. It was definitely a boy; loads of dark hair and the mirror image of myself. I don't remember if Mum had a phone at that time, as not many working people did. But however I got the message, I was told that Shirl had been taken into St Mary's Hospital at the Archway.

Usual state of affairs, I was potless, so I said to Mum, 'Lend us two bob for the bus fare.' She just shook her head, 'No.' 'What do you mean, no? It's your first grandchild – I want to see my baby.' She wouldn't budge. 'If you won't work, don't expect me to pay your way.'

I stormed out and ran miles down to Shirley's friend Diane at

Haringey. By this time it's twelve o'clock at night. She's stuck her head out of the window and I've given her the story. Down came half a crown, and when she asked me about the baby that I hadn't even seen, I took this picture straight out of my head. 'He's smashing, black hair and looks just like me.'

This was October, so I couldn't even nick a bunch of flowers on the way, and I arrived empty-handed. And there she was, my princess, looking tinier than ever under white sheets, and clutching a little ginger-haired bundle. I've gone up the wall. 'Who the hell is that?' I've shouted at her. 'It's our son.' 'Not with that lot on top of his head, he ain't.' By now I was upsetting her, but I couldn't stop myself. 'There's no redheads in your family, and definitely none in mine, so turn it in.' She'd just been through hours of pain to give me this wonderful gift, and I was acting the prat. I should've been ashamed of myself.

After a bit I calmed down, said I was sorry and of course he was mine – but I still wasn't too sure, and the next morning I was telling my dad how I felt. He burst out laughing. He actually laughed at this terrible dilemma I was in. Then he said, 'Don't you remember your uncle, my brother Pat who lives in Ireland?' I'm looking blank, so he reminded me of being out with him when he'd got into a fight. Jesus, yes, this memory flooded back from nowhere. The trauma of that day had wiped out what I saw as though it had never happened.

I would have been a tiny dot, and Dad and his brother had taken me out. We were on the bridge that spans the A1 just up from the Archway when some trouble flared up. Dad pulled me to one side while Uncle Patrick, who was a Goliath of a man with this shock of ginger hair, picked up this geezer and held him right over his head. Then without warning, he flung him straight off the bridge. I didn't know it then, but this bloke hit the bank, rolled down into the road and broke his arms, legs and back. It was horrific, with all these people shouting, screaming and fighting, and I just stood there quietly crying to myself. My uncle got two years for that, and I don't remember seeing him again. In fact, had obviously forgotten all about him until Dad reminded me.

Looking back over the years to that conversation reminds me of a gesture of Dad's that made me chuckle inside at the time, but which now I find quite touching. He said to me, 'Son, you're a family man now. You've had some ups and downs; now I hope you'll straighten yourself out.' He put his hand in his pocket, pulled out what was obviously the only fiver in it and gave it to me saying, 'There you go, Mike, make a new life for you and Shirley.' New life? I could drink that much in a couple of hours. But bless him, his heart was in the right place.

We named the boy Michael, and I was like a dog with two tails. Now I had to get us all together as a family.

Like waiting a couple of hours for a bus, then three turn up together. While Shirl was still breastfeeding the baby, she found she was expecting again. Living like we were, hand to mouth in a tiny flat, she wasn't ready for this and nor was I, so she had it terminated. Again, I've got to hold my hand up to a certain amount of naivety. When a woman didn't want a baby, she found someone to do the business and that was that. What I never considered was the physical damage or the psychological effects it could have. Bit of a nuisance out of the way – back to normal. I would love to be able to say that at those times I was extra caring, considerate and aware of just what terrible ordeals Shirl must have gone through. But to my shame, I can't.

This didn't just happen once, it happened a number of times, and I don't recall taking too much notice. I had other things to think about, like making a living.

Considering that I never sat around on my arse, we always seemed to be struggling to make ends meet. My bit of club work brought in about eighteen shillings a night, and the scrap game could earn me a good lump one week, then nothing the next. So something had to go, and that was invariably the rent.

We moved as regular as clockwork from one miserable flat to another. At that age, I still hadn't funnelled my vision into the fact that whatever happens, home comes first, and I have to admit I was pouring the little money we had spare down my throat. For a long time I practically lived in the Queen's Head up Turnpike Lane. Looking back, I must have been mad. Morning, noon and night, pissing it up the wall, and Shirl at home looking after the kids. I could have lost her. One time I really thought I had, and that pulled me up short.

Because of money problems, we were both desperately unhappy. You know how it is when things aren't going right – you take it out on the one nearest to you. The flat we were in was a piss-hole, and selfishly, I was never there. I've got to say it doesn't give me any pleasure to remember those times, because when I did show myself I was moody, argumentative and generally acting lousy. One night she looked at me and said, 'Michael, I don't love you any more.' It wasn't said for effect or nothing, I could see she really meant it. I was devastated – absolutely knocked back on my heels. Nothing was said for the rest of the night, and when I woke up in the morning she was gone. I've had a lot worse days since then, but looking round that empty flat counted as one of the worst so far. I consoled myself with the fact that she hadn't taken all her gear. Sure enough, she eventually came back and I vowed that things would change, but I soon slipped back into the same old rut.

Funny really, after the scare that gave me, not long after I threatened to leave her – though it was more for effect than with real intention.

Old Bill pulled me in for something or other, and when they've dug out my record of unpaid fines I was carted straight off to Brixton Prison. I should have had my name on one of the cells, the amount of time I spent there.

Once Shirley found out where I was, she came up and I told her, 'If you don't get me out of here, we're finished.' Considering her stroppy character, it's a wonder she didn't say, 'Well, stay there then!' but she didn't, and trailed this way and that knocking on doors, calling in favours to raise the cash to get me out. If we were skint before, now we were on our uppers.

Then Shirley got a bit off colour. She'd been to one of those back-street abortionists some time before, but that was all in a day's work, so it couldn't be nothing to do with that. In retrospect, I cannot believe my ignorance of what that entailed – yeah, all in a day's work!

She kept on asking me if I could smell something. I went all round the flat, but apart from cooked cabbage and damp washing from the other tenants, there was nothing. Then she insisted it was on her, and I had to draw the line there. She was then, and still is today, fastidious about personal hygiene, and no matter where we lived, wrecks or not, you could eat off the floor. I began to wonder if the way we lived was getting to her, and she was having a breakdown.

Then one day, and I don't want to be indelicate here, Shirl was standing at the sink and without warning, *whoosh* – she had this terrible discharge from down there. I can't begin to imagine what that young girl went through at that moment, when she found that she had passed the remains of a twin from that earlier termination.

Our upstairs neighbours got her to hospital and, without going into detail, she was sorted out and home in three days. One, she was lucky the law didn't get involved because abortion was illegal then, but second, and most important, luckier still that she hadn't died. She swore then that even if it meant having ten kids, she'd never go through that again.

Subsequently four months later she was pregnant again, and this one was for keeps. It wasn't the right time, and wouldn't be for many years, but having accepted the inevitable we were both over the moon.

By coincidence, a couple of weeks before this I'd been looking for a bit of scrap over Wanstead, and had seen a house for sale that really took my fancy. Me, a property owner? Wasn't really feasible, but when you're young you have more hope than sense, so I'd made an enquiry and it was priced at four thousand eight hundred for a quick sale. I dreamed about it for a week, then knocked the idea on the head. But with this Sergeant Davison virtually running me out of town I said to Shirley, 'We've got to move somewhere, so why don't we give it a go?'

At that time councils used to give a hundred per cent mortgages to young couples as long as the property was valued by them at below five thousand pounds. I went down to the offices, filled in a load of forms with total bollocks about my earnings, paid over five pounds for a survey fee and waited.

Now that the seed was planted I was desperate for this house, but worried about the survey, so I phoned up every day. 'When's he going? When's he doing the survey?' Two weeks I suffered that, then they told me he was going to Wanstead at one o'clock on the Tuesday.

I slipped over in the lorry and sat outside, and when I saw this suited geezer go up the path, I gave him ten minutes and followed him in. By that time he was coming out, so I introduced myself and asked him what he'd come up with. 'Lovely property, Mr Reid. Unfortunately I value it at five thousand, five hundred pounds, so I'm afraid you'll have to look elsewhere for a mortgage. You understand the council's limit.' I was gutted.

He walked away and I was telling myself, 'Think, Reidy, use your loaf.' I caught up with him and said, 'You're a working man, same as me.' He looked up and down at my scruffy work gear, then reluctantly agreed. 'Yes I am – in a sense.' 'Well, guv'nor, it's no skin off your nose what you put in your report, and I've got twenty-five quid that says this property is worth less than five.' He reddened up, so I went for it. 'Please, I'm begging you. One scribble of that pen and you walk away with five and twenty,' and as I'm speaking I tucked the notes in his top pocket. He just got in his car and drove away. Three days later we got our mortgage offer, and all those piss-hole flats were behind us.

Coming out of furnished places we had nothing, so we moved in with a load of orange boxes I picked up from the boys in Covent Garden. We used them as little cupboards, chairs and tables. We slung mattresses on the floor for the kids and us and we were set up.

Five years it took, before we could even consider putting carpet on the stairs. The contrast between what it was then and what it was to become is so great it's beyond comprehension, but I have never forgotten and I'm eternally grateful that fate, if that's the right word, has seen fit to bring me to the position I'm in now. Once again, 'Lucky old boy'.

That first council mortgage cost me about six and a half quid a week. Laughable, that; today it doesn't even cover a couple of days' fags, but then, even though it was less than Joe Gurber and most of the others were charging, it was a struggle to find.

Funnily enough, it was while we were living in this place that I set something in motion that even today is still causing aggravation to Wanstead Golf Club. My mate Ernie, who, with his missus, was a witness at our wedding, was a bloke after my own heart when it came to a bit of poaching and that sort of lark. He was a lighterman, working the barges on the River Thames, and I first met him when I was resident compère at the Elm Park Hotel. I'd spoken to him a few times, and although he wasn't a bloke who said too much, when he did he could talk for hours about shooting and ferreting in a very knowledgeable way.

I said to him one night, 'Ernie, I'd love to come out rabbiting with you sometime.' He gave a big sigh, like it was some effort to even consider it, then said, 'OK. Meet me outside the pub at half-five tomorrow morning.' I dug out my poaching outfit and turned up with all the gear on – the lot. Big old jacket with loads of pockets, loops and game straps, gun, game bag and my trousers tucked into long woolly socks. Ernie was waiting for me, dressed in his work clothes and a scruffy duffle coat. He just looked me up and down – never said a word. Then one of his mates turned up, Skittles, still alive today and a proper ducker and diver. He took one look at me and said, ''Allo, we've got ourselves a great white hunter.' I felt a complete prick. They took the piss rotten, and even when I bump into him today Skittles still calls me the White Hunter.

I thought I knew a lot about the countryside and all that, but it was nothing compared with what Ernie knew, and he taught me so much. One thing I picked up was keep well out of the way when someone's pointing a shotgun around.

We'd stuck a ferret down a hole on this big grassy mound, but we didn't know where the rabbits were going to come flying out. I'm on one side; Ernie's on the other. One ran out, scampered away from me then doubled back. Ernie's got it in his sights, followed it round and shot me in the leg as it went past. Hospital job – hours picking the pellets out, and in case I forget that day, I've still got some lying next to my shin bone to remind me.

Another time, we heard they were going to flatten the old arsenal at Woolwich, so we decided we'd go and have a look at the rabbit situation on these acres and acres. There were thousands of them, and we caught no end.

Now in the park next door to where I lived, you might expect that it was heaving with rabbits, but there wasn't a single one. Plenty of disused holes, but not a single sign of life. So I had the idea of bagging up live ones from Woolwich, then releasing them in the park. They'd breed, and I'd always have a bit of meat on my own doorstep. It worked a treat, only those randy little sods didn't know when to stop, and the last I heard was that Wanstead Golf Club is absolutely overrun with rabbits – all down to White Hunter Reidy.

I was still bringing in a few shillings with the singing and gags, but nowhere near enough to say I was making a living in show business. Us club turns were ten a penny, though without making out I'm Mr Wonderful, I was top of the tree. There was always work for me if I wanted it, and I always came up with what I was paid for, even if that pay only amounted to fifty bob a night. And to be honest, Shirl and me could kill that stone dead over a meal in the Queen's Head.

The scrap game was up and down, so when I wanted serious folding, all my ideas of keeping on the right side of the law fell out the window. Not completely, though. I still played devil's advocate when Frankie or one of the firm came up with something I thought was too heavy. I mean, banks then were a pushover. No grills, no security, you could run in mob-handed, wave a pickaxe handle around and walk out – everybody was at it. But not me.

I remember Frankie setting up this job to turn over a branch bank out in the sticks. I didn't exactly say I wasn't up for it, just made some excuse or other. Give them their due, they pulled it off, but as they'd gone eight-handed and come away with two hundred and seventy-two quid, that came to thirty-four each. Why that sticks in my mind is because that was the exact sum I owed Joe Gurber for back rent when I lived in Lordship Lane. Considering the company he kept, he was either going to have my legs broken or take me to court. Either way, I had to find it. Frankie knew this and though I wasn't even on the job, handed over his take. A lovely gesture, but one that I paid back a hundredfold as the years went on.

I mentioned the sausage-skin caper. Well, the same situation cropped up, but this time with tea. Swings and roundabouts – we did the same to other firms if we got the whisper. Though that didn't make it any easier to swallow when it was done to us yet again. We were absolutely livid – good money paid out and nothing back.

Word came back that it was Derek Smalls and his firm that had turned us over. Derek eventually made a bit of a name for himself as the first and biggest supergrass, but by then he was known as Bertie; God knows why. So we've got him and his lot down for a good hiding.

We knew they were going to be in a certain flat, so we've slipped over there, parked up and crept up this long alleyway. Me in the front, Frankie behind me, then Frank Wheeler, Indian fashion, dead quiet, creeping along the fence. All of a sudden bang, bang, bang; a load of blinding flashes. A lump came out of the fence by my head and some- thing whistled between my legs. As I found out later, it's done the same with Frankie and downed Frank at the back. He's taken one through the calf muscle, so we just grabbed him and dragged him to the motor. We dumped him in casualty and buggered off without being seen, and when the Old Bill turned up, Frank kept shtoom and swore he didn't know who'd done it, and that was the truth, really.

Bertie had won the first round but we couldn't leave it alone. We were in our drinker when a fella we knew came in and told us this Smalls was in the Unwin, just around the corner about a quarter of a mile away. There was four of us, and we all rushed out and jumped into our identical Ford Zodiacs and tore down to this pub.

As I always seem to be skint, I'll explain the motors. At that time there had been a change in the finance regulations that allowed dealers to sell cars on HP without a deposit. What a godsend to potless young men! Literally, all you had to do was sign a paper and drive away, and did we take advantage. I was like a millionaire. I changed my car as often as my shirt. Never paid a penny, just dumped the old one outside the car lot and moved on to another. So, copying film gangsters, we'd got these Zodiacs and had three of them sprayed silver and yellow to match the one Lenny Hornby had got first.

So we steamed down the Unwin, screeching the tyres as we pulled up, then jumped out hollering and shouting. Now what our informant had neglected to tell us was that Smalls was in there with twenty of his firm, and they've poured out of the place and into us. I was kicked from arseholes to breakfast time. They stomped on my face, my ribs. I remember getting to my feet and Derek coming at me. I said, 'C'mon then, just you and me, let's have it.' Next thing someone's done me on the back of the head with a bottle. I went down and the boots came in. I was rolling round in circles and I felt my ribs go, so

I thought I'd play possum. I'm dead or spark out, whatever they want to think. Then *whomph*, someone's kicked me in the stomach. Playing dead might work if a bear collars you in the woods, but believe me it don't work with some would-be gangsters. So I've stuck my arms in the air. 'OK, I've had enough', and they packed it in.

Two of our firm had driven away as soon as it went off, leaving me and Frankie to face it. Now he was nowhere to be seen, so I drove off to where he lived with his wife Mary. I don't know how I got in the house, I was in so much pain. My Shirley was there and her and Mary cut my shirt off and cleaned me up.

What I didn't know was that the mob had chased Frankie up the railway embankment at Hornsey Rise, caught up with him and caned him with a club hammer. When he eventually crawled in, his missus fainted because he looked so horrific. From head to toe he was dripping blood, and he left a trail across the carpet as he came in. The girls took him to the hospital and got him stitched up. Never mind those film beatings where they go after the baddies two minutes after regaining consciousness. Frankie and me lay in his place for a full seven days before we could even go for a piss without groaning, and it was a month before we could even think about getting our own back.

If they got away with it, our cred would be down the pan, so us two roped in Tony Davis and went after them. We heard that most of the mob was at a party in this basement flat, so we got ourselves over there. Tony had his own piece, I lent Frankie my silver pigeon shotgun that Shirley had bought me for my birthday and I had my twenty-eight-inch Greener – the one with the hair trigger I mentioned.

Totally, totally irresponsible, flying around with firearms, as we had no intention of shooting anyone, but there was a principle at stake, and they'd taken the piss.

When we arrived at the flat we could see the front room through the window, and it was packed with people dancing and larking about. What do we do? Burst in and blow the ceiling out? While I was thinking, my gun went off. I had it pointing down the steps and bang, two dustbins have blown up in the air. With that, the other two have let their guns go – wham, bang, the dustbins went up again, and the glass fell out of the front door.

The total panic from inside was frightening to listen to. Unintentionally we'd done what we set out to do, so we ran off double quick. We weren't spotted, but that firm got the message not to fuck with us again.

Tony Davis came from a big family of Davises out of Edmonton, and was a very tough guy. I hadn't seen him for years, then he rang me up out of the blue and asked me to do a spot in a club he'd just opened in Stoke Newington. Without being flash, I was quite a big name then, but not too big that I couldn't help a mate out.

After my turn, we were talking at the bar and some geezer kept interrupting us. Tony was polite at first, then he got the hump, picked this guy up, threw him up the stairs then calmly beat the shit out of him. I'm thinking, 'Tony, old son, you haven't changed one bit from the old days.' If someone had told me he'd been shot to death I wouldn't have been one bit surprised, but considering the life he led, he died in a strange way.

About eight or nine years ago he went out early to pick up the Sunday papers and came across two geezers knocking seven bells out of each other. He's gone, 'Hold up, fellas – no need for that,' and broken them apart. Minutes later, he came out of the paper shop and one of them threw a jar of acid in his face. Burned his throat and lungs, and he died right there on the pavement. All because he tried to do a good turn.

Not long after the shooting at the flat, my relationship with Frankie went belly up. We didn't fall out, and it wasn't the last time I saw him, but it was the end of our association, and with that the firm as we knew it, as well.

It's only speculation on my part as to what happened, so it's not for me to say, as it may not be true, but one afternoon Frankie opened his front door and somebody shot him. One in each leg, then jumped on a motorbike and away. Hard as he was, and they don't come much harder, his bottle went. Apart from his own life, and the legs were probably just for starters, he had his wife and kids to think of, so he packed up and moved to Manchester. I wouldn't say for a quieter life, because by the time I caught up with him he was into something that absolutely terrified me.

Why is it that when other people's kids are born it usually goes without a hitch? Newborn babe, proud mum and dad, smiles all round. But when it's Reidy's turn, something has to go wrong.

Shirley had gone her full term and eventually she was taken into the hospital that had at one time been Gracie Fields's house. What a place. It was in The Bishops Avenue, where Hampstead runs into Finchley, and the road was known as 'Millionaires' Row', because all the big houses in it were fantastic. Anyway, during the war, Gracie had taken off to Capri and before she went, had given her home away to be turned into a maternity hospital.

So when I got the word I went flying up there. I copped hold of this black nurse, told her my name and she took me over to a glass-fronted room. We've gone down this line of babies until we came to mine, and he was swaddled top to toe in this white blanket. I couldn't wait to see him. The nurse uncovered his face and I went, 'For Chrissake.' She said, 'What's the matter? He's beautiful.' I said, 'I can see that, but he's as black as the ace of spades. No offence to you, darling.' She looked at a little band round his wrist and said, 'Baby Reid – yes, definitely yours.'

I've gone straight into one. The venom that sprung up in me was terrible. I found the room Shirl was in, stood in the door and shouted, 'You cow. How could you and me knock out a black baby?' She was well used to me flying off the handle, and all she said was, 'Shut up, Michael. All babies are dark right after they're born.' And she pulled back the sheet and showed me little Mark lying on her chest. Can you believe, two Reids in the ward at the same time? We laughed about it after, and still do, but my heart didn't stop banging for hours.

As I held my son for the first time, I couldn't have known the pain and tears that little scrap would cause us in years to come. Just as well we go into the future with our eyes shut, because at some point me and Shirley were going to suffer grief beyond imagination that would change us both for ever.

But right then I was bursting with pride. I had two healthy sons of my own, and two other kids who were mine in every sense other than the biological one. Unfortunately I didn't have much time for bonding, as they call it today, because I'd signed onto a cruise liner as Entertainments Officer, and I was leaving that same night.

Getting into this game was a combination of things all coming together. With my family growing up and Mark on the way, I told myself I'd lived on the edge too long, that it was about time I packed it in before I got myself into really serious trouble. It was getting beyond the stage of being a 'rascal', having a lark, when I could pick up a shotgun to settle a difference without a second's thought. And Frankie getting shot gave me the shits for weeks. I could've been next. I wasn't thinking of giving up the ducking and diving and picking up a bit of knocked-off gear – just the heavy stuff. With Frankie moved on and the firm less active, the temptation wasn't there anyway.

My bit of cabaret work took a turn for the better when I teamed up with a guy by the name of Danny Ray. We were doing an act where we got pre-recorded feedbacks to lines we were throwing out. In one sentence the act sounds about as exciting as watching paint dry, but believe me it was very funny, and we always got a good hand. We took this act all over the place. It was incredible experience for me because timing was everything – absolutely crucial, and that stood me in good stead in the years to come.

The only drawback with this routine was that it meant carrying bloody heavy amplifiers and tape equipment to every venue, and that's what brought this popular turn to an end. Carrying a couple of these hundredweight amplifiers up the stairs in one of the clubs, I slipped and fell to the bottom with the two bastards on top of me. I didn't break any bones but damaged a couple of vertebrae, with the result that I was advised by the doctor to pack up the lifting, which in effect meant knocking that particular act on the head. One little slip on those stairs, and I'm still paying for it today. Not only with back trouble but also in a lessening of my height.

Also, during the intervening years I'd done more trips in the merchant navy, and had been all over the world. So combining the fact I wanted to straighten myself out, my experience at sea and my bit of show-business work, everything seemed to come together when someone suggested I put myself forward as Ship's Entertainer.

At least, that's what I applied for, but once I got through the rigmarole of paperwork and interviews I came out the other side as Entertainments Officer. Posh title for the guy that does all the running around for the Cruise Director, who on my ship went by the name of Ray Savola.

The day my Mark was born I went flying off to New York. That's how it worked; the firm flew us out, then we picked up the liner at the other end ready to go to work. All the other times when I'd gone to sea, it had either been with the Castle Line that did South Africa, or with a big New Zealand company with their 'Rangi' boats. *Rangi Tana*, *Rangi Toto* and *Rangi Tiki*, which was the one I was on. This time it was completely different, and I was going to work on a luxurious liner that had been completely refitted at a cost of millions.

My side of things was a doddle. In essence, we were like holiday-camp redcoats and me being the top one, if you like, had to make sure everything was pulled together. But at the end of the day, if there were any problems they weren't mine to worry about. That was down to Ray Savola, and I wouldn't have had his job for a million pounds. I don't think I ever saw him when he wasn't pulling his hair out. Everything, but everything, had to go through him, whether it was the menus, the line-up for the cabaret or the layout of the tables. He spent the whole time with his head in his hands going, 'Oh, my God. Oh, my God', as he tore about from this deck to that deck.

We sailed out of New York mainly on seven- or ten-day cruises, and as the ship could strap up thirty knots, if we left in the evening we'd be docking in, say, Puerto Rico at five o'clock the next morning. We did all the West Indian islands and the Virgin Islands, places like Martinique and all that game – most of them at that time completely uncommercialized.

I must have visited about fifty of these islands, and at first it was a great novelty. As before, as soon as I'd done my duties I'd hire a bicycle and do the grand tour of all the bays and coves, checking out the wildlife and scenery; up and down the coastline, seeing how the people lived and absorbing their culture. Remember, this went on for about three months, and once I'd taken in a particular place the novelty wore off and I lost interest. After that, I'd either lie on my bunk reading for the day or, when that got too much, walk off the ship as far as the first bar at the end of the dock and get rat-arsed.

I was getting regular letters from my Shirley, and as time went on the tone was changing and it was obvious she was getting a bit pissed off with me being away 'enjoying myself', while she struggled to look after four kids.

I had to finish the time I'd contracted to do, but once that was up I decided not to sign on again and got myself home. The money was shit, anyway.

CHAPTER FIVE

ONE OF THE PROBLEMS SHIRLEY HAD TO PUT UP WITH WAS young Jimmy. He must have been about fourteen then, I suppose, and the little sod was running wild. Talk about take after his dad – me that is, not Jimmy Collins. The coppers were always knocking on the door over nothing. Stupid kid's stuff; broken a window here, nicked the odd motor there.

To be honest, I thought it was bloody funny, but as I had a responsibility I couldn't let him see that, so I was always giving him a talking-to. I remember one time four coppers came to the door looking for Jimmy. He'd been seen in some car, or something. It wasn't that, though; these four were pissed out of their brains, staggering, glassy-eyed and they'd driven up in a police car. I told them all to bugger off. I said, 'You've got two minutes and I'm phoning your nick.' And away they went.

Didn't do myself any favours, though, and I got no end of aggravation with them always chasing me up for no tax or speeding, or wanting to see my insurance papers.

As I said, it was crap money on that ship, and although I really did have the time of my life, that didn't pay the rent, so after about three months we were feeling the pinch again. So much so that I began to think I'd have to pull something off, even though I'd backed away from that sort of thing.

Then I got a letter from Shanos Lines, asking me to go to their offices in Shoreditch. I thought, if they want me to sign on again for pennies they could stick it up their arse, because it wasn't worth the earache I got from my old woman. I got myself up there anyway, and you could've knocked me down when they offered me the position of Cruise Director on the *Amerikanis*. Ray Savola had moved on to the *Franconia*, and it seemed I was their first choice to take over his position. I couldn't take it in. Me, Reidy, taking over this luxurious liner. OK, I wasn't going to be Captain, but even so, Cruise Director was an important job with terrible responsibilities, at least judging by Savola's carry-on it was.

When they said the money would be double what I was on before I almost signed on there and then, but I said, 'I'll have to speak to my wife', which I did, expecting her to go up the wall. Here was my newborn son nearly seven months old, and I'd seen him for less than half that amount of time, but in essence all she said was, 'A man has to do what a man has to do.' She pulled a face when she was saying it, but agreed it was a good move.

From the moment I phoned up and accepted until I actually started the job, my stomach was upside down. I was in constant dread of what I'd committed myself to and frightened that I'd make a total prat of myself two minutes out of dock. Silly really, to undersell myself, though I couldn't help what I felt. If I'd stopped to think, I was well qualified.

Outwardly I was full of front and confidence. I got on with everyone, I'd had experience and, as I think I mentioned, when it came to compèring or telling gags I was top of the tree. So if I'd given it any thought, my upcoming job would be a walkover. And it was. Oh, my God was it. It turned out to be farcical. That Ray Savola had either built up the apparent stress to make himself look like the President of America, or he was nowhere near the same calibre as I was.

All I had to do was delegate. Let's face it, all these individuals doing whatever it was they were doing knew the job inside out. None of them were monkeys. When the chef brought me the daily menus, all I did was sign them. I knew he wasn't going to serve up swill. Same with everyone else – 'Yes, thank you, that's fine. Carry on.' Piece of piss.

I had my own beautiful cabin, breakfast in bed and my own steward. A long, long way from that first trip I made with Dave and Kevin.

Although the *Amerikanis* was a comparatively old ship, the refit had made it almost brand new, so at every port we called into all the local dignitaries were invited on board for the grand tour. The mayor, chief of police, local politicians, everyone. One of my duties was to do what they called the 'port lectures', which is when I told the bloods what to see or what to expect on whatever island we visited. On top of that, on the understanding that I got a kickback, I'd recommend this shop and that store. Jewellers, fine ceramic places, carpets – you name it.

The most unbelievable store on my list was Reece's, on the Isle of St Thomas. It was then, and probably still is, the biggest liquor store in the world. It covered half an acre and sold every brand of booze that's ever been made.

In those days, it didn't matter if you were two or a hundred and two, every American was allowed one gallon of booze, duty free, to take back into the States. So if you had a family of five, that was five gallons going back.

Most of the time I had something like two thousand passengers, so you can imagine, Reece's looked after me like nobody's business. They asked me what my favourite drink was, which happened to be Rémy Martin, and after that, every week without fail I'd find six cases stacked outside my cabin. I could put a fair bit away but even I had my limit, so this stuff built up and built up. So much so that when it came to embarking, even though I gave a case to every officer, every dancer and all my mates, I still had to drop thirty cases of prime booze over the side to sink to the bottom. I couldn't take the risk of getting it off the ship, and I'll bet it's still lying there to this day.

One of our best ports of call was Puerto Rico, and what a place of contrast that was. You saw two totally opposite environments. The old part was riddled with poverty. Beggars, slums; terrible place. One step across the road, and you found yourself among magnificent beautiful buildings, and one of these was the El San Juan Hotel. Unbelievable – it had three thousand rooms and eight themed restaurants: Chinese, Japanese, Hawaiian, the lot.

I think it might have been one of the first times we docked in Rico, and because it was the biggest island, we knew we were going to get everybody and his auntie turning up for the bash we were throwing. So they asked me to lay on a special show. Every week we'd have different nights, i.e. a Parisian Night, a Moroccan Night, and so on. This night I decided we'd go Greek, because that's very lively with loads of dancing.

One of the team was Marti Webb, a young girl then and just starting out. She was a solo singer and lead dancer. Even to this day my old woman will swear that I gave her one, but she's wrong. I'm not saying I wouldn't have if the situation had arisen, but it never did. We were just mates, and she had this way of putting her head on one side when-ever she spoke to me. 'Hello, Mike. How are you?' 'Lovely, darling, lovely.' Nice girl, and a massive star now, doing musicals with Elaine Paige and other big names and when she's not doing those, she's very popular in the clubs and holiday resorts. Norman Collier was another one of the turns trying to make a living, and him and me would meet up some years later and make names for ourselves, but that was beyond our imagination at the time.

So I organized this show, and it was performed not only for the passengers, but about two hundred local dignitaries. The main chore-ographer and dancer was Greek himself. He went by the name of Paris, and was as bent as a nine-bob note, which has nothing to do with the fact that he got all these top people up and taught them all that Zorba stuff. Broken plates everywhere, but it went down better than we could have hoped for.

I did my bit, which to me now was like falling off a log, and all in this American accent I'd had to take on. About ninety per cent of the bloods on board were out of the States and I got tired of repeating myself. You'd think I was talking some foreign language to them. They'd go, 'Pardon me? Sorry? Say again?' and I'd be thinking stupid bastards on the inside, but with this big smile on my face. So to save myself getting wound up, I took to cutting the corners off my voice, and after a while could drop in and out of it as easy as breathing.

These people were so impressed by the do we gave them that they invited me and a load of officers to a big show that was going to take place in their pride and joy, the San Juan. Frank Sinatra and Dean Martin were going to do a one-night stand, so it was going to be well worth seeing, particularly for me, as Frank was one of my biggest heroes.

We turned up at the hotel and were taken to this enormous cabaret room. It had a vast ceiling covered in lights that looked like stars, brilliant chandeliers and a stage with marble steps leading down to the floor where all the tables were set out.

I'm just settling down, thinking, this'll do me, a front seat to watch these megastars, when the guv'nor came over to my table and asked me if I would honour them by compèring the show. OK, this was a bit of arse-kissing on their part because of all the business the ship was going to bring them, but nevertheless I was knocked out and didn't have to be asked twice – I was up and straight into my spiel. It was like sticking on a comfortable overcoat.

One minute I'm plain old Reidy – and this has applied all my life – the next, I'm Mike Reid the compère with all the gags and the timing. I introduced myself, then briefly talked about the *Amerikanis* and this beautiful hotel we were in and, 'Haven't we got a spectacular show for you tonight?' Funnily enough, I never let it show for a second that the two guys behind the curtains intimidated me.

The guv'nor took me backstage and introduced me to the regular compère. This fella himself was a black comic out of America, and a big name in his own right. The name Bill Cosby comes to mind, but memory being what it is I could be wrong. Either way, when the guv'nor said I was taking over for the night, I could tell he was well pissed off. He looked me up and down and stormed off without so much as a kiss-my-arse. Bollocks to him, this was my night.

First off, I brought on Dean Martin and he came on with a glass in his hand. I've got to hand it to him, he was as smooth as silk. What a showman. Straight into a number, and never faltered until he'd sung eight songs, which was surprising considering halfway through every one of them he crooned his way to the side of the stage, stuck his hand through the curtain and swapped his empty glass for a full one. I don't know about 'little old wine-drinker me', this was neat bourbon he was pouring down the hatch.

While he was on, I spent some time backstage with the man himself, Frank. Strange really, years later I was less nervous of shaking hands with the Queen than I was shaking hands with this worldwide legend. I'd love to be able to say that we discussed our individual careers, that I cracked him up with a few gags, or that he gave me some hints on how to pull the birds. But the truth is, everything that came out of my mouth was an unintelligible, stuttering mumble, but he was kind to me and told me I was doing a great job out there. I just stood there thinking, if only that lot in the Queen's Head could see me now.

With Dean finished, I went out and introduced Mr Sinatra, and he put on this routine to the backing of Axel Stordahl that I can see in my head today. It was magical.

Before he left, he gave me a photograph of himself signed, 'To my friend Mike', and I've still got it among the few bits and pieces I have kept. What would be nice would have been to have had a picture taken, arms round each other like two old pals, but I was so in awe of him I was too frightened to suggest it.

Tucked in the same suitcase, I've still got a certificate stating my qualifications as a 'Cruise Director', and God forbid I ever have to, but if I presented myself to any shipping company with that piece of paper, I'd be taken on immediately.

Once again, another string to my bow. I don't know what this says about me, but all my life I've looked to adding new skills to my repertoire. I suppose if I analysed it, it's some sort of unconscious fear of ending up on my arse. Each time I've learned something or had a go at something different, like the cruise game, I've come away with the thought that at least I can fall back on whatever it was.

Today, me and my family are very comfortable. By anyone's standards I'm successful at what I do, so it's ludicrous to even consider having to deliver coal, scratch around for a bit of scrap or get back into ducking and diving. But no-one knows what's around the corner, and I found that out at a point in my life when I was on the crest of the wave and, as I thought, financially secure. Within nine months I was wiped out. All I was left with in my pocket was dust. And although I didn't end up back on a car lot, it was close, and I would've done if needs be.

As it was, without any help from anyone other than my missus, I pulled myself back up by grafting my plums off twenty hours a day. That's why, no matter how it looks from the outside, I never become complacent about the position I find myself in today.

Back then, though, while I was pleased to have had that experience of being Cruise Director, and more than enjoyed myself in the process, I was even more pleased to be back with my family. I was holding folding, so I weighed out Shirley, kitted out the kids and bought a fridge and other bits and pieces. Didn't stretch to carpet on the stairs – that would have to wait for another couple of years, because I had my eye on a beautiful powder-blue Plymouth.

The word wasn't used then, but I was going to be a right poser, surrounded with all that chrome and pointed wings. Forget the HP, this was serious cash money. The motor was brand new, and if memory serves, I'd clocked up less than a hundred miles before it got smashed to bits.

I was sitting in our front room when I heard a crash. I've run out, and there's the Plymouth crunched up against the lamppost with a big old Bentley sticking out the side of it. When Old Bill turned up they practically had to lift this old doctor out of his car because he was too pissed to get out by himself. Never had a bump on him, but stank of booze and couldn't walk, let alone talk. They patted him on the head, took him home and then came back to tell me I was being nicked for having no lights on a main road. Welcome home Reidy.

I suppose it was lucky that I had insurance for a change, otherwise I'd have been pulled for that. But as it was only third party, all I could do was wipe my mouth and walk away from it.

It's funny really, if that's the word, but until I got myself established in the business where I made a name for myself, my life was full of contrasts. I took it all in my stride but time and again, perhaps as I was driving along in my lorry covered in shit, oil and grease, I'd think, was I really shaking hands with Frank Sinatra only a year ago? Or, if it was pissing with rain, I'd think of those tropical islands and all those birds with flowers in their hair.

I hadn't given up the idea of going to sea again, but I was settled enough doing my bits and pieces, so I'd no plans for getting back in that game for the foreseeable future. I suppose 'foreseeable' is the word – like I said, we never know what's round the corner.

I was knocking about with a fella called Bobby Cardew, who strangely enough had been one of Bertie Smalls's mob when we had that dust-up. That was all forgotten about then, and me and him got on well, and we'd go to the drinking clubs together. We ended up in the Regency and Bobby ran out of money. I'm saying, doesn't matter, I've got enough for both of us, and he's insisting that we go back to his place so that he can pick up some of his own. We're wasting drinking time by arguing, so in the end we've jumped in my motor and shot off to where he lived.

The Plymouth was just a memory then, and I had a Chevy Impala. Just as impressive, even though it was on the knock. It was well known all over the manor, and that's what got me in a mess.

While he was indoors getting his wedge I parked in the yard next door, watching a beautiful big dog that was sitting in the passenger seat of a greengrocer's lorry. As Bobby climbed in beside me, just for conversation I said, 'See that big chow in the lorry, I've heard they're really vicious when they get going.' He looked at me, looked at the dog and said, 'Fucking vicious? Leave it out.' And to prove his point, he's got out of the car, opened the cab door on the lorry and flung this chow out into the road by the scruff of its neck.

As the dog's gone yelping up the road, its owner came flying out of one of the houses shouting, 'Oi, what's going on?' Now Bobby's a bit of a handful, so he's told the geezer to piss off back indoors. As he turned he mumbled 'Wanker', or something, so Bobby's made a grab for him and caught hold of his coat. Of course, this slippery bastard's wriggled himself out of it and run off down the road. Bobby's slung his jacket on the ground and we've driven off laughing.

We slipped back into the Regency, had a good drink and I thought I'd better head for home. As I turned into my road I could see four squad cars outside my house, so I did the quickest three-point turn you've ever seen and took off.

I gave it a couple of hours before I rang Shirl to see what was going on. I was in two minds. One, I was shitting myself, but two, I knew I hadn't been up to anything for about a month so there had to be some mistake.

When I got through, Shirley started screaming at me, 'What have you done? They want you for robbery with violence.' I could hardly speak, but I managed to say it was all a misunderstanding. 'Well it's a bloody big one then,' she said, 'because the bloke says he was beaten up and his jacket nicked with all his money in it. Somebody got your number, and they're still outside waiting for you.'

Standing in that phone box, my legs went to jelly. 'Sweetheart,' I said, 'I promise you I'd nothing to do with it, but I'm between a rock and a hard place. If I tell them what happened I'll be grassing up Bobby Cardew, and I can't do it. Look, don't worry. I'm going to slip away for a bit until it gets sorted. I'll be in touch soon.'

Am I in the shit or what? Robbery with violence don't come any worse unless it's with a shooter. With my MO I could be facing a ten. Shit, shit, shit. I couldn't think straight. All I wanted to do was get away as far as possible, so I drove into town using all the backstreets, parked my too distinctive motor in a mate's lock-up and jumped on the first train out of Liverpool Street.

It pulled into Grimsby of all places, in the early hours of the morning. Without even stopping for a cup of tea I headed straight for the docks and signed myself onto the first available boat. Straight off the street and into a job. And no wonder: who in their right mind would volunteer to spend time on a fishing trawler heading for Iceland? Pity I hadn't got on a train going to Southampton – I could've ended up in the tropics.

As it was, I ended up living in one of the worst nightmares of my life. Every one of the crew was a hairy-arsed jock and as tough as nails. I hadn't learned much from my very first trip in the merchant, because I still thought I was prick the bishop. I thought I could have a fight, but for the first few days I was knocked from arseholes to breakfastime. 'Hold up, Jock' – bang. 'Piss off, Hamish' – bosh.

First off, my nose was bleeding from the good hidings I was getting, then once I'd learned to keep my gob shut it was bleeding from the cold. I'd be gutting cod at twenty below, rub my nose and down would come the claret. All the hairs in my nose had frozen and turned to needles.

Five o'clock in the morning: 'Reidy, Reidy – de-rig, de-rig', which basically meant de-ice the rigging, so I'd have to fall out of my bunk, grab an axe and chop inches of ice off every surface it had built up on. Didn't matter if the boat was pitching and tossing or there was a force-nine gale, it still had to be done or eventually the weight would turn us over.

If that trip taught me nothing else, at least it made me look at a plate of cod and chips with a different eye, and by the time my twenty-four days were up, I had learned to respect those trawlermen for the tough life they have to live.

First thing I did when we tied up back in Grimsby was to phone up my Shirl, and she told me to phone the detective in charge of the case. All the way into port that morning, as we came in sight of land, I can remember looking through binoculars shitting myself in case the police were lined up on the quay.

I rang the detective and it turned out I knew him. He told me to come home because it was all squared up, but I wasn't so sure. 'Yeah, I come home and you'll be waiting to nick me.' 'Reidy,' he said, 'do yourself a favour. I'm not playing games with you here, it's all been cleared up and there'll be no nickings.'

Was I pleased to get home. What had happened was some kids had found the jacket and naturally pinched the money that was in it, but this didn't come to light for a few weeks.

A lot of people said I was an idiot for running off when it could've been sorted, but I don't know. At the least, I would have been locked up for nearly three weeks, and at the worst I wouldn't be the first person to go down for something he didn't do. That really woke me up. No, more than that: what could have happened terrified me, and I made up my mind that this time I really was going to straighten myself out.

At about this time, I got an offer that excited me beyond imagination from the man who'd been getting me work for years. This was Benny Palmer, the biggest one-night booking agent around. I'm not talking major stars here, but if there was a turn wanted for any function, stag dos, dinners or clubs, he was the man everyone went to. He knew what I was all about, not only as a comic and compère, but that I could be relied on. So he pulled me into his office one day and told me that he was going to expand his interests, move into new premises, but best of all, he wanted me to go in with him as a partner.

Suddenly everything was coming together at last. I told Shirl that finally all my years of grafting, being reliable and tearing about being the funny man had been recognized, and the only way from now on was up. Me an agent, suited and booted and working out of a plush office? Incredible.

It never happened. Weeks and weeks went by without a word from Benny, and the next thing I heard was that his new business was up and running without me. Gutted doesn't put over how I felt. It was as though I was of so little account he'd shit on me without a word of explanation. With my dream flying out the window I was terribly disappointed, but more than that, I was hurt by the fact that he could have done that to me.

Then I got angry, and made up my mind to fight back. I kitted out our basement with a desk, filing cabinet and other bits and pieces. I stuck a phone in and said to Shirl, 'Go on gel, get on that blower, we're going into business ourselves.' And that was the start of the Goodnight Agency that took away fifty per cent of Benny Palmer's acts and clients. No, not took away as such, they followed me, because they knew I could get them better deals.

While we kept it going we made a good name for ourselves. But like a lot of things in my life, when something has run its course the edge goes off it and I walk away. And that's what I did. But I'd proved myself, and made a point in the process.

My life has always been a series of doors closing and others opening. And shortly after the agency venture, a pal of mine suggested that I had a go at the film extra game. He'd done a fair bit, and reckoned it was the easiest money he'd ever earned. Why not? It might be another string to the bow, and I wouldn't have to go away from home for months on end.

He was right – it was marvellous. Seven and a half hours sitting on our arses, then half an hour poncing about in the background of whatever they happened to be shooting. It had its moments, though, and one of these nearly ended me in the film business before I got started.

I was working on the Michael Bentine show, and we'd all been bussed down to Southsea to do a couple of scenes. There were four of us extras and we had to do some silly stuff in the sea, splashing about and all that, while he did his bit on the beach. It was summer, but freezing cold, and while we were doing one of these endless takes I couldn't help noticing a huge oil tanker going by about two miles out. Nothing out of the ordinary, so I never gave it another thought.

They called 'Cut', and the other three extras got out of the water and followed everyone else up the beach. For some reason I was further out, so I was a good bit behind them. I'm just getting to the shallows when a wave picks me up and smashes me face down on the pebbles. What no-one could've expected was that this monster of a ship had sent out a terrific wake and I'd been caught in it.

All the breath was knocked out of me and before I could move, the undertow dragged me backward straight into the path of the next wave. Whoosh. I was lifted up again and crashed back on the shingle. Three times this happened, and by then I was barely conscious. The fourth time I was dropped back, something scraped across my chest on the way down and I instinctively clutched at whatever it was. I was completely wasted, so I don't know where the strength came from to hang on while the sea tried to rip me out again. Then it stopped as suddenly as it had started, and it went all calm.

I just lay there for a couple of minutes, and when I got enough energy back to raise my head I found I was holding onto an inch-thick three-foot reinforcing rod sticking out of the shingle. I looked at the deep graze across my chest and realized that a fraction closer, and I'd have been impaled on it like a kebab, yet at the same time it had saved my life.

Remember I mentioned earlier about my brushes with near-death? The time I fell out the tree, and when the chimney collapsed? Well this was another one that made me think that whatever's up there was looking after me. Did I get a ton of sympathy from the crew? No. Somebody shouted, 'Oi, Reidy, stop pissing about. We're waiting for you on the pier.'

I worked for a long time on those Michael Bentine shows, and because he was a real goon and it was all about comedy, I tried to be funny myself, and this was never, ever, ever, ever appreciated by the star of the show. I'm not singling him out in particular, because I came up against it time and time again. What was the matter with these people? Were they so far up their own arses they thought everyone else was a mug?

I stress, I don't make myself out to be better than anyone else, but if the cleaning lady said to me, ''Ere's a good joke Mr Reid,' I'd listen, say thank you darling, and if it was crap I'd forget it. But just because I'm a professional doesn't mean that I've got a monopoly on telling gags, so if it had any merit at all I'd turn it around, add this, add that, make it my own and stick it in the act.

Unlike many other comics, I've never made a secret of the fact that I'd nick anyone's material. But to be fair to myself, I have to say that once I've given it the Mike Reid treatment, they wouldn't even recognize it themselves. I've never paid for a gag in my life, but it hasn't stopped me working for over forty years.

I treated the film extra job the same as everything else I've ever done: do it well or pack it in. I was always punctual, did what I was told to do, and because of that I got loads of work. I never looked like a choirboy, so all my parts tended to be villains, policemen or some tough guy or other. I mean, this wasn't acting by any stretch of the imagination, even though I got to say the odd line here and there, but I've always delivered the goods and my money was bang on the nail every week.

The mob I worked with over and over again, the other extras, were a mixed bunch, and that's what being an extra's all about. Doesn't matter how old you are or what you look like, you're there to fill a gap behind the main action. Don't get me wrong, I'm not knocking any one of them, but most of them weren't my cup of tea, so I found myself drawn to a group I could identify with.

These were the stuntmen and, I suppose, due to the nature of what they did they were like me, Jack the Lads. Not when it came to work, because that was taken very seriously, but off camera, in the long waits between scenes, they were always good for a laugh and a bit of a lark about. They were a great bunch of guys, confident in what they did and not a bit worried about sharing tips and experience with an up-and-coming young fella. In contrast to some extras, who were so desperate for a little bit of glory they would jump in front of you so their face was on camera and not yours.

Hours and hours I spent with those guys. Not that I was in their crew, but like I said, they were right up my street. We played cards, and I had them rolling about with gags. I don't remember how it came about, but out in the back lot at Shepperton a couple of these stuntmen were rehearsing some moves with a motor. Not on camera, just trying out a few things to see if they'd work.

I think you'll have gathered by now that cars are an abiding passion with me. If they look the business and have got something under the bonnet, I can't resist them. I have just got to get behind the wheel. And that's what happened on that film lot.

I'd obviously never mentioned to these fellas that I'd been driving since I was eight and nicking cars at eleven, so I don't know what they expected when they made sure I was well strapped in, but I've got to admit I did a bit of showing off. I took off like a dose of salts, screamed down this stretch of concrete, stuck the handbrake on and spun it in two circles, ending up facing the other way. I stuck my foot to the floor again, roared towards the stunt guys and drove on two wheels up a ramp, tilting the car in the air so I was driving at forty-five degrees. Dropping back down, I gave it another spin and parked up by the lads.

I made some crack about look out for your jobs, Reidy's taking over, but instead of laughing it off they said, 'Why not? You're a natural.' And that was that. A bit of flash driving and I was stringing that bow up again.

It didn't happen overnight, and it was some time before I actually performed stunts for real. I carried on with the 'extra' work, but during the long gaps I learned as much as I could. How to fall, how to roll; because what was drummed in endlessly was that safety came before anything, and that was down to no-one but yourself. Check your padding, check the scaffolding, check everything, then do it all over again. This is why you very rarely hear of stuntmen getting hurt or killed. It does happen, but considerably less often than, say, in the boxing ring.

The very first TV film I got roped into was nothing to do with cars. This was an episode called 'War Machines' in *Dr Who*, the one my old mate Roy Castle starred in with Peter Cushing. This was really a good earner, not so much for what we had to do but for what we were put through in make-up. I think the characters we were playing were some sort of alien soldiers, so we wore blond wigs, had our eyebrows dyed and the hair shaved off our chests and legs. And that sort of personal attack on your body merits double money. Us lot were blown up with the Daleks, so there was a lot of diving up in the air and all that.

One of the longest films I ever worked on was *The Dirty Dozen*. It just went on for ever, and the expense and waste was incredible. It put me in mind of when I had been in the merchant navy and seen whole sides of beef or crates and crates of fruit being slung over the side because they'd gone a bit trumpy. Stuff 'em, it's not my money – away you go. Same with this film.

For three months we were on standby, and did nothing except play cards and drink. That in itself gave me a sore head, and it was nothing to do with the booze.

Me and another couple of the boys were playing cards in one of the trailers. We'd been at it for about half an hour and Lee Marvin came in holding a bottle of Jack Daniel's. He sat there watching us, and all the time he was knocking the drink back. Then he invited himself into the game. Every time he played a hand he took another mouthful of the bourbon, until eventually he was like the character he played in *Cat Ballou*, slouched in his chair slurring his words and getting a bit stroppy.

We were only gambling with silver so it was no big deal, but because of the state he was in I don't think he won a hand. One of the lads who was sitting it out made coffee for all of us, and stuck this mug in front of Marvin just as I'd done him with a straight flush. Poor loser? That old bastard picked up the hot coffee and poured it straight over the top of my head. I shouted, 'You fucker', and jumped up so quickly the chair went over. And this geezer is so pissed or laid back all he does is belch and say 'Oops'. I wanted to punch his lights out, but I wasn't stupid. Imagine the headlines: 'World famous film star beaten up by minor stuntman'. No thanks. So I wiped my mouth – and my head and the front of my shirt.

Sober, Lee Marvin was as good as gold, and next morning I doubt whether he even remembered doing it, and I wasn't going to mention it.

As I said, the film went way over schedule, and that didn't get any better when the main set burned down. If you've ever seen the film, you'll know what I'm talking about. If not, look out for the French chateau.

The idea was that the dirty dozen were going to storm the place, so in the can they had all the scenes leading up to this, all the action, jeeps driving up and all that.

The night before they were due to film the final push, the chateau burned to the ground. Well, a mock-up of a chateau anyway, and it was going to take two weeks to rebuild. Nearly all the stars were from the States, and to put it mildly they were already cheesed off with this film. Two of the leading actors, Clint Walker and Trini Lopez, said, 'That's it. We're going home', and they did. So in the film, these two are in a jeep ready to go to work and then they disappear. No rewrite, no explanation that they've been vaporized in a bomb attack – nothing. Look out for it.

I'm as sensitive as the next bald guy when it comes to my biscuit, and over the years I've come to realize that if anyone's going to take the piss it'll be somebody with a head of hair like a mop. And that's what Roger Moore found when I was his stand-in on one of the Bond movies.

Outside the film game I'd done a bit of underwater work, so when I stuck that on my cv I was bound to get roped in somewhere along the line.

The scene I was in was shot at Crystal Palace swimming baths, because they've got portholes round the sides that were perfect for filming through. I had to do my stuff underwater, then as I climbed out the shot would cut to Roger. He'd had a bucket of warm water gently poured over him, so it appeared that he'd just got out of the tank. Between repeat takes he was sitting by the pool, and naturally his hair was a bit plastered down.

I was a young man then and had a lovely head of hair, and I'll swear it was done in all innocence, but while I was standing behind him I happened to say, ''Ere Rog. Going a bit thin on top, old son.' The way he reacted, anyone would think I'd slapped him. He jumped up, gave me a look to kill and stormed off. Never said a word – didn't have to. It might have been a coincidence, but I was chucked off the set the next day.

The list of stuff I've worked on is endless, and most of it is uncredited. Like my part as a policeman, of all people, standing outside court in that classic film of its period, *Up the Junction*. Although my name did come up on screen when I was a compère in an episode of *Steptoe and Son*.

I like to think I made a good job of whatever I did, whether I made a name for myself or not. But whenever cars were involved it was always the same thing: 'Get Reidy in'.

A major film springs to mind, and that's *The Devil Rides Out*, where they used a lot of vintage motors. These were hired from private owners, and as they were expensive and rare, invariably I was the one selected to nurse them around. I could be trusted, and that meant a lot to me.

One thing I never did, and have never done, was to brown-nose my way into a bit of work. If you were that way inclined there were always opportunities at Pinewood or Shepperton Studios to slip into the bar last thing and rub shoulders with producers or directors. Push yourself forward, give a bit of flannel, stroke these people up the right way and you could be down for some work on their next film. Not me. At the end of the day I was in the motor and off home to my family. If somebody wants me I make myself available if the price is right, but I'll never kiss anyone's arse so that I can earn a crust.

Anyway, the film work was my day job. At night I was doing stag functions all over the place. That meant I had to tear home from the studios, rush upstairs, bath, change and then just have time to kiss Shirl and grab a sandwich she'd put on the banister ready for me.

At different times when I didn't have a car for some reason, I'd use the lorry. I'd be out all day picking up scrap if the stunt work was a bit sparse, then, same thing. Home, quick sandwich and off. It must have been comical to see this geezer driving a beat-up old lorry, five tons of shit and metal on the back, while wearing a dress suit.

I even used to give the strippers a lift home in the same rig, and they didn't give a monkey's. They weren't earning fortunes, and a free lift was better than a kick in the arse, whatever it was in.

These strippers were gorgeous girls, and though my old woman might not have believed it, I never went near one of them. I was there as a compère, not to look at their tits. Most of the time I looked after them in case the punters got a bit lairy, so they trusted me.

The northern club circuit has always been a great area for work. Doesn't matter what's going on in the world, people in that part of the country will never miss their nights out at the club. So when work got a bit thin on the ground in the south, I found I was taking on bits and pieces all over Bradford or Manchester.

First of all I tried driving up, having a couple of nights, then driving back home. But it was knocking me out, and with petrol and lodgings to pay for I was only just breaking even. But I didn't really have too much choice. If you want to be in this game, you have to be where the work is or forget it.

A couple of other comics were in the same boat as me, away from home and backwards and forwards, so we decided to pool our resources and rent a flat between us. Bryn Phillips was a big guy and a good comic. Dave Swan was Welsh, same as Bryn, and a very funny man, so with the three of us webbed up together we had a load of laughs. It was like being single again, always out on the piss when we weren't working.

Every penny I earned, once I'd paid my share, went down to Shirl and the kids, so most of the time we were skint. The old woman wasn't too happy with this set-up, because while I'm having a laugh with the fellas she's stuck at home, and she must have got a bit lonely.

We took our bookings where we could get them, and the arrangement was whoever was working bought the grub. I think we had one white shirt apiece, and none of us had a clue about washing or ironing, so each time we needed to dress up we'd get a toothbrush, stick a bit of Surf powder on it and scrub just the collar and cuffs. To dry them off we got a wire coat-hanger and stuck it in a little slot in the ceiling where the paper had peeled back, and hung our shirts round this bare light bulb.

This set-up with the flat went on for months, and I was having a rare old time away from the responsibilities of home. In fact, I didn't show myself for so long I got a letter from Dad giving me a bollocking. This was similar to what Shirl had written on a couple of occasions when I was away on the ships. 'Get yourself home, son. You're not a single man any more, your family need you.'

He was right. Though I was only away to earn a few quid for Shirl and the kids, I suppose I was stretching it while I was enjoying myself, so I packed up and went back with my tail between my legs.

While I'd been sharing with the boys money had always been critical, and once I moved out it got worse for them, and subsequently they couldn't pay the rent and were kicked out. Bryn took off back to Wales, but Dave, who had to stay in the area for some reason, gave me a ring and said he was in the shit. I don't know what he expected me to do about it, but I did like the fella and tried to help him out. That meant a trip back up to Manchester to have a word with my old mate Frankie and his missus.

I'd seen him on and off while I was up there, and he'd been round our flat, so he vaguely knew Davey. So when I asked him to put Dave up for a little while he agreed to do it for my sake. Nicely sorted, I went back to whatever I was doing.

A month later Frankie's on the phone and he's going apeshit. 'Your mate's robbed me. I'm sorry, Mike, but I am going to kill the bastard when I find him.' And he meant it. What had happened, and I can understand desperation when you're a bit short, was that Davey had broken open Frankie's gas meter and nicked the money, which couldn't have been worth more than five or six quid. What got Frankie, more than the fact that he'd taken this bloke in and fed him, was the utter pettiness of what he'd done.

'Mike,' he said, 'if he'd stolen a grand off me I could half respect him, but for a bit of silver? He's nothing but a piece rubbish.'

I'm pig in the middle, and next thing it's Dave's turn to get on the blower. 'Mike, I think I'm in trouble.' 'Dave,' I said, 'don't think it, you *are* in trouble – the worst kind.' I put him in the picture. He made his living in the clubs and pubs, and I guaranteed him that the Frankie I knew would scour every one of them until he found him. By now he's crying down the phone. I told him I couldn't make any promises, but I'd do my best to turn it round.

I got back on to Frankie, called in all the favours I could think of, and, to cut a long story short, he agreed to forget it if Davey had the guts to apologize face to face.

When the three of us met up I was shitting myself, and it was nothing to do with me. Dave, though, looked like death warmed up. He was convinced this was a set-up and he was going to be shot. He stuttered this apology out, swearing he'd meant to pay it back, and Frankie shook his hand with his right. And with his left he gripped the back of Davey's neck and squeezed very slowly. If ever a squeeze spoke volumes, that one did. He said, 'If you ever, ever turn someone over for pennies again, I will come after you. Be lucky.' And that was the end of it. Cost me a lot of time and a lot of aggravation, but I did it for a very good friend – a friend, it would turn out, that when it suited him had the memory of a goldfish.

Back home, as time went on, life was pretty stable. The kids were growing up. Shirley had put a nice home together and what with earning regular, we'd even managed to carpet the stairs – something that had bugged the missus from the day we moved in.

Best of all, her and me were getting on better than we'd ever done. It wasn't always like that and, like I said before, could we have a row when it came to it.

I got into a game of cards one night with Reggie, Ronnie and a couple of others on their firm. I was playing a blinder – poker I think it was – and as the evening wore on this pile of money in front of me is growing and growing. It got to two o'clock, three o'clock, and I was still ahead. But I was in a bit of a dilemma. Do I say to these fellas, 'Excuse me, chaps. I'd better ring my wife and see if she'll let me stay out late', or do I go against the unwritten law of card-playing and walk out holding the large bunch of folding I've taken off these blokes?

I wasn't sure which option scared me most, her indoors or the Twins. I've looked at the two of them, given it half a second's thought and played on until about six in the morning. By then they've nicked most of my winnings back off me so they're well happy, but I'm in the shit.

My old woman used to get these funny ideas that I was putting myself about. Seven o'clock I tried the front door and it was locked. So I stepped back and called up to the bedroom window. 'Sweetheart, darling, I can't get in.' Wallop. The window opened and down came my best suit, then my shirts, followed by everything else I owned. She's screaming, 'Bastard. I know what you've been up to', and curtains are flying back all up the street. I grabbed my gear, stuck it in the motor and pissed off.

She cooled off eventually, but even today she's the most un-reasonable woman to have an argument with. I don't mean a fight; I'm talking about differences of opinion. I'll say, 'No, darling, this is the way it is.' 'Not listening.' 'What you've got to understand —' 'Not listening.' 'Please, Princess ...' 'Bollocks.' God, she wins every time.

If I make a move towards her she'll chuck herself back in an armchair, kick her legs in the air and pedal away like she's riding a bike shouting, 'Don't you hit me, you big bully.' I never have and she knows I wouldn't, so we always end up pissing ourselves laughing.

One time, I took myself off in a rage. This was in the early days, and I'd got the hump over something, so I'm chucking all my stuff into bags and telling her, 'That's it, we're finished.' I didn't have much so it only took me two minutes, then I took off to Mum's or Frankie's. I must have just come in from work because I had my boots on.

When I came to get dressed up to go out, I've only got one shoe of the only pair I had, so I had to polish up these oily old boots and suffer them when I went up the club.

Three days, and I'd had enough and wanted to go home, but I was too proud to admit that I'd been in the wrong. In the end I went round to our house on the pretext of getting this shoe. As soon as she opened the door I told her I wasn't coming back, all I wanted was this shoe. Do you think I could find it?

Time went on and she said, 'You might as well have a bit of dinner.' I had that, then carried on looking as though my life would fall to pieces without that piece of poxy footwear. In the end I must have worn her down and she said, 'Are you staying, or what?' Funnily enough, I had all my belongings in the motor and it was inside in half a minute.

CHAPTER SIX

D URING 1967, I WAS WORKING ON THE SPOOF BOND FILM *CASINO Royale*, when I got a letter that changed the relationship between Shirley and me. It was my divorce papers, 'absolute' as they call them, and this meant that the mistake I'd made as a teenager with Sheila was put right and I was free to marry Shirley.

She was never one of those women that keep on about tying the knot and proving my commitment. But once I had that piece of paper in my hand, I didn't have to think twice and I said to her, 'Sweetheart, when this film's out of the way, how do you fancy getting married?' Her face lit up. All she kept saying was, 'Do you mean it? Do you mean it?' and I knew I'd made the right move.

Thirty years later, even though we've had our share of problems, I still reckon that was the best day's work I ever did.

As it turned out, it led to more than just bringing Shirl and me closer together. Things that happen in your life have a knock-on effect. Turn left, you go one way – turn right, complete opposite direction. So by getting married, going where we went, doing what we did, that led us to a change in lifestyle that then was beyond our wildest dreams.

This was February, though, and it was wet, cold and miserable, so we settled for August to do the business. That meant Shirl only had six months to get a dress sorted. In two minutes, she was into the catalogue and laying out a tanner a week on a little white dress with red spots on it that cost two pounds two and six. I can still see it now. In fact, if I went upstairs I could see it for real, because it's still in her wardrobe, and even today she can still fit into it without breathing in.

Come the day, we turned up at Redbridge registry office with a couple of our mates, Ernie and Sally, paid the fee, did the honour-and-cherish bit and it was all over in ten minutes. Not the most romantic of set-ups, and we didn't even have a camera, so the only memories of that day are in our heads.

It was going to be nearly twenty-five years before my Shirley got the wedding day she should have had then, and that was when we retook the vows in our little local church. Believe me when I tell you that she was as beautiful then as she was back in 1971.

Once the formalities were over, we couldn't wait to get down the Redbridge Arms and push the boat out – and did we. By the time we fell out of the place, Sally and Shirl were paralytic, giggling, falling over – a right state. Ernie and me weren't half as bad, though I doubt we'd have passed a breathalyser if they'd had things like that then. Don't ask me why, but Shirl got in the front with Ern, and Sally fell in beside me in the back. They were probably so pissed they couldn't tell the difference between the two of us.

Off we went, and they're laughing and screaming. I should have guessed what was going to happen when Sally went quiet, but I didn't. We did another half-mile, then she turned to me with a funny look on her face and vomited all over me. I'm covered from neck to ankles and shouting, 'For Christ's sake, Ernie, stop the motor.' I'm pissed off about my suit, and he's got the hump with the mess in his car, plus the fact that the girls are wetting themselves with hysterics, so we slung them both out. I've still got this picture in my mind, looking back as we drove off, of those two, with their heads in the gutter and their arses stuck up in the air.

They both turned up at home a bit later in a taxi, and we had a good laugh. What a start to twenty-eight years of married life – but I wouldn't change her for the world.

I won't call it a honeymoon because when you've been together fourteen years, got four kids and have been through hell and high water together, the word doesn't sort of fit in, so I'll say we took a holiday in Folkestone.

Jimmy was nineteen by this time, and much to my relief had moved in with his girlfriend sometime before. I mean, I loved the boy as my own, but I've got to say he brought a load of aggravation to the door, what with the law and bits and pieces he got up to. Nothing worse than I got up to at his age, but I was trying to get away from all that, so with Old Bill watching him, they were watching me as well and I didn't need it.

Angela was thirteen and too grown-up to take a holiday with Mum and Dad so she stayed with a mate, leaving Michael and Mark to go off with us.

We booked into a hotel, and to put it mildly the two boys were a bit boisterous. Going back to my own childhood, I always felt that my mum had kept me on a tight rein. In hindsight that was wrong, but that didn't alter the fact that that's how I remembered it. I made up my mind that it would be different for my own kids, so to this end I gave them their heads until they were about eight years old. After that it was a case of OK, you've had your formative years without too much aggro, now it's time to step into line. Michael was a year past this benchmark, but Mark was only six and the two put together drove the people in the hotel mad. I suppose I should have checked them, but I wasn't too old myself, and didn't see any harm in a bit of high spirits.

Different today, though. If I'm staying somewhere and there's kids playing up, I want to tell the parents to keep their children under control.

Upshot was, straight after breakfast on the first morning the manager asked us to leave.

I've slung everyone in the motor and just taken off. Didn't have a clue where we were going, but I just loved driving and getting my foot down. We did about a hundred miles in no time, and I said to Shirl, 'Another hundred and we could be in Minehead. How do you fancy going to Butlin's?' She's up for it, and the boys are shouting, 'Yeah, yeah.'

We got there, were given a lovely chalet, and the kids could get up to whatever they wanted without bothering anybody.

On the Monday, I noticed on the posters all round the camp that apart from 'Best Looking Granny', 'Knobbly Knees' and a beauty contest, there were a couple of competitions, one for singers and the other for comics.

With nothing to lose, and the chance of winning a couple of quid I stuck my name down for both of these. For the singing one I did that song they use for the TV series *Birds of a Feather*, 'What'll I Do'. I walked it. For the comedy routine the next night, I did a cleaned-up version of what I'd always done in the clubs. Not my stag material – if I'd cleaned that up I'd have only been left with, 'Hello, I'm Mike Reid'. I walked away with that first prize as well.

I'd only entered these things for a bit of a laugh really. Whether the details weren't on the posters, or I was a bit slow I don't know, but what I didn't realize was that there was more to be gained than a ten-pound note and your name in the local paper.

One of the organizers took me to one side and told me that although I'd won two competitions, I'd have to choose one or the other if I wanted to carry on through the heats. I said, 'What do you mean? I thought I'd won and that was that.' 'No,' he said. 'If you want to carry on either as a vocalist or a comic, but not both, you'll come back here for an area final. If you win again, you'll go through various other finals, and with a bit of luck end up at the main event that's held at the London Palladium. You've got a good voice, and though there's no guarantees, you could end up with a recording contract, so think about it.'

That night in bed I said to Shirl, 'Bloody hell, this is a turn-up. What do you think?' She said, 'You'll win every one of them – go on, give it a go.'

I weighed up all the pros and cons, and came to the conclusion that there were too many singers out there who were far better than me. But good comics were a bit thin on the ground, and without blowing my own trumpet I was a good comic, so I went for that.

I passed every contest through every Butlin's camp, and if memory serves, there were about nine back then. I went back to Minehead, then it was Jaywick down Clacton way. Caerphilly in Wales, Canvey Island, Barry Island and the others escape me.

Winning every one was a feat in itself when you consider the numbers of people there were involved. Summer seasons are shorter now for some reason, but then they were twenty-six weeks long.

Every contest took in roughly sixty people every week for the whole season, and without going into all the mathematics of it, by the time it came to the grand final, the entrants had been up against nearly twenty thousand other acts.

Another thing I found, and it still applies today, is that amateurs never get further than halfway along the line. What happens, and who can blame them, is that pros and semi-pros go to these camps with no other purpose than entering the talent contests. So what chance has Uncle Fred got singing 'Lonesome Cowboy', or some young kid telling corny gags?

By the time I reached the London Palladium, I've got to say I was very nervous and up against stiff competition. I was nervous, because although it had all kicked off as a bit of a laugh, as time had gone on I'd started to think about where it all might lead. I'd always had that burning desire to make something of myself in whatever I tried to do, but when it came to it, I worried about whether I really had what it takes.

Anyway, we had rehearsals and I was well pleased with how my bit went. I did my comic routine and finished off with a song. Afterwards Hughie Green, the main man and one of the judges-to-be, came up to me and told me that I had something. But he suggested I drop the song and make sure I stuck rigidly to the five-minute slot we were allocated. OK, he knew more about the game than I did.

We did the show and another comic knocked me into second place. If we're talking professionals here, Joey Kay couldn't kiss my arse as a performer, and that's not green-eye because he beat me – it's been proved, because he's never been heard of since. One of the reasons he got the edge on me was that he went against the instructions we'd been given by going two minutes over his time and finishing up singing, 'Scooby Doo, I Wanna Be Like You', that number from *The Jungle Book*. Now, audience reaction has got to swing the judges' vote one way or another, and this fella had brought coachloads of his mates down from Liverpool. Reidy? All he had was his mum, dad and missus cheering him on.

Diddy David Hamilton was another one of the judges, and wasn't he full of himself. He came up to me pointing his finger, going, 'Oh, you're such a rude person.' I just ignored him.

When it was all over, Hughie Green got me on my own and said, 'With your great talent and my know-how you could go a long way in this business, so for a start I want you to appear on my show *Opportunity Knocks*.' I went, 'No thanks.' He said, 'Michael, you don't understand – I'm talking about television.' I was polite, but I told him I wasn't interested.

Three or four days later I got a letter from HG Enterprises, on posh green paper. 'Following our conversation the other night – very talented – long way to go – star in the making – blah, blah, blah.' It finished with, 'This is an official invitation from ATV for you to appear on *Opportunity Knocks*.' I ignored it. But he wasn't going to let go of it.

A couple of days later he phoned me up. He gave me the same old flannel, then out of the blue he said, 'If you're worried about the show, I'll repeat, with your talent and my personal backing, I am sure you will win.' I couldn't honestly put my finger on what it was, but an inflection in his voice made me think he was trying to suggest a bit more than just the words he was saying. I told him I'd think about it, and I did.

I said to Shirl, 'I might be picking this up all wrong, but if I can't make it in show business under my own steam, then I don't want to know.' Sounds a bit moralistic, considering I'd been a ducker and diver all my life, but this was important and I meant it.

Years and years later, one of the papers was running a list of all those people who'd made it after *Opportunity Knocks* – Freddie Starr and all the others. And up the top they've got Mike Reid. I phoned them up. 'Whoa – excuse me, not Reidy, old son,' and they rubbed it out.

Right or wrong, I'd heard rumours on the grapevine that once Mr Green had kick-started someone into the limelight, or should I say before he gave them a start, he wanted a signature giving him a percentage of future earnings. Whatever, there was no way I was going to run the risk of putting myself in the position of being owned by anyone.

I don't knock the show, though. It was a fantastic showcase for talent that otherwise might never have seen the light of day. Since it came off the air there has been nothing to replace it – nothing. And that saddens me, for the entertainment industry as a whole. Because when it comes to all the major jobs that new talent should be fronting, it's left to all the old faces – Jim Davidson, Mike Reid, Jimmy Tarbuck and others like us. It grieves me that youngsters haven't got the chance we had of being seen by millions.

I've had my day, made my luck and a fortune at the same time, and I'm still there because no-one else is getting a chance to come through. OK, there are people out there saying what about Ben Elton, Eddie Izzard and others like them. But I'm not convinced, after watching these alternative comedians, as good as they are, that any one of them could fill a pier in this country throughout a summer season. Perhaps I'm too old to understand the humour, but in my opinion you cannot beat a good old-fashioned comic.

So I stood on my moral high ground and kicked myself in the bollocks, but it didn't worry me a bit.

I may have said it before, but I think our lives are mapped out for us. If something's supposed to happen, it will.

I'd enjoyed the months of all the heats, and proved beyond any doubt that I was more than good at what I did.

A footnote to that earlier story about my good friend Dave Swan is that, a while after me and him parted company, he was fortunate enough to win *Opportunity Knocks* twice. Television being the wonderful medium it is can make you famous overnight. Be seen on that little box and half the country knows your face. A hairdresser might have a two-minute slot doing an interview or whatever, and suddenly she's a celebrity, if only locally. 'See you on telly the other night', and all that. So in a bigger way Davey's exposure on *Opportunity Knocks* slung him straight into the limelight.

I was in Manchester for something or other, and I noticed he was appearing at a big club, The Nightspot in Chorlton-cum-Hardy. The place was packed out to see this new talent that had been on television, and give him his due, he went down a bomb. I love to see people making a success in any walk of life, but in this case, because we'd been through some tough times together, I was doubly pleased for him.

He came off stage and I was standing there with a drink in my hand. As he came towards me I put my hand out and said, 'Dave, that was brilliant. You're doing well for yourself, son.' He ignored my hand, got my cheek between his two fingers, gave it a little rattle and said, 'Eee, everyone's come to see me tonight,' and carried on walking past with his nose right up his own arse.

I was really hurt. Then I was angry and I thought, 'You stuck-up twat. I should've let Frankie kill you.' I never saw him again from that day to this, though I understand he's still working the smaller rooms in Vegas.

Still, what goes around comes around, and not long after that Granada Television put on a new comedy show. This turned out to be a new concept that no way followed the old pattern of a talent contest or nothing like it, but was a show made up of unknown comics from all over the country.

Up to that time, although I had great ambitions to make something of myself, I never really thought I had enough ability to go on TV. At the same time, I had it in my head that you had to be something far more aspiring than I was, so I never considered pushing into that medium. That was until I watched the first run, and realized that I was at least the equal of any one of the acts.

I had actually done quite a lot of TV work, but being hidden under a hairy mask, or to be seen for two seconds being blown up in the air, wasn't really in the same league as standing all alone in the spotlight doing a routine. I thought about it and thought about it, talked it over with Shirley, then made up my mind to give it a go and get myself onto this TV show.

I got hold of a phone number, and got through to one of the studio offices and came up against a very professional girl by the name of Lucinda. Her job was to make sure people like me went through the proper channels, and I was getting nowhere. So I turned on the Reidy charm. Once I got her laughing I was halfway there, so I said, 'Give us a break, darling. Just tell me how I can get hold of the main man', and she gave me a number.

I got straight on it, stuck a plum in my mouth to get past another secretary, and waited and waited and waited. I was just thinking, I'm getting the old runaround here, when this geezer came on the line sounding like he'd run up ten flights of stairs. I jumped in and told him I wanted a slot on his new programme, and he went up the wall.

'Who are you? I was in a very important meeting. How did you get this number?'

Normally, if someone hasn't got the manners to talk to me with a bit of civility, I'll tell them to stick it up their arse, but having come this far I kept my cool; told him I was Mike Reid, a comic, and that Lucinda had given me his phone number.

He burst out laughing. 'Well,' he said, 'if you can get through her you must have something. Give me a couple of gags.' Dropping into this was as easy for me as it is for other people breathing – bang, bang, bang. I've thrown four jokes straight at him, and he went, 'Whoa – that'll do, you're in.'

Some time after, I showed up at their Manchester studio to do the business. Now this was the second series, so almost all of the other fellas had been through it all before. Yet in my innocence I really did think that we were all in the same boat – nervous, excited, and hoping that this was going to lead to the big break. Well, I thought we were all in the same boat, but it turned out that muggins here was in the water. Because not one of those other guys wanted to give me the time of day. They were all from the northern circuit, had made a name from the first series and I was given the cold shoulder because, it seemed to me, I was from the south, and in their opinion one of those flash bastard cockneys.

It wasn't the first time and wouldn't be the last that I would be stereotyped as a gangster, conman or someone who'd nick your watch at the first opportunity, simply because of the way I talked. I thought, 'Stuff 'em', did my bit, which went down well, and grinned to myself all the way back to London.

Perhaps I was wrong about why the other guys appeared to shut me out, because once my first show was in the can, I've got to be fair and say their attitude changed. Frank Carson was the first one to break the ice when he came up, slapped me on the back and told me he thought I'd done well. After that, the other fellas soon came round and there was never any more friction.

Getting back to normal at home, I didn't have a clue as to what a monster this show was going to be for me, or how it would affect my life and my family. I had to wait three or four months before it hit the screens to find out.

In the meantime, I got the last nicking I would ever get, other than for motoring offences.

Our Jimmy came round one night with a very nice television set, and asked me if I wanted to buy it for thirty quid. Knowing what my stepson was like in those days, I had to ask him if it had been thieved. He looked at me as though I had said something out of order. 'Dad, would I offer you something that was hot?' A couple of days later Old Bill are banging on the door looking for this telly. Turned out it was nicked, and the geezer who'd had it away was lifted for something else, grassed up Jimmy and pointed the law at my house thinking he lived with us. What could I say? This thing's blaring out in the corner of the room. They've taken it away and me with it, and two weeks later I got a heavy fine for receiving.

Could have been worse. A few months later the TV people would've gone boss-eyed and totally kicked me into touch. My television debut would never have happened, nor the stardom that followed. That was before I was a name, yet strangely enough, if it happened today it wouldn't affect my career, and I'd go so far as to say it might enhance it.

Whenever I have been in trouble and there's been a bit of a spread in the papers, if I'm appearing in a club the same night the audience go wild when I walk on stage. 'Eheheheheh – Reidy! Reidy!' and giving it all that bowing, arms waving 'we're not worthy' stuff that youngsters seem to do these days. It's just to show that they're right behind me, no matter what crap has been printed in the dailies.

What is funny as well, is that back then you could go on stage and tell gags that would not be tolerated now. Nothing was sacred. No such thing as 'political correctness', and half of us would be doing ethnic jokes that would get us slung inside today, and they weren't only accepted, they were applauded.

I'm not saying it's wrong that that sort of material has gone out the window, but in essence, it was never vicious or intended to provoke – just funny. And I'll bet you most of these minorities laughed as loud as anyone else.

I do remember watching that first episode of *The Comedians* that I was appearing in, and being well pleased with my performance. I wasn't camera shy; I was full of myself, and every one of my gags went down well. After that, and for the rest of my career, I don't think I watched myself on television. Bits and pieces here and there, but like most performers, I've never seen the point of getting wound up over a performance where it's too late to change a fluffed line or mis-timed gag.

Even on that first night, I still thought this was just another bit of work, and couldn't imagine the impact it was going to have. It was a phenomenon, and as time passed it got bigger and bigger.

There was a story in one of the papers that, according to their infor-mation, twenty-four people were killed in road accidents directly related to *The Comedians*. People were rushing and tearing about in their cars so they could get home and watch the show. That's the sort of draw it was. Massive.

Overnight we all went from relative obscurity to being recognized in the streets. Though it took a while for our names to be on everyone's lips, and for a couple of years I'd get people coming up to me and saying, 'You're Wallop, ain't you?' or, 'You're that geezer T'rific on the telly.'

I think an exception to this was Charlie Williams. He was a black comic with the broadest Yorkshire accent. 'Eh, lad. Eh bah goom', and all that – never been seen before, and he caught on straight away. I used to stand in the wings and watch him and think, 'Jesus, this fella's got magic.' He had a marvellous rapport with the audience, and they just loved him. I'd say he was the mainstay of the show, and we all came second-best to him.

Like I said, once the other guys got to know me, all that giving me the elbow went out the window and we got on well. But it took a long while to break down the Liverpudlians, because as far as they're concerned, no other city in the world comes close to being as good as Liverpool, and they are so proud of the fact. I have to agree that great humour has poured out of that place, but they do have a tendency to go over the top with their opinions.

Once the show hit the air the phone never stopped ringing. Though it was the TV that stuck my name up front, you have to remember that this was only one night a week. It was the spin-offs that really brought the work and the money in, so I was all over the country appearing at this club and that club.

Whenever I was in Manchester I'd either call in and see, or stop over with, Frankie and his missus. I think he was going through a bad patch, and though nothing was said, in so many words I was always pleased enough to dip my hand in my pocket and come up with a bit of rent.

When we'd been knocking about with the firm in Tottenham, he was my closest friend. So when I knew he was running a bit short of the readies, I never gave it any thought, other than in the back of my mind I kept remembering the thirty-four quid he'd generously given me to pay off Joe Gurber.

Then one time his missus asked me some favour or other on behalf of her old man, and I said, 'Sorry, darling, I'd love to help but right at this moment I'm over my head with work.' She tore into me like a wild thing. 'Fucking good friend you turned out to be', and all that. 'You've soon forgotten what my old man done for you now you're a big star.' I was gutted, hurt, and needless to say, our relationship came to a shuddering halt.

Frankie's missus had gone down the path that all my old friends were eventually going to take. I swear I never changed from when I made two quid a week until I was earning hundreds, but suddenly I was pushed away by everyone I'd grown up with. I walked away in the end, but I wouldn't have done if I hadn't been pushed.

I got tired of the constant ridicule and of being dug out. 'Oh yeah, new suit. How many you got now?' 'Hello, 'ere comes old money-bags, he'll get this round in', and so on. I thought, 'Bugger it – I don't need this', and moved on. But that's not to say I wasn't hurt, and that even to this day I still miss my old mates.

Even now, I can be doing a bit of work and somebody will come up and ask me if I remember them from the old days. Yeah, I do. We shake hands, have a natter, then once we've run out of 'Do you remember this? Do you remember that?' it all goes flat. We've got nothing in common any more, no conversation – we're worlds apart. Great shame, but it's a fact of life.

Going back to Frankie: we never fell out as such, but he went his way and I went mine, and the phone never rang.

Though what I did hear some years later was that he went down for a ten-stretch for something he never did. I think I've used the term before, what goes around comes around, and that's what happened to Frankie. Or, as the law might put it, poetic justice, because as far as they were concerned he was owed a bit of time for the things he'd got away with over the years. His boy pulled off a job with shooters and all the rest of it, very professionally done, but with one slight slip-up – he pulled this caper using his own motorbike. Someone took the number, and Old Bill was round his house within twenty minutes. Frankie swore his son was innocent, and gave him a solid alibi. So the law said fair enough, then it must have been you, dragged Frankie in and banged him away for ten.

Like I said, work was coming from everywhere, and for the first time in our married life me and Shirl didn't have to scrimp and save. It was about time our financial struggling turned the corner, and it was all down to that phone call I made to Lucinda.

I believe you make your own luck. I've worked extremely hard all my life, and I'm very proud of it. I've never once signed on the dole, even when we could hardly stretch to a pint of milk and a loaf of bread. No matter what, I always rose to the occasion to bring money in for my family, though as you've seen, too many times it meant stepping over the line.

Now that I was earning real money legitimately, it made me feel bloody good.

I was appearing in a club up north, and Bob Monkhouse spoke to me after one of the shows. He was appearing in another place locally, and he invited me to have breakfast with him the following morning. Eight o'clock sharp the next day I was banging on his hotel room door. I stood there like a lemon for ages, then the door opened a crack and Bob stuck his face out and demanded to know what I wanted. I was a bit taken aback because he seemed to have the hump, but I said, 'You asked me round for breakfast.' 'Breakfast?' he said. 'Breakfast? It's only eight in the morning. I meant around eleven o'clock.' How was I supposed to know? In my house, that would've been nearly dinner time.

He opened the door a bit more and he was in a silk dressing gown. He said, 'You'll have to come back later', went to shut the door, stopped himself and asked me how I was finding the clubs up this way.

I said before how pleased I am when somebody gets on. Well, I found then, and still find today, that the feeling isn't always recipro-cated. It might be a new car, a decent bit of work or some bit of luck – whatever, I run off at the mouth. I'm not trying to prove that I'm the big man, but if I'm chuffed and excited I want to share it, and hope other people get a kick out of it like I would if it was them. Bad move most of the time, but something I didn't learn to control for many years.

So when he's asked me, I've opened up. 'Wonderful, marvellous. It takes some getting used to that I'm picking up twelve hundred notes a week without getting my hands dirty.' If I'd punched him in the mouth he couldn't have reacted more. His eyes opened up, his face went red and he shut the door. I knew straight away that I'd made a ricket, because his attitude told me that it was pretty obvious that his bit of scratch was nowhere near what I was picking up. Golden rule in this business – never, ever divulge what you're earning to another performer.

This sort of arrogance has never ceased to amaze me, and hand on heart, it's something I've never aspired to. I've always been too grateful for the position the public have put me in, or too secure in what I do, that when I see or meet young kids on the way up, I want to help them, not kick them down.

Not too long after I made a name for myself, I was booked for a show business do at the Lancaster Hotel. It was a meal and a cabaret, so there's all these celebrities at tables around the stage. To one side of me was a man who, like millions of others, I absolutely worshipped – Eric Morecambe. He was with Ernie and their wives. Mike and Bernie Winters were on another table, and all around were loads of faces whose names escape me. But right in front of me was Bruce Forsyth and another major comic who I shan't name, because what happened wasn't down to him.

As if on cue, as soon as I went into my routine Bruce started talking and laughing at the top of his voice, and just went on and on. It was extremely difficult for me to concentrate, particularly when you consider the company I was in, but I struggled on with my act thinking, 'How dare you be so rude. How dare you ridicule one of your own people who's trying to make a living.' I'll never ever forget it. If he wasn't interested, or didn't like what I was doing, he should have gone outside. OK, we've all slipped up getting carried away with a conversation, but all it takes is a quick *shhh*, and it's hands up – sorry, sorry. But not him. He gave me a hard time, made it very difficult and I can never forgive that.

Looking back at all those comics that hit the big time alongside me, I'm eternally grateful that I was given other breaks along the way that's kept my name up in lights. Otherwise, like most of those fellas, I might have disappeared without trace, same as them.

Take Ken Goodwin. Very funny man, and even twenty-eight years later you can still hear people saying, 'Eh-heh – I'm too good for this place.' That phrase of his always brought the house down, but at the end of the day, that was his act. Fifteen minutes, and it was great. But it couldn't be sustained after that, and if he tried, you could see the audience starting to fidget. It wouldn't be fair to say he shuffled off to the sound of his own feet, but people certainly got bored with him playing the idiotic, silly child for half an hour.

He was another one who believed his own publicity material for a spell. Every night he used to come past my dressing room, stick his head in the door and say, 'Hello Mike, got a drink for me?' I'd give him a nip of brandy, and that's the last I'd see of him until the next night. And if I did see him, he would totally ignore me and walk past, nose in the air.

To be honest, if I thought anything about this at all, I found it amusing that he felt he had a right to get up on his high horse.

I must have mentioned it to my Shirl at some time, and one night she happened to be there when he went through the routine. Tot of brandy – now you can piss off. He came past me, up went the nose, and my old woman shouted after him, 'Oi, you.' He stopped and said, 'What's the matter, Shirley?' She said, 'What's up? You blown-up-never-come-down sow's bladder – how dare you treat my husband like a piece of shit?' I'm going, 'It's OK, sweetheart, it's OK,' but she wouldn't have it. 'It's not OK. Who does he think he is?' Jesus, did she tell him his fortune. After that he was as good as gold, but what had been going through his mind in the first place, to act like that?

Dave Butler, a Somerset comedian, was another one that was

always on my neck for a drink. Never bought one back, but I didn't give a monkey's, there was always plenty in the cabinet. His forte was as a holiday-camp redcoat. You know, gee everyone up. 'Hello everybody – Hello, hello.' Great as a five-minute slot on TV, but not enough to make a career of, when you think you might have to do an hour in a club or two on the pier. Still, he made a few quid while it lasted.

Somebody told me that once he was making good money, he bought a house just outside Blackpool. Big place with an acre of garden, and the first thing he did was have the acre ploughed up and planted with potatoes. When they were ready for digging up, he sold them to his brother-in-law who had a fish and chip shop. I couldn't get over it, him digging up a beautiful garden for the sake of a few quid.

Or take Jerry Marshall, dead and gone now, I believe. One of the best one-line comics I ever heard in my life. Think of a word and he'd make a gag out of it – tremendous gift.

Off the top of my head I can only think of two other guys with that singular talent, and that's Billy Connolly and Bob Monkhouse.

Never mind Bob giving me a blank all those years ago. I've got so much admiration for his skill, and think he's one of our greatest comics.

Billy, though, is a one-off, and I'd say I was his most ardent fan. I watch everything he does with my mouth open, he's so brilliant. I've never met him, but I spoke to his missus a couple of times and she told me that he'd said I was his favourite comic, and that meant so much to me.

Colin Crompton was always taking the piss out of me because I was losing my hair, and back then my bald spot was no bigger than a tanner at the back of my head. But him, he was virtually bald. What he did was comb what was behind his ears right over the top. And he's standing there, cool as you like, saying, 'Aye, Reidy, you'll have none left by the time you're forty', as though I couldn't see what he'd done with his own.

Here and there I seem to be digging out other comics as though I've got no time for them, and that is far from the truth. What I'm pointing out is how, in some cases, that bit of success went straight to their heads. Putting that aside, whatever their attitude might have been towards me, and indeed many people they came across, doesn't take away from the fact that, without exception, they are all working in the most difficult area of show business. Every day, year in, year out, they've got to go out on that stage no matter how they're feeling and put nothing but their own self up for offer. Whether they go down a bomb or fall flat on their arse is all down to them. Unlike a lot of other areas in the business, if it all goes wrong they can't blame the songwriter, the scriptwriter, the director – anyone. Everything they do rests or falls on their own personality, and I've got to take my hat off to every one of them because they've got the balls to make a living in the loneliest and hardest game in the business.

The comics that I have the utmost admiration for, my heroes if you like, whose talent I hold in total awe, would fill a book on their own. I'll mention a few, but that doesn't disregard those there isn't room for. George Saunders – wonderfully disciplined comic. Mick Miller from Liverpool – one of the best one-liners I've ever come across. Mick Pugh – real staunch guy. Jimmy Taff – absolutely hysterical. The black comic Ian Irvine. Harry Scott, John Cassidy, Dave Wolf, Stan Taylor – president of the Golf Society. The more I think about them, the longer my list gets. Keith Okeefe – one of my dearest friends, and a man I put right up there with Billy Connolly, because he's got that special something of being able to make a gag, or indeed an act, out of incidents that, to be honest, I wouldn't even see a chuckle in. I'll give an instance. Me and him flew over to Jersey in a 757 to play golf. Big plane, small airport, so it has to hit the runway early. One minute you're in the air next – bomp – you're on the ground. We checked into the hotel, played nine holes, came back to the complex where Keith was going to do a cabaret and six hours after the wheels touched the tarmac, he did a hilarious, non-stop, thirty-five-minute act on nothing but that landing. I was just amazed, as always, by his comic brain.

These fellas, and many others who I haven't mentioned, are not what you might call household names, and that's no reflection on their enormous talent. There are two reasons for that. One: as I said before, there's not the showcase any more for stand-up comics on the box. The other reason is that these guys are perfectly happy working the clubs where they feel comfortable, have a huge following and pick up a very nice living.

Referring only to the fellas who made their names through *The Comedians*, apart from myself there's only been two other survivors from those days and that's Bernard Manning and my friend 'It's the way I tell 'em' Frank Carson.

After a bit of a fraught beginning with Frank, the same as with the others at the start of *The Comedians*, we became very close. He's not only a great family friend, but also godfather to one of my grandchildren. They all call him Uncle, and I do myself although he's only a year or two older than I am. He can still pack them in during the seaside summer season, but you see hardly anything of him on the box because times have changed, and the TV shows that he would shine in are very few and far between.

Bernie Manning didn't give a fuck for anyone. I'm convinced he set out to be Britain's answer to American Don Rickles, who made a career out of attacking and ridiculing everyone. People as big as Frank Sinatra would go to his shows for the honour of being singled out for a bit of piss-taking. And if that's what he aspired to, I've got to say he succeeded.

I used to watch him, thinking, 'You can't do that, they'll boo you off the stage.' I was wrong, and the punters loved him, even though he called half of them c—ts. It was his stock word, and one that I only used once on my very first video, and that was a mistake, in the heat of the moment. I never ever used it in my stage act, I just thought it was too offensive and completely unnecessary.

After eight, nine or possibly ten years, I can only surmise that what with everyone moving into this political correctness stuff, producers got frightened of booking him, because they never knew what he might come out with next. I've got to admire his attitude, he must have known it would keep him off the box, but he was what he was and wouldn't change for anyone. On top of that, I have to say that today there are not the vehicles on TV for the older-style comics. Nothing to do with lessening popularity or lack of talent: times have changed, that's all.

Give Bernie his due, he can still pack a club out. Though I don't know why he bothers, because he must be a multi-multimillionaire. He's always had this club in Manchester that he calls the Embassy Club and that I call an ashtray with seats, because I think that's all it is. But what I do admire is his loyalty to the punters that support his place. When he was working in London, he always insisted that he opened the show at eight o'clock. He'd do his forty-five minutes, then get straight in a motor to show his face at the Embassy by eleven-thirty. He never failed – never let his punters down, and I take my hat off to him for that.

Once the cash was rolling in and I could see that this was going to be regular for years ahead, me and Shirl had the pleasure of spending some of it. The very first big layout was an agreement between the two of us that we would set our parents up in houses of their own. Forget selfless act: the pleasure we got in being able to repay our mums and dads just for being there was absolutely immeasurable.

Shirl's mum and dad, Ted and Gwen, were easily sorted. We found a place, they loved it, moved in and that was that.

Mine were different, or should I say, Mum was less easily satis-fied. Dad would've been happy wherever he was. We'd get them fixed up and two, three months later, Mum started. This was wrong, too far to the shops, neighbours were no good. OK, let's find some-where else. Trailed her all over until we found the right place. 'Yes, Michael, this is the one.' All the upheaval of moving again, and months later everything was wrong with it. No problem. Might as well be happy, so off we went again. It took three properties within the year before she was satisfied, and cost me a bit of hair I couldn't afford to lose.

Isn't it sad that we don't understand our parents until it's too late? Sitting here now with a lot of years behind me, I realize that perhaps I should have tried to understand her overcarefulness and been a bit more tolerant. I know she explained why she was like she was, but I always told myself that that was just her excuse for being mean. And because I hadn't taken her reasons on board, I allowed myself to be wound up right up to and even after she died.

I can remember feeling so angry when, once we'd buried her, me and Brian found she'd left us fifteen hundred each. Three grand – an absolute fortune in her eyes. But in mine, and I'm sure in my brother's, all it amounted to was a year's car insurance or a couple of months' boozing money. And for that she'd gone short and scrimped and saved, while in her later years she could've spent that money on a cruise, which even though she'd had a couple of strokes, she was quite capable of doing. But worst of all, over the years she'd fallen out with people and lost friends because she couldn't bear to part with a copper coin. My sense of loss at the time was overtaken by my feeling so infuriated at her obstinacy. Yet now, I think I should have just accepted that she never knew any other way and left it at that.

We'd lost Dad some years before Mum, and when he went it was a blessed release for him. I was fortunate enough to have enough money to put him in a Harley Street clinic, where they found he was riddled with cancer. The picture has stayed in my mind, of me walking into his room with my Brian and seeing him sitting in bed like a wafer, head to waist in bandages. He looked up and said, 'Son, please let me die.' That hurt – really hurt. But he'd had enough, and just wanted out.

Not too long after, an inexplicable thing happened that I've never tried, or wanted to try, to analyse. I was on a sea-fishing trip with my mate Ted, and thinking of nothing in particular. The sea was calm, I'd cast my line and was just taking in the view when there was Dad, right in front of me. Larger than life, he looked at me, gave that big old grin, then faded away, leaving me feeling strangely comforted.

We lost Dad about fifteen years ago and buried him over at Hatfield, where we were living at the time. Ten years later we placed Mum's ashes beside him, and it's nice to think they're both together, because even though they had their differences in life, they always loved each other.

Still, that was a long way in the future, and once we'd got the house business all settled, we considered having a move ourselves.

As usual, most of my work was up north, so I stuck a pin in the map, somewhere nice and central, and came up with a place called Sutton-cum-Launde, near Nottingham. That put me within half an hour of any of the clubs.

Before we'd put our names down for this place, I'd considered moving to Scotland. Crazy really, because I would've spent my life driving to work. But with plenty of folding and delusions of grandeur,

I'd found a castle for sale in the *Exchange and Mart*. Imagine Reidy, the ducker and diver, taking over a turreted castle with thirty bedrooms. Not only that, it had two thousand acres, and two and a half miles of its own shoreline.

It was on the north coast of Scotland just above Ayr, and I couldn't wait to view it. I took a few days off and me and Shirl drove up there – and it rained and rained and rained, non-stop. All we saw of the castle was a grey lump through the mist and driving rain. I looked at Shirl, she looked at me and we both burst out laughing, turned round and went home.

Once we'd moved up to Nottingham I really did feel I'd made the grade. I didn't have to worry about where the next quid was coming from, we had a beautiful house and I was where I always wanted to be – in a nice little village surrounded by fields and woods.

One thing about the game I'm in is you can't turn round to the bookers or your agent and tell them you're giving it a miss for a while. 'Sorry, fellas I've got plenty of dough. Give me a call in about six months.' It can't be done. A month, two months, they'll be going, 'Mike who?' In effect, you get stuck on a treadmill of your own making.

So I'm all over the place; show here, club there. But always, always, I tried to get home to sleep in my own bed. It wasn't always possible, but I did my best because I just loved the country life.

I'd taken my little Jack Russell up there with us, and not long after, bought a beautiful long-haired German shepherd. It was pure bred but looked like Lassie –lovely dog. They both were. I'd be sitting in the armchair, and they wouldn't take their eyes off me. If I fell asleep for an hour, when I woke up they'd still be gazing at me.

At every opportunity, I'd take them out into the fields for hours, and all the pressures of work just faded away. We had a big old lump of ground with the house, so one day when I couldn't find them I never thought anything of it, but after a couple of hours I started to get a bit worried because usually they never left my side. I stuck the boots on and went everywhere, calling the two of them. Outside the grounds, up a lane, across that ditch, until I found them a couple of fields away – shot dead. My beautiful dogs were lying side by side, dried blood around their mouths and flies buzzing in and out. I could've cried. No, to be honest, I did – I sobbed my heart out.

It turned out that a local chicken farmer had spotted my dogs in his field, and with that God-given right that all farmers have that nothing should be on their property without permission, he'd killed them. He never even had the decency to come and give me one warning to keep them off his property. And if the truth be known, he did it to have a dig at this upstart Londoner who'd dared to move into the country. Townies. 'Oh, here come the townies', implying that, given the chance, we'd turn them over.

Yet with one or two exceptions, in my opinion, as a mass of people there's none more cunning, sceptical, mean and unfriendly as farmers – those slippery bastards would nick your last penny. And I've hated them ever since that incident.

What I should have done was got him on his own and kicked the shit out of him, but mindful of the fact that I was a face now, I did it the right way and took him to court. What a waste of time! I spoke for myself in court, and with a bit of advice I was asking all the right questions and the judge dismissed everything I said as 'not relevant', so I got no joy.

It could've sickened me for the country life, but there were a lot of good people in the village that we were very friendly with – one a bit more friendly than I would've liked.

Same as any village anywhere in the country, the first person to come banging on your door is the local vicar. Now Shirl's already met him somewhere or other, so she knew what to expect. Not only is his name John Thomas, but he's got a bugle about two foot long. I could imagine he spent his life telling people, 'No, I haven't been telling lies.' If it wasn't for the fact that he'd specifically asked to see Michael and Mark, probably to talk them into going to Sunday School, Shirl would have tied them up and hidden them under the stairs. Because there was no way those little sods wouldn't make some comment about his horrendous hooter.

When he turned up, Shirl was on tenterhooks and nervous, not only because she'd never entertained a man of the cloth before, but she was dreading what the kids might say even though they had been warned. She put the kettle on, came through with the cups and a few biscuits and – this is the honest truth, even though it sounds like a line out of a sitcom – she said, 'Do you take sugar with your nose, vicar?'

Apart from him, who never showed his face again, we got on with most people in the village. Most of our neighbours were well-heeled, so we were nothing special. Just Mike and Shirley to them all. We got involved in whatever was going on, and I even went to the extent of offering to finance the fella in the local pub so he could stick another bar on the side.

Don't get the impression that I was being a flash bastard and chucking my money around – it wasn't like that. Apart from its being a business deal, I liked the guy and wanted to help him out.

As a contrast to some of the times Shirl and me had been through together, most of the time I had to pinch myself to make sure it wasn't all a dream. Those piss-holes of flats and rooms, going out robbing, coming home knackered every night and scrapping all day for two bob: It was all behind us. But it doesn't take money to make you happy, and though I can only put my own point of view, I did think that me and Shirl had been happy together at least ninety per cent of the time, no matter how tough things had got.

CHAPTER SEVEN

I DON'T CARE HOW MANY TIMES I SAY IT: SHIRLEY HAS ALWAYS been a very attractive woman. I've watched geezers over the years, hundreds of times, thousands, as they've given her the eye or tried to pull her. I'm a fella; I know what it's all about and I know what their game is. She always had two stock phrases to put down any guy trying to come across with it. 'Piss off', or 'Get lost'. It's never failed. I might be a good distance away at the bar, or sometimes even on stage, and I could tell straight away if she'd given somebody a knock-back. They'd go all stiff and rock back like they'd been smacked, then take off, tail between their legs.

Having witnessed this time after time over the years, I thought I understood her, and trusted her implicitly and without question. I would rather have been stabbed in the stomach than ever consider she would be unfaithful to me, and when I found out that she had, that's just what it felt like.

I'm talking about a period here when I was in great demand. It was crazy: bookings were coming from all over. I could be in Wales one day, Scotland the next – Bournemouth – Brighton. I didn't know whether I was coming or going. When I did get home, instead of relaxing I'd be thinking about where I had to go next, so I was tired and, if I'm truthful, irritable. I might have been so wrapped up in myself that I didn't know what day it was, but if Shirley was acting any different from normal, I really didn't notice.

As far as I was concerned, home was an oasis in my hectic life, and she was always there for me – same as always. OK, we had rows over nothing, but we always had done, and they never lasted five minutes.

While I was away, Shirl had to make the best of it, what with looking after the kids and the house on her own. But as far as I knew, she was fine with that. She was friendly with loads of people in the village, and they'd be in and out of the house. If she wanted to socialize away from the house the pub was virtually next door, and being a country place, the kids could go with her and play in one of the rooms.

I had a few days off, was getting relaxed and looking forward to going to a local function. Nothing fancy: a few beers, bit of a dance, all in aid of something or other. Shirley's mate from London was staying with us for a few days, and we were going to make a night of it.

Why did this friend Pam do what she did? I asked myself that a hundred times, yet I think I knew the answer all along. As I said a few lines earlier, I'm a fella and I know the score. I hadn't spent most of my life involved with women without learning to know when one of them is giving me the old come-on. And this is the vibe that was coming from Shirl's supposed best friend. As far as I could see, she wanted some sort of relationship with me, and obviously thought the easiest way to get what she was after was to stick a knife into my missus. I'm not just referring to that particular night; this had been going on every time we saw her. I won't say it made me feel uncomfortable; blokes aren't like that. Buzz to the old ego, perhaps, but if you're not interested, it can't go any further. And I definitely wasn't.

We went to the do, had a few laughs. I danced with a couple of the local ladies and eventually gave Shirl's mate a spin round the floor. I was enjoying myself, and about a minute away from my whole world caving in. Suddenly this friend Pam came out with, 'Mike, I feel I've got to tell you this. There's something going on with Shirley and Reg from the pub.' I went 'Excuse me?' and she said, 'You've got to know, she's having an affair.'

It was like being hit between the eyes with a sledgehammer. I stopped dead, shoved her away and looked over to Shirley standing at the bar. She knew. She knew straight away that it was all out in the open. I couldn't think, I felt sick, so I pushed my way through all the people and ran out the door and through the village towards home. First, though, I went through the pub door like a maniac and caught hold of this Reg Turner, the landlord's nephew. He started to say, 'I know what this is all about', but I punched him so fast and so hard in the face he was spark out before he hit the floor. He didn't even hear me call him a piece of shit.

I needn't go into all the tears and recriminations, but it goes without saying that it was a terrible time for both of us. I knew it was true, but I wanted to hear it from Shirl's own mouth, and when I asked her, she put her hand up to it and admitted she'd had a thing going with this fella for some time. Her excuse was that I was at it myself when I was away from home. It seems unfair that it's only my side of things that's being put forward, because I'm sure Shirley could come up with many reasons to justify what she did, and some of them would be very relevant. And people on the outside not personally affected by it would say, 'Yes, it's understandable', but I couldn't accept any excuses at all.

If I was paying too much attention to dancers or showgirls I met in the clubs, that was all part of the game I was in. Not that she would have known whether I was or wasn't up to anything. But I never immersed myself in affairs with anybody. I never, ever got into that. I was too busy on the road and working very hard. And though that may have been the main cause of my neglecting her, that very fact was why we were living in a big house with two cars and everything money could buy.

The whole thing hurt me beyond anything I can ever remember. I don't think I was ever that egotistically naive to think nothing like that could ever happen to me, but when it did, I found it very difficult not only to get it out of my mind, but also to trust my wife, for years afterwards. I'd go away working, and there was always a niggle in the back of my mind about what she was up to. My insides were ripped out of me, but there were two sides to this, and Shirl was not only sorry for what she'd done, but completely devastated by how things had turned out. What had begun as a mild flirtation had got out of hand and I feel sure that if Pam hadn't blown the whistle, it would have faded away and I might never have known about it. And when

I think of the gut-wrenching pain it caused me, perhaps that might have been for the best.

Regardless of all the trauma that was tearing us to bits, I still had to go to work, and in my state of mind I was pleased to get out of the house, even though nothing had been resolved between us.

The next thing I knew, I'd got a call and Shirl was in hospital. To get her through the days and nights she'd been swallowing pill after pill, with the end result being a slow build-up to an overdose. If she'd wanted to do away with herself all she had to do was empty a bottle of tablets, then go to bed. But because it wasn't deliberate, she'd got in the car to go somewhere, been overcome at the wheel and drifted off the road, just managing to stop before she went unconscious. I wont even presume to say what was going on in her mind, but once she was in hospital, she kept ripping out all the tubes that were in her arm and up her nose.

Thank God she pulled through, came home, and then it was up to the two of us to start repairing the damage and building bridges between us.

It was a terribly slow process, and being a bloke, with a typical bloke's thinking, I tortured myself with images I shouldn't have done, which didn't help one bit to get things back to normal. Fortunately we managed to keep what had happened within the family. Yeah, Turner getting knocked on his arse in front of a dozen customers left room for a bit of gossip, but then villages thrive on that sort of stuff.

The last thing I wanted was for anyone to know about it. I was aggrieved and ashamed that some sort of weakness on my part had let it happen. As well as that, I didn't want fingers being pointed at my missus, because it was nobody's business but hers and mine.

So our time in Nottingham had run its course. I won't say events drove us out – it was on the cards anyway, because I'd been offered a show in London that was going to run for some time.

By this time I was turning over a colossal amount of cash, and my philosophy was that if I was going to graft my plums off earning the dough, I was going to take great pleasure in spending it. So I splashed out on a mansion in Hatfield Peverel that had been offered to me by a property dealer, who just happened to be the husband of my manager at that time.

Now there was a woman, Eve Taylor. One of the best, but one of the toughest managers and agents ever. I'll never forget her telling Lew Grade to fuck off, and back then he was one step below God in the entertainment business.

Anyway, this house was a piece. It had belonged to Ford Motors of Dagenham, and they'd used it for visiting American executives, so as you can imagine, it was a bit special. It had three floors, fourteen bedrooms and was set in six acres, with a sweeping drive. At the beginning of the drive there was a lodge house that had its own walled garden of half an acre. It made sense for me to have someone pottering about the place doing bits and pieces, so we moved Shirl's mum and dad in so that Ted could take over the job. Though he'd always earned his living as a driving instructor, like my own father he was very clever with his hands, so this arrangement suited us both.

I'll never forget the first time I took my dad to see the place. He got out of the car and I showed him all round. The house, the garden, the biggest private swimming pool in the country. I pointed out the real silk wall coverings. He never said a word. When we got back to where we'd started he just turned and gave that grin of his and nodded. He didn't have to say a word – that grin spoke volumes, absolute volumes. He was proud of what I'd done for myself, and I was proud that I'd done what he'd suggested when I was a lad. He'd said, 'Son, I don't care what you do in life as long as you strive to do better at it than I have.'

I'd not only achieved what he wanted, but in great style, and he loved that. He also loved the fact that I was a public figure, but he kept it all inside, unlike my mother, who trumpeted about her son to whoever would listen. And in the early years I couldn't get enough of that, because it doesn't matter who you are or what line of show business you're in, we're all tarred with the same brush, wanting to be famous and be recognized. Never mind all the bollocks about doing it for art's sake, at the end of the day it's about being a 'face', or you wouldn't be in the game. That was certainly my motivation when I was younger.

Not too long ago, me and Shirl were invited back to that house in Hatfield. It's an old people's home now, and once we'd been shown all the changes that had been made, they couldn't wait to show us that beautiful silk wall covering – it's still there after all these years.

Once we were nicely settled in this house we both really wanted to make an effort to put the past where it belonged and move on. But life always likes to chuck a fly in the ointment.

When I first became a bit of a name I got some advice from the wonderful actress and very dear friend, Anna Karen, who'll always be remembered for her performance as Olive in *On the Buses*. Now of course she's often on the screen as Peggy Mitchell's sister in the soap. When I refer to her as a friend, I use the word with great emphasis, because Anna is one of the most genuine and loyal people that me and Shirl have had the pleasure of knowing. She's always in and out of our home, the kids and grandkids all call her auntie and we think the world of her.

Anyway, as she'd been in the business longer than I had, and I trusted her judgement, I should've listened to her when she told me to be very wary of all journalists. Five minutes later, too innocent or too stupid to take on board what she'd said, I went trapping off at the mouth to the first journalist who brushed up my ego and asked for a meet.

How was I supposed to know that all that friendly show-biz interview stuff was going to set in motion something that was going to crucify me and Shirl? If I hadn't been so naive and eager to get a bit of publicity then what followed might never have happened. But it seemed my piece coincided with the fact that the paper had been given a whisper that we'd had problems up in Nottingham. Perhaps one of our neighbours from the last place had phoned up with a juicy story like 'Mike Reid serves up punch in local hostelry'. The editors must have loved it. 'Oh, thanks very much, here's fifty pounds. Now we can have a go at that smug bastard who's climbing the ladder too quickly.'

Shortly afterwards my worst nightmare came together when my wife's affair was splashed all over a daily paper. Can you imagine what that did to me and Shirl when our relationship was so fragile?

I felt I'd been made a fool; of my missus and family were torn up and my relationship with the press was soured from that day on. Soured because the newspapers never gave a thought to the pain and humiliation they knew they were going to cause us. I got wind that something like this was going down and begged them to spike the story. Begged? I cried down the phone. Yeah, tough old Reidy, brought to tears, asking for a bit of compassion. And I got nothing. They knew what it was going to do to me and they just didn't care.

So why now twenty years down the line do I want to rake up all that pain from a short period in mine and Shirley's life? Terrible gut-wrenching pain that I want to forget and never talk about? The simple truth is I meant what I said about telling the truth warts and all. No good me pretending that our lives were like some Mills and Boon love story, because we're ordinary people and we've had our ups and downs same as everyone else. But what I really want to show is that even though these things happen in life, we can rise above them and come out the other side even stronger.

The whole experience changed me, there's no doubt about that. It made me harder. Not towards Shirl, but generally in the way I thought about things. Yet on reflection, if the same thing happened today I'd go 'So what?' I might be saying that in the firm knowledge that there's no way it could, but I'm much older now. I've seen a lot of life, and come to realize that sex is superficial. It's not important. What is, is a close relationship, and above all, trust. And we've certainly reached that state of play after all these years.

Having come through that and a whole lot more since, I don't know anyone that has an affiliation like we do. I tell her and she tells me 'I love you' a hundred times a day. The kids all take the piss as though we're too old to kiss and cuddle and all that caper, but I think they're all aware that they've been fortunate enough to grow up in a warm, loving relationship and a happy atmosphere. I've said we're both very volatile, but that means nothing. It's our way of blowing off steam and no-one takes any notice of it.

Getting back to work immediately after the heartbreak was very hard. In fact, I had to stick on the clown's face to hide what was inside for longer than I care to remember. But I was proud that I was always professional enough never to take my personal life on to the stage. Every single person in an audience has some sort of problem, and they've paid out hard-earned money for me to help them forget whatever it might be. They're not there to listen to mine, or to see me with a face like a donkey's dick.

Time after time, after that business, I'd be in the spotlight giving it plenty and my mouth in overtime, yet I'd be miles away, thinking of something else. So in a way, when I was offered the chance of fronting a new kids' quiz show I jumped at it, because it was an exciting break for me and wouldn't leave me much time for brooding.

Colin Nutley, a director for Southern Television, had bought the idea of a children's show from America. It was a totally new concept as regards any show for kids, and so far ahead of its time that I can say without fear of contradiction that all the stuff you see today involving flashing lights and gunge tanks all stemmed from that earlier programme.

It was an eye-opener. What was phenomenal was the incredible speed with which it was produced. From buying the scripts and a few tapes to actually hitting the screen took eight weeks, and that's moving. Even today, when everything's computerized and it's rush, rush, rush, you're talking a minimum of six months' production time. Doesn't matter if it's a play or a variety concert.

Everyone from the director down studied the demo videotapes and then made the best of it we could. Consequently, nobody quite knew what they were doing. We copied the Americans and hoped for the best.

If you're of a certain age group, you'll know what I'm talking about. If not, the basic premise was, we got five kids from one school and five from another, then the audience was made up half-and-half with their supporters. This got a bit of excitement going with all the competitive cheering and shouting. The idea was that it all took place inside something like a circus ring, and in effect I was the ringmaster, though unlike *Starburst*, I didn't wear the gear. I stood in the centre with these ten kids, asked them questions then gave them three answers to choose from. Once I shouted 'Runaround', they had to run off and stand in front of a board that had on it what they guessed, or hoped, was the right answer.

What knocked the excitement up was that they had three seconds to change their minds, so to confuse the opposing team they might deliberately go to the wrong answer, then jump over at the last moment. Those kids that got it wrong were out of the game, so they were gradually whittled down.

The prizes for that time were unheard of: bikes, televisions, and naturally this generated excitement for the kids viewing, even though they weren't getting the prizes, and the show just took off. Its popularity wasn't even gradual, like most shows. It went from a standing start to vertical in three weeks.

That first show was a nightmare because no-one knew how it would go, or indeed how the audience of kids would behave. All their parents were invited as well. On top of that, the researchers went to every school in Hampshire and asked all the teachers if they'd like to come along and see what their pupils could well be doing in the future. This was done because they knew the show would run for a long time – which it did.

Consequently, that first day the studio was heaving. People were standing on gantries, in the aisles and all round the studio floor. In fact, there were so many bodies the producer brought in thirty or forty extra firemen to cover regulations.

Although it was pre-recorded, we were told that all mistakes would be left in and the show would go out billed as live. And that turned out to be the actual joy of the programme. All bitty, with me making cracks about the things that went wrong.

As time went on and we got the hang of what it was all about, we'd start recording at four o'clock and by half past it would be done and dusted.

But that first day, with so many people in, we started at two p.m. Before and between each question, I'd do an interview with different people from all walks of life. So if the person was a baker, for instance, one of my questions might be, 'What is a baker's dozen?' Some of these interviewees were interesting; some were boring.

So I've tried to explain everything in the first five minutes, but no, the kids haven't picked it up. Cut – do it again. Get that right, and the cameraman makes a right balls-up. Shots dropped, shots missed, and it was all going wrong. I mean, badly wrong. By the time everyone's got the hang of it the kids are bored – their concentration span, as we all know, being virtually zero. Now it's three p.m. and all we've covered is one question, and it's time for the first interview with a shepherd.

To add to the interest, they've opened up the back of the ring and shunted in about fifty sheep. We're in the middle and all these animals are milling round us. I've done the business with this geezer, turned to the audience: 'There you are kids – that's a shepherd's life. Give him a big hand.' And they all went 'Raaaaaay', and every one of those sheep shit itself. Not one – all of them. There was crap from one side of the studio to the other, and every drop had to be cleared up in case anyone slipped over, broke a leg and sued us. It took an hour to sweep up and wash down.

By this time the kids in the ring have forgotten the rules, so the next runaround took half an hour instead of two minutes.

Ideally, next up should have been a goldfish breeder or a flower arranger, but no – they want to make an impact with the first show, so they trundle on an elephant, of all things, and its trainer. I stood facing the trainer with the elephant behind me. The whole time this bastard thing had its trunk round my plums, up my arse and sniffing my neck.

Behind the guy I was interviewing there was a monitor, so that I could see what was going on and, if I thought it necessary, change my position. I'm keeping my eye on this elephant when all of a sudden this monstrosity of a cock starts to unfold – it was like a four-foot roll of lino. I'm dodging about so that this thing is hidden from camera and it decided it wanted to piss, and sprayed about twenty gallons everywhere.

Cut – clear it up, blow-dry the floor and carry on. Now it's half past eight in the evening and everybody's completely pissed off, including me. Kids, teachers, parents – none of them have had a drink or anything to eat. They're tired and the novelty's worn off, and we still haven't finished.

The last interview was with two police motorcyclists who thought they were something out of *CHIPS*, that American TV series. They drove into the ring and sat there with all the gear on and were as cocky and pompous as they come. 'Yes, we do this – never do that – safety is paramount', and so on.

'Traffic police, kids,' 'Raaaaaay.' To exit, they circled in different directions, aimed for the gap to take them off set and smashed into each other. Blood, oil, snot, petrol, firemen running in – absolutely horrendous. I just collapsed.

At twenty past nine we came to the last question before wrap-up, and we're all knackered. Two weeks prior to this, Francis Chichester sailed round the world, and it was big news. I did a quick interview with a sailor, then asked the kids was Chichester a footballer, a mountaineer or a yachtsman? They all ran around, lined up in front of what was indeed the correct boards and 'footballer' flashed up. I went 'Footballer? Ffffucking footballer?' There was a sharp intake of breath all round the studio. I just ran off stage.

The producer's pulling his hair out and telling me I've got to go back out and straighten things up. I stood there in front of these hundreds of people trying to look contrite and said, 'Ladies and gentlemen, boys and girls. Uncle Mike is very sorry.' Probably the first time in their lives that these Hampshire kids had ever heard the eff-word, and I'm trying to smooth it over by calling myself Uncle Mike.

Needless to say, we got that first show in the can and after that it got smoother and smoother. The viewing figures were phenomenal. So much so, that in the terminology of the business it was a 'wipe-out'. If they had included kids' shows in the ratings of the top twenty programmes watched every week, which they have never done, *Runaround* would consistently have been in the top three.

Even today, I get people in their thirties and forties coming up to me and shouting, 'Runaround'. And I go, 'Yeah – nice one', as though they're the first person to have chucked it at me since the seventies. Nice to think it's remembered so well, though.

People used to tell me I was a bit hard on the kids, but I had to be, otherwise they'd have run wild.

I had a couple of breaks to take on something else, and Leslie Crowther took over. He rang me up and said, 'Mike, I can't do it. The kids are like animals; they're ruining everything. How do you keep them under control?' What could I say? Leslie never had the authority that I'd picked up doing the clubs.

Next time I was away Stan Boardman had a go. Stan's a very talented comic, and if he'd stuck to being himself he would have made a great job of it, but his mistake was he tried to be me. He'd been shown tapes of the shows that I had done, thought, 'Yeah. All I've got to do is copy the style and it'll be a piece of cake.' He had a roll of paper with the questions on, but between every one was his own script telling him what to do, so it made this rolled-up tube a bit bulky. Now my style has always been aggressive, but because I was dealing with kids, or was in front of them, I toned it down. So with a big smile I'd say, 'Go on, get off', or give a gentle shove here and there. Stan's obviously clocked this.

He was interviewing a kendo fighter with all the sticks and chains they use, and as he's finished he's said to the geezer 'Right, clear off', and given him a bang with his roll of paper. Instinctively this fighter's gone bosh, and cracked Stan round the back of the head with his stick. The kids thought it was hilarious, but he didn't, and told me a long time after that he had a lump like an egg on the back of his crust.

I can remember when Stan first started, or more truthfully, when he got his first break. Funny how things come round. I'd kicked *Opportunity Knocks* out the door in no uncertain terms, and yet some years later I turn up as one of the judges. So there I am at the London Palladium, and for the life of me I can't remember who else was judging other than David Hamilton and Freddie Davies, who was always billed as 'Parrot Face'. It might have been Shirley Eaton again. I forgot to mention she was a judge on the show that I appeared in.

The only two serious contenders out of the bunch of contestants were Stan and a singer I've never heard of since.

Everyone did their turn, and we retired to the green room for a glass of wine and to add up the score cards to see who'd won. Stan Boardman came out number one, no question. Yet the other judges, for whatever reason, didn't want to give it to him. They agreed he was an excellent comic, but tried to convince me that it would be more beneficial if the singer got the vote. I wouldn't have it, and told them. I said, 'Hang on. Just wait a minute. The cards say that man has won it, never mind all this shit about what you think should happen. This is supposed to be a democratic vote, and if he doesn't get it I'll kick up such a fuss you'll wish you never even considered stitching him up.' Half an hour this took, before they gave way and accepted the right decision. All this time the competitors were biting their nails to bits on stage and the audience were getting restless. Stan got it, and I was well pleased for him.

Over the road from the Palladium there was a club used by agents, artistes and anyone in the game. Every year after the contest they held a party for everyone involved. We've gone over, the judges and everyone else, and I'm standing with my Shirley when Stan came down the stairs with his entourage. He hadn't hit the bottom step when I went forward and said, 'Stan, congratulations. That was a great show.' He didn't even look at me. Just went 'Hmmm', and walked past me. His mate who was right behind him put his face close to mine and said, 'Fookin' better than yow, ain't he', and carried on. I thought, I can't believe this. I've stood there arguing my nuts off for this boy to win, and I get treated like that.

Me and Stan have got quite chummy over the years, but I never told him the story of how I fought so hard in his corner for him to get the win he'd earned.

While I was doing *Runaround*, I was invited into a nice gentle comedy show called *Yus My Dear* with Queenie Watts, Arthur Mullard and Helen Keating. This was my first acting part, and though I wasn't camera shy, on reflection I was bloody awful. I just couldn't stop laughing and giggling my way through it. I played Benny Briggs, while Arthur and Queenie were my mum and dad, Wally and Lily Briggs.

Queenie was a one-off. Slight and with jet-black hair, she was a proper cockney. She wasn't only one of the best character actresses around at the time, she was also a great singer. Even before I worked with her I used to go once every week to her pub and listen to her. In those days every pub had at least a piano, bass and drums, so it didn't matter where you went, there was always some sort of entertainment. She was a legend, and loved by everyone in the business, yet strange and sad, when she died I was the only face at her funeral. I expected her send-off to be ten deep with showbiz people, so was astounded that I was the only one that turned up.

Arthur was a diamond. He always played himself, and you never got a 'yes' out of him. It was always 'yus', and I'm sure that's what gave the scriptwriters the idea for the title.

Helen Keating helped me out a lot, because she was an old hand at the sitcom game. She played Val, my tarty girlfriend. You name it; she'd been in it. No disrespect to her because she's a lovely girl and we're still mates, but if ever the part called for a blonde tart or a barmaid with plenty of bust, she got a call.

Like I said, this show wasn't my finest hour, and I'd never want to see it again, but it got me seen by people who matter, and that's what this business is all about.

Before I jumped into anything else, I made the most of a brief lull in my work and me and Shirl shot off to Spain for a couple of weeks. We'd made up a bit of a group and gone out there with my best mate Ted Pearmain, his wife Marge and two other very dear friends, Val and Terry. As far as holidays go that's all it was, a nice break from the pressure of tearing about – the old cliché, sea, sun and sangria – apart from one incident.

This particular night, Val and Terry had gone for a walk or something while the rest of us slipped into a local club. We were having a nice drink when a bit of trouble flared up. I was standing with Shirl and Marge, and Ted was talking to a group of fellas at the bar. One of them, who was giving it plenty of old trap, was built like a brick shithouse. I heard him say 'Man United' or some team, and Ted mumbled something and walked away. He may have said 'Rubbish', or he might have just been going for a piss.

Either way, this geezer raised his arm and went for Ted's back. I never even thought, jumped forward and planted one right in his boat. He shook his head like a dog coming out of water and flew at me. This time Ted gave him a bang. He staggered back, and before any of us could do anything my Shirl's shoved us out of the way, whipped her shoe off and gone at him like a terrier. Same as with the Maltese guy years before, she knocked four lumps out of this geezer's face before he could shove her off and gear himself up to belt her. I saw it coming, and gave it everything I had. I pulled my arm as far back as it would go, then hit him with seventeen stone behind the punch. He went down, smashing tables on the way like something out of a western. At the same time, local plod burst in and we were nicked and whipped off to the station.

The upshot was we were kept in all night, fined for public disorder and that was it. No mention of the punch-up.

What we didn't know was that the big fella who'd got a good hiding was a minder for the Kray rivals the South London Richardson family, and he hadn't pressed charges because he'd made up his mind to sort it in his own way.

We got back to England and I got word from different people that I was marked down for some serious aggravation. I was pretty well known by then, so it hadn't been too difficult to find out who I was or where I could be found.

I won't pretend I was a hero; truth is, I was shitting myself. I've faced guns, I've faced knives and I could have a fight if it came to it, but never ever without being frightened.

There are only two men I've known in my life who honestly didn't know what fear was. I don't mean bravado or plenty of front, but genuine lack of fear – and these were Lenny McLean, who everyone knew as The Guv'nor, and Roy Shaw. Both of these guys were bare-knuckle fighters, and though Lenny smashed Roy senseless and nicked the title of Guv'nor, I wouldn't have wanted to face either of them in my worst nightmare.

I never actually met Roy, but I did bump into Lenny more than once, and on one of those occasions I gave him a bit of advice that I'm pleased to say he took. We were both visiting Reggie Kray in Maidstone Prison, and afterwards when we were having a chat I suggested he try his hand at the acting game. This wasn't just to make conversation, I genuinely believed that his character and personality would make him well sought after. Sadly, he died just after making a name for himself as an actor, but I was pleased to see in his auto-biography, written just before he passed away, that he credits me with putting the idea in his head.

Anyway, to go back to my bit of aggravation. To make up for my being scared shitless, there is another side of my character that forces me to face up to whatever problem I might have. So as these stories of what this geezer's going to do to me got wilder and wilder, I thought, this is ridiculous, got in touch with a local face and arranged a meet. At least once he'd knocked seven bells out of me I wouldn't have to keep looking over my shoulder.

I stood at the bar of the club where I said I'd meet him, and he turned up after about half an hour, and I'm sure he was twice the size of what he had been in Spain. When he saw me he said, 'Mike, old son, how you doing? What's the problem?' I'm stuttering about being out of order for decking him, and he's shrugging it off saying, 'Forget it – let's have a drink.'

This was virtually the same result I'd got some years earlier with another bit of aggro, and funnily enough, what brought me and Ted closer together.

Always looking for a bit extra to supplement my piss-poor wages, I'd taken on a job as a bouncer at Room at the Top, Ilford. Ted was on the door with me but I didn't know him too well, we just worked together. I'm on one side of the stairs; he's on the other. Suddenly there was a bit of a scuffle, I heard him go 'Agh', looked over and he's crumpled to the floor. A geezer's just stuck a knife in his neck.

I leaped over and floored this guy before he could move, then to get him out of the way so I could attend to Ted, I picked him up and flung him down fifteen steps to the landing. I presume his mates carried him off, I don't know. I was too busy sorting my mate out.

I thought he was going to die on me, but once we got him to the hospital they found that though the blade had gone in one side and out the other, it had missed his jugular by a hair and he survived.

To get to the point, once it was all done and dusted Reidy found himself on the death list of a local 'family'. 'Lucky old boy' must have deserted me, because the fella I'd slung down the stairs couldn't be any old punter; he had to be related to the tastiest firm on the manor.

Before either me or my house got shot up I decided to front them up. Same thing again. I found out which drinker they used, and one Sunday morning walked in with my cheeks firmly clenched together. Talk about OK Corral. As I pushed the door open, everything went quiet except for a growl going right round the place. I walked over to the corner where the faces were sitting, put my hands up and told them I'd come to apologize. Should have been the other way round, really. Their bloke nearly killed Ted and only ended up with a few bruises, but I was there to save my own neck, not argue the toss, so I would've said anything. The main man looked me up and down and said, 'You've got some bottle, son. Sit down.' At the end of the day we shook hands, and it was squared away.

But my method of fronting trouble didn't always work. Back in the days when I was knocking about with Frankie, there was another geezer who wanted to kill me. He'd had a row with his girlfriend, and to wind him up she'd thrown at him, 'Oh yeah, and another thing, Mike Reid's been giving me one for weeks.' He's gone apeshit and I'm in trouble. It was completely beside the point that I'd never even been near his bird; he thought I had, so it was up to me to face him and get it sorted.

Frankie and me went to see him by the arches near our café. And never mind 'You've got bottle', or 'Let's have a drink', this geezer pulled a Luger pistol out of his jacket and shot at me from about five yards. He missed, and before he could get another one off, Frankie took the gun and beat him senseless with it.

Going back to Ted Pearmain, after that stabbing caper our friendship was cemented. Later on when I made myself a name on *The Comedians,* he came with me as road manager, though I would much prefer to call him personal assistant because he drove the cars, booked hotels, saw people and looked after me all the way. But it was more than that; he became my best and closest male friend, and over the years, they've been few and far between.

Strange, when you consider how gregarious people are in show business, but I've always been a loner, and getting up in front of an audience never changed that.

Frankie was a mate, and a very close one, but when you're young, life's a bit of a game and there's no time for any in-depth thinking.

When I met Ted I was older, that much more mature and I found I could discuss and talk to him about things I couldn't share with anyone else, not even my wife. Most fellas are frightened to talk about having a close relationship with another man, but I'll bet there are not many who wouldn't admit, if only to themselves, that there is nothing like a real solid man's friendship.

We went all over the world together. We played golf; we got pissed and spent hours in each other's company. Then, at age fifty-three, Ted died of a heart attack and I was gutted – totally bereft. First I was hurt, then I was angry. His dying bordered on offending me. How dare he fucking leave me? If anyone thinks that sounds a bit soft, man or woman, then all I can say is either they've never known the joy of a good friend, or they're completely insensitive.

I'll tell you, there was nothing soft about Ted. I mentioned Tony Davis who died with the acid in the face. Well, one night he had a row with his missus, and she buggered off. When he was pissed he didn't care who his mates were, so he got himself a skinful, went looking for his wife and ended up banging on my door hollering and shouting. Ted was there that night, so he opened the door and Tony pushed his way in, stuck a pistol in Ted's throat shouting, 'I want my missus. I know she's here.' I've said, 'Hang on, Tone, you're out of order', but Ted never batted an eyelid, just said, 'Go on then, pull the trigger, you fat bastard. Let's see how hard you are – you've got the gun.' Tony said, 'Yeah, I have', and fired a full cylinder up the passage. He missed a murder charge by two inches. As he let the gun go, my sister-in-law opened the kitchen door and this spray of bullets went over her head and into the wall. Ted took the gun and decked him, and next day Tony had forgotten all about it.

It was a long time before I found anyone to replace Ted because road manager, PA, whatever term you use, is not just a job. Whoever takes it on, for me anyway, has to be father, brother, friend and a thousand other things. So it's not a case of becoming a friend of whoever it is, but giving the job to a friend, and for three years another guy, Peter Swanson, and me were very close, then he had to move on.

I've never gone through life looking for someone to confide in. I'm perfectly happy with my own company. Nevertheless, when I do meet someone who I can empathize with, it's a great thing. So when I met Bill Reilly, the other 'Lucky old boy', and we found we had a lot in common, I was well pleased. And to this day we're the greatest of friends. He's an Irishman, a real Paddy, yet we are very much alike, down to the fact that he talks the same as I do, and in many ways thinks like I do because he was born in London and has only been back to the 'Ould Country' four times in his life. He has an outlook on life where everything is either black or it's white – no in-between. I've learned so much from him because he has this way of analysing things that makes me stand back in amazement thinking, Jesus, he's right. So I feel privileged not only to have him as a mate, but grateful that his insight and advice has kept me from going wrong on many occasions.

Going back to my work, I remember I did a pilot show for the BBC that never came to anything, which was a shame because there were some lovely people in it, all of them dead and gone now. They were Jimmy Edwards, Arthur Askey and Kenneth Williams, whom I loved and admired so much.

I was sitting in the green room with Arthur Askey – tiny little man but a wonderful character – and he was having a go at me in a grandfatherly sort of way. I can see him now, up on tiptoe, wagging his finger saying, 'You lot have it too easy; you haven't learned the trade the right way.' I've gone, 'What do you mean?'

And he explained that in his day, when he was a young man, him and all the others used to travel from one end of the United Kingdom to the other, year in, year out. Every town had at least two theatres, so they'd do twenty minutes or so in each, then move on. Like painting the Forth Bridge; it might take them a year to come back to where they'd started. Same act, same material – they didn't need to change it because after a year, the punters have forgotten what they did the last time. Piece of piss.

And I've got his finger waving in my face as he tells me, 'You youngsters. Five minutes on television and you're big stars.' I thought, 'Yeah, and that's five minutes worth of material that can't be used again.'

He got my back up, really, though I didn't say anything because he was a legend and I had so much respect for him. I thought, if only you knew what we had to do nowadays to get a laugh, you wouldn't believe it.

It wasn't their fault, but these old fellas were well out of touch.

I was compèring at the Royal Lancaster Hotel, and Tommy Trinder did a turn. When he finished he went off with his catch-phrase, 'You lucky people'. I've stood there, looked at the audience, and in the aggressive manner that was expected I said, 'You lot lucky? Fuck off.' Backstage old Tommy's nearly collapsed. Fuck off? He'd never heard nothing like it in his life. Things had changed – completely different world.

One of the shows I got wrapped up in that was very, very popular was what they called *Seaside Specials*. Michael Hurle, a director at the BBC, ran them, and every week they'd be set up at a different venue. Southsea one week, Bournemouth the next. Each time they'd move the tent from one resort to another, because in essence it was a variety show under a big top.

I was all dressed up in the red coat, top hat and all that goes with being a ringmaster. One day, we'd done all the rehearsals and I was having a break sitting on the steps of a caravan, which was my dressing room for the day, and all I was wearing was my underpants. A skinny-ginger haired fella came up to me and went, 'Ey oop.' I said, 'All right pal, how's it going?' He said, 'Where's t' director?' I pointed out the mobile control unit where he usually hung out, and this geezer said thanks, walked away then stopped and came back. 'Hold that, chummy,' he said, and gave me a little suitcase and his jacket and walked off again. I'm top of the bill, and I thought, who the hell's that? It turned out to be Paul Daniels, the magician. That was him just starting out.

Another two were Cannon and Ball. This was going to be their first big TV show. They'd been trying for years to get a break, and obviously thought that being on my show was going to set them on the road.

Because of this, the pair of them were so nervous it wasn't true. They were shitting themselves. I took them into my caravan and tried to reassure them that they'd be OK. Don't worry about this, don't worry about that. If it goes wrong, we can always re-shoot it, and so on. Two hours I've spent with them before they went on, and to be honest when they did, they died on their arse. Terrible.

Months later, once they'd got a grip on themselves, they started to come through, and eventually for a short time became one of the biggest double acts in the country.

Now Colin Crompton died of cancer, and Johnny Hamp, who produced *The Comedians* and several major shows, got in touch with all the comics he'd been involved with. Would we please be part of a tribute to Colin at the Lakeside Country Club?

I was the compère, Tommy and Bobby were top of the bill. You wouldn't have recognized them. All through rehearsals they ignored me, looked right past me as though I was nothing. To crown their behaviour, just before they went on I was standing in the wings, and Bobby Ball was over the other side wearing his coat like a Batman cape and clicking his fingers at me. 'Oi, you. Yes you – over here.' I didn't want a row, so I pretended not to hear him and walked on stage to introduce them.

I didn't see anything of them for about a year or so, and when I did it was in a restaurant used by all the showbiz people. This time Tommy gave me a blank. I went, 'Hi Tom, how are you?' Nothing. As far as he was concerned I wasn't even there. I said, 'What am I, invisible? You ignorant prick', and a lot more. Cor, did I tell him off.

Funnily enough, only recently Barbara Windsor and her boyfriend bumped into the pair of them while she was spending a few days in Ireland. I think they were on tour or in a pantomime or something. I suppose with me and Barbara being good friends, and together at the studio every day, my name had popped up in conversation. Tommy and Bobby both asked her to give me a message. 'Please tell Mike we're sorry for how ignorant we were all those years ago.'

Fair enough. I've been around long enough to understand that human nature being what it is, a bit of fame can go to people's heads without them realizing it. I might make allowances for that kind of behaviour now, but personally I find it completely alien, unnecessary and a trap I've never fallen into. And I defy anyone to contradict that statement.

Mind you, it doesn't take very much for stories to go the rounds. Only the other week I was out for a meal with my missus and some bloke came up to me, well pissed. He said 'I know you, you're Mike Reid, a member of Worley Park Golf Club.' I said, 'You're right, I am.' 'Well,' he said, 'the last time I saw you and said hello you went "Bollocks". I was infuriated.' I said, 'Excuse me, you're bang out of order and a fucking liar. I've never said that to anyone who's approached me, so I know I never said it to you. I don't know you, and you certainly don't know me, do you?' He said no, so I said, 'Well piss off, then.'

It's not fair. For years he's probably been telling his mates that I told him 'Bollocks' when he approached me, and now without explaining why, he'll carry on telling them I told him to piss off.

I never abuse people. I might if they start it, because you can only take so much from a whippersnapper. I'd think, 'Hang on a minute, pal. I'm a human being here. I don't need to be talked to like that.'

But as regards my public (if I can use that term), I'm never anything but as polite as I can be, because I'm always conscious that if it wasn't for them, I might still have the overalls on.

Funny though, even with that attitude of mine, people are wary of me and won't come up to me. Not because they don't want to, but it's down to the fact that I can look a bit serious, and that could be off-putting.

When I appear at different venues, invariably the bouncer, or whoever, will come up to me and let me know that there are a couple or three people at the door that want my autograph. The place might have been packed to the rafters, but only a few people have got the nerve to ask. Yet if before I leave the stage I make an announcement, 'Now listen, tell you what. If any kids out there want an autograph, or you fancy one yourself, I'll be in the dressing room for the next hour – you're more than welcome.' Queues? You've never seen nothing like it. Invariably I don't put myself up for this because I'll have a long drive home. But when I do, it's usually to prove a point to someone I've mentioned this phenomenon to. Never fails.

Something that makes me laugh inside but not out, is when I'm standing at a bar and the geezer next to me clocks who I am. I know what's coming, and it's usually when they've sunk a few. 'You're Whatsisname, ain't ya, do us a gag.' 'Pardon?' 'Tell a joke – make me laugh.' 'Excuse me, pal, what do you do for a living?' 'I'm a cobbler.' 'OK. Do you fancy making me a pair of shoes while we're standing here?' Stops them dead every time.

Golden rule of mine: never accept a drink off a punter, especially if they've had a few, which usually they have before they approach me. It was a lesson I learned the hard way. One drink, fine, two and they think they've bought you for the evening – then the insults start to creep out. 'That show you did on telly, it was crap.' 'Thanks mate, just what I needed to hear.' 'Not much of a singer, are you?' More than one geezer got a dry slap before I learned to avoid situations like that.

In a sense, I'm not what you'd call a natural comic. When I was a kid and a young man I was as silly as arseholes – would make a joke out of a sink plug. But as a professional, the humour I put across is a trade that it's taken me a lifetime of hard work to perfect. I can switch it on. I don't mean what I do isn't sincere, it is, but I don't carry it on twenty-four hours a day.

Frank Carson never stops. Stan Boardman never stops – they probably crack gags while they're asleep. It's the way they are. I've got to hand it to them, they're both extremely talented comics who see and make a joke out of every situation all day long. I haven't been that way since I left school, and now I'm quite a mundane character.

Away from the camera I've become very laid-back and in some ways quite introverted, and that's down to the things that have happened in my life that have moulded my character.

I've spoken of people being wary of me; well, I've found myself being wary as well – and because of this it's suppressed my natural personality. I suppose what I'm looking for is the word trust. I don't trust easily any more. Because of what life has dished up for me, and being streetwise since I was six or seven, I do have the ability to suss people out. Give me ten minutes with whoever, and I've got them. I'm rarely wrong, and that's what education in life does for you.

I shouldn't have to do it, though. I should accept people as they come, but we're all concerned about what people think of us, so I'm asking myself, what do they want? If I'm too bubbly or too gushy, I'm a cocky bastard. If I go the other way, I'm a miserable bastard – no-win situation. Which is why, at my age now, I surround myself with my immediate family and a very few close friends, because they accept me for what I am.

Mentioning the drunk who reckoned I couldn't sing reminds me of doing a show at some club or hotel. I couldn't get my motor right up to the door where I would've liked, so I stuck it in the car park among a hundred others. On it was my own very distinctive personalized number plate, JOKIE, so it didn't take the Brain of Britain to work out whose it was. Show over, I got back to the car. Window smashed, tape player ripped out and about fifty tapes nicked – all except one. Sitting on the dash, just behind the steering wheel so I couldn't miss it, was a cassette I'd made. In other words, those toe-rags were telling me that my voice was so bad it wasn't worth nicking. Cheeky bastards.

I've always loved singing. The old ballads; easy-listening stuff; all the songs I'd grown up with.

After *Runaround* I was signed to Pye Records, and the guv'nor was

When Dad saw our house at Hatfield Peverel
he never said a word – but his grin spoke volumes.

A long way from nicking other people's cars!

When Prince Philip got to the end of the line and it was suggested, 'You know Mike Reid,' he said, 'No, I don't,' and walked off.

My one and only panto, with Helen Shapiro. Love the whistle.
John Alexander Studio

My best friend, Ted. I still miss his company.

Mark and me with Michael and Kirsty Anne – proud father, proud grandad.

This is how we remember Mark.

Pam St Clement taught me so much when
I joined *EastEnders*. BBC

Early days on the soap with my
TV family Ricky (Sid Owen) and
Diane (Sophie Lawrence). BBC

Flogging old bangers at my Rainham car lot was a wonderful rehearsal for
my TV role as Frank. BBC

Me and my screen mum, Mo (Edna Dore). *BBC*

Peter Dean, Bill Treacher and me.
Don't ask! *Ali Liddle*

Barbara Windsor and I sparkle together and
bring out the best in each other.
Doug McKenzie

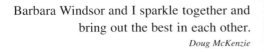

My son Michael – a chip off
the old block.

We could never accept the
loss of our Mark, but together
we gradually came to terms
with it. *The Sun*

Occasionally, when I look at little Michael, memories come to the surface and I wonder, what if?

S. Lewis © The Sun

Me and my princess. Forty years and still in love.

My family, although a few are missing – I love them all.

My utopia – literally roses round the door.
The Sun

Sir Louis Benjamin, who was also managing director of Moss Empires that owned the Palladium. At that time Tommy Steele had the title role in a Hans Christian Andersen that was on at the Pally. Somebody on the firm took the score of this show to Pye Records, and asked them if any of their artistes would like to have a go at some of the numbers. My producer Terry Brown checked them out and asked me if any of them appealed to me. Funnily enough, I was doing one of the songs in my act already, so I said go on then, stick me down for the Ugly Duckling.

Doing impressions was never my game, but I used to tell a few boxing gags, then sing this song as though it was Terry Downes doing it.

We got into the studio where Kenny Woodman had already laid down the backing track, and I said to the producer, can I do it my own way. He gave me my head and I went straight into it. Not as Terry Downes, but as myself – proper cockney, and chucking in all my own bits and pieces. 'Wallop, he went; Have some of that, he said; T'rific, I'm a swan.' It went a blinder. No pick-ups, no retakes, got it in one first time. Right at the end I said, 'I think I'll wobble off down the road and have a look at some of these Christmas dinners.' All they had to do was snip out the word Christmas so it wasn't seasonal, and it went to number three in the hit parade.

What a turn-up – Reidy on *Top of the Pops*. I stuck a little old soft hat on my head and did the show three times in all. I put my heart into that, and it paid off handsomely, which has been another philosophy of mine. Always do your best, because you don't know where it will lead.

Just like on the cruise ships, I got stuck in and ended up being offered Cruise Director. Another example is when I was asked to do a Christmas show by director/producer John Schofield. He was a great director, and one of the most prolific in the early years with major shows.

Behind his back he was known as The Prince of Darkness. That wasn't a criticism, it was down to the fact that he was handsome, wore his black hair swept back and stalked the corridors of the studio with his coat draped over his shoulders. This, plus the fact that he had charisma and a great air of authority.

It would be wrong to say we were frightened of him. It was more a case of being nervous, because we all wanted to do the very best for him.

He'd booked me to do *A Christmas Carol* with Christopher Timothy, the bloke from the vet's series. My manager, Tony Lewis, had written into my contract that I had to be given a day off so that I could do a voice-over on a commercial that had been signed up prior to this engagement. As the time got nearer I said to Tony, 'Can you put that voice-over back a bit, I don't really want to take any time off from rehearsals.' He did, and I gave it a miss. When I turned up for work on the day I shouldn't have been there, Schofield got up from his desk, came over to me and asked me what I was doing in the studio. Remember, I was nervous of the guy, so I said, 'Well, sir, I realized that I need rehearsals more than any of the others, so I put off my other engagement.' He looked me up and down, went 'Hmm', and sat down again. He never mentioned it again, just gave that thoughtful grunt.

We eventually did the show, and it was a great success. Afterwards Schofield took me on one side, congratulated me on my performance, then said, 'More to the point, you impressed me very much with your attitude in rehearsals,' referring to my showing up on my day off. 'It showed true professionalism.' Talk about praise from Caesar, I was knocked out.

Down to that, he offered me the job of compèring what was to be the last of the big variety shows to be made in this country – *Starburst*. What a show it turned out to be. This wasn't work for me; I think I should have paid them for giving me the opportunity to be involved with all those major stars – Shirley Bassey, Jack Jones, Tony Bennett – the list is endless, and they were all backed by a forty-piece orchestra. It was a dream come true for me to be fronting these people, introducing them and doing the funnies.

The first sixteen shows were made at Elstree Studios by ATV, then the BBC bought the studio and the whole lot moved to a brand-new place up in Nottingham. So in effect I worked on the last show ever made by ATV at the old studios, and the very first in the new building up north.

Now I've come full circle, because the original lot is now where *EastEnders* is produced.

Because this new studio was a major enterprise for the industry, they had to make a bit of a splash, so they got Prince Philip to open it. I was no stranger to the Royal Family, because I'd made no end of appearances in front of them. In all, I did four Royal Command Performances and countless birthday parties. Prince Charles, Princess Anne, Margaret, Diana and so on. It was a great honour to be asked, but to be honest, I never felt that I came over at my best, because I was always conscious of the risk of stepping over the line and slipping into my normal act. On top of that I did many, many charity functions that the Royals had an interest in. But after a while these requests for my time got a bit much, and I had to tell myself, this is nonsense. There I was, tearing all over the country, three hours there, three hours back, plus the function. For what? Basically a kick in the bollocks for nothing, because invariably I was treated like I was nothing by the organizers. Considering I never got or expected a penny piece out of the deal, they acted like they'd bought me for the day. Stand here, sit there, wait in the back room until we're ready for you, and so on. So I began to become very selective about where I showed my face.

Don't think that I was giving the charities a knock-back, because I wasn't. As far as that went, on my own account I could hold my head up knowing that over the years I'd done more than my share. In later years, with much gratitude for what I had myself, I willingly put myself forward as patron of many hospices and kids' hospitals.

Going back to Prince Philip, I remember a time when me and Shirl were invited to a do for the Queen's birthday, that was held in a marquee in the grounds of Windsor Castle. I was having a wander around and I came across the Prince having a swift one on his own in one of the tents. Normally the Royals don't drink in public, but they like a drop of turps, same as anyone, so while his elbow was going up and down I took advantage of him being on his own and nipped in for a chat.

I've got to hand it to him, I know the press give him some stick, but speak as you find, he struck me as highly intelligent, and knew his stuff no matter what we spoke of. I suppose we talked for about twenty minutes, and I was impressed by how clever he was at finishing with one subject, then flowing straight into something else.

He was coming to the opening of the new studio. Unfortunately, about four or five weeks prior to this, a new sensation for its time had hit the TV screens, in the shape of *Spitting Image*. With rubber puppets the show ripped the piss out of the Royal Family – ridiculed them. I can't imagine royalty getting tied up with contracts, so Philip could have told the TV company to stick the tape-cutting up their arse, because this man really had the hump with anyone or anything to do with television because of that series.

He showed anyway, got on the microphone and did what he was there for. I could tell it was a bit fraught when he didn't crack his face once – no gags; no banter. Then he made a few cutting remarks about *Spitting Image*, and finished up saying how he and the family were a bit upset.

It passed off, and they gave him the tour of the studio, told him all about the show, which was now renamed *Entertainment Express*, then walked him right down a line of all the people involved. He didn't look happy, and he didn't hang about. Quick handshake – next. I was last in line, because I was the top man as regards the show. As he got to me the director of ATV said, 'Of course, you know Mike Reid', and he went, 'No, I don't', and rushed off. So everyone else shook hands with him and I got the elbow.

I've got a nice photograph of me shaking hands with Her Majesty framed and hung up in my snooker room. This room stands on its own and is away from the house. It's surprising the number of people who question why something like that is relegated to the garden, almost suggesting that it should be hanging over the fireplace. Don't let that give the impression that I'm not extremely proud of that picture. Reidy the ducker and diver, who wobbled over the edge of the law too many times, being presented to the Queen of England. I mean, who could ever have imagined such a thing? A guest in one of her prisons, yes, but not face to face with her.

But these images of my past, like that and others that hang alongside it, I seem to have outgrown. It's all in my head, and I don't need things to remind me of what I've achieved, no matter how proud or chuffed I was at the time. In fact, apart from a few pictures, I don't think we've kept anything relating to my past work. My old woman reckons she's got a box of videos tucked away upstairs, but I've never set eyes on it, and I've yet to see her dig it out.

Same with autographs. I won't say I wasn't tempted in the early days, but when you're with a megastar like Frank Sinatra, there's always that tendency to think you're making a prat of yourself for asking. As it turned out, he gave me a signed picture, but I don't think I would ever have asked.

Although I've been doing it for years, I still wonder why people want my name scribbled on a piece of paper. I always oblige, and gladly, but never fail to think, why? I'm just a working entertainer, for Christ's sake. Even my Shirl doesn't understand it. Her memory's not that short that she can't remember how things were back in the days of the one-room flats, and she often says to friends, 'I don't know why these people want Mike's autograph, he's only my old man.'

Funnily enough, only the other week she was sorting out the cupboard and she pulled out a photograph of me opening a shopping centre – Lakeside, or somewhere like it. I'm stood in the middle of about five hundred people, and everywhere there's arms waving pens and paper. Unbelievable, yet I've never come to terms with it.

Referring back to my singing, there was a time when I knocked it on the head, and that was all down to one woman. I had a show called *Mike Reid Makes Music*. There was Kenny Lynch, Harry Fowler and the girl in it was Helen Shapiro. Who, although she had a smash hit with 'Walking Back To Happiness' and loads of other pop songs, was at heart really a jazz singer. And that's how we always kicked off the show, with a real nice jazzy number, big band – lovely, it was.

We had some laughs and I did a few numbers with Ken and Harry, and to finish off I'd sing something nice and slow, accompanied by Laurie Myer, who was a beautiful pianist. Then it was, 'Goodnight, ladies and gentlemen'.

We had bags and bags of letters every week from people thanking us for giving them a chance to hear all these great old numbers again. Of course, we'd all dive into the papers to read the reviews or what have you, and almost without exception they were kind, except what was written by a hack named Nina Myskow. She tore me to pieces – not the show, me personally. Week after week after week. She was writing for the *Mail* at the time, so was kindly informing God knows how many readers all over the country that Mike Reid was absolute rubbish. 'I can watch it until he opens his mouth, then I have to switch it off. I hope he loses his voice.'

Some of the things she said! Bang, have this – bang, have some more. In the end I said to the producer, 'I'm not going to sing. I'll do the funnies, but forget the songs.' And I did. My confidence was kicked into touch when I began to think she might be right, perhaps I did sound like a frog. And as always, if I can't do something well, scrub it.

She destroyed me. Easy for people to say I shouldn't have read the paper if it bothered me, but knowing I was getting coverage every week, I just couldn't stop myself having a look, perhaps hoping each time that it might be different.

I still enjoyed singing in the bath, around the house, and if I was at a party a good piano, bass and drums always got me up. But in public, it took me years before I could force myself to get back into it – all because of a few pages of self-publicizing, self-opinionated garbage.

Because she got a name as a critic, this woman got herself onto a talent show fronted by Marti Caine. The idea was that amateurs or semi-professionals would do their act, then have to stay on stage while they were judged with the camera full on them. I can't remember who else was judging the show, but generally they were fairly reasonable. Not her, though – nine times out of ten she would crucify these people. She would insult them by commenting on their dress sense or looks, which had nothing whatsoever to do with their talent, even if it was slightly dubious in some cases.

I used to watch it and seethe with anger. I'd say to Shirl, 'How dare she do that to people trying to get a break?' If it affected them like it did me, no doubt a lot of them took her advice and went back to hairdressing or bricklaying.

Who are these people? What right have they got to put down someone who is trying to better themselves? Gary Bushell, there's another one. Nothing but a jumped-up copywriter and a man who has made it a personal crusade to rubbish 'Fwank', as he calls me, and to dig me out personally at every opportunity. There's nothing about my appearance that he won't have a go at. My ears, my nose, my thinning hair – nothing. He sets himself up as a professional TV critic in one of the biggest national papers, and his reasons for slagging me off are so pathetically childish it's almost laughable. At one time he reckoned I was the best thing since sliced bread: 'Mike Reid – Top comic – Great guy – Mr Showbiz – Never fails to make me laugh', and so on. Then he got his own television show that was so wonderful, they stuck it on in the small hours of the morning to put insomniacs to sleep. He was desperate for me to appear and liven it up for him, but genuinely there was no way I could fit it into my schedule, and I had to give him a knock-back. He never forgave me, and from that day to this he's never missed the chance to have a go. Should I be surprised at anything from a man who agreed with his readers when they voted him one of Britain's best-looking men? C'mon – if he's on that list, my arse should be up there in the top ten.

It's my firmly held conviction that at the end of the day this man is nothing but a frustrated entertainer. He'd like to be able to get up on a stage and do the business as an actor or comedian, but having no skills in that direction he makes a name for himself by rubbishing talents that he can only dream of.

I've seen it time and time again. When it suits him to have his face plastered all over the middle pages of a tabloid, grinning like an idiot with his arm round a well-known personality, he's Mr Wonderful. Then, bang, once he's promoted himself, the Judas in him creeps out and that personality is suddenly relegated to 'no-talent-of-the-week', and they have absolutely no comeback. Which is why, if anyone thinks I'm getting a bit vitriolic about this guy, I'm taking the opportunity to dig him out on behalf of all of us in the business who are tired of his self-congratulating abuse.

One of these days I'll have an even better showcase for putting him in his place. God help us, but if his TV show is ever resurrected a national newspaper has offered me the position of being their television critic the day after each transmission. Believe me, I'm going to grab it with both hands.

Has he or Myskow or any of these so-called critics ever done anything that gives them the particular skills to judge other people's work? Been a comic, a singer, or written a best-seller? Have they bollocks.

If someone in the business like Nigel Hawthorne or Billy Connolly said to me, 'Mike, that acting you did last week was crap. You were stilted and your timing was out'; if that was the case, fair comment, from very talented people. I wouldn't be offended. I'd have a look at whatever I'd done and probably go, 'Yeah, you're right, I'll sharpen it up next time.' Because those two and others like them have proved their worth over and over again, and I could respect their opinion, so I'd try and aspire to take on board whatever they suggested.

In all, I suppose there's about three or four television critics who deserve the name. They don't dig people out, they give constructive criticism, and that's acceptable. But the others, all they do is abuse and abuse. I'm not talking about when this sort of crap is directed at me, because quite honestly I've reached a stage in my career when I just don't care. I've made a success of myself and nothing said or written about me can ever take that away, but some young actors or whatever could be destroyed for the rest of their lives. 'Did you read what Bushell said about so and so – they're rubbish. Don't book them, get someone else.'

What can be annoying, and it goes to prove that these people haven't got the talent or decency to concentrate on serious criticism, is when they have a go at a physical defect or someone's mannerisms. Writing comments like, 'His nose is bigger than his talent', 'Her voice is as flat as her chest', and so on. It makes me furious, because not only is this sort of thing both stupid and unnecessary, it's completely destructive.

CHAPTER EIGHT

ONLY THE OTHER WEEK ONE OF THESE WRITERS MADE SOME remark about Frank Butcher's new teeth. I didn't read it; somebody mentioned it on set, so I don't know what else was said, though I should imagine it was something a bit sarcastic. Bloody marvellous. I look after my teeth every day of my life, then get a knock-back because they look like three grand's worth of dental treatment.

I've got to thank Mum for that, because she plagued the life out of me, making sure I cleaned them every five minutes. You'd think they were her teeth the way she kept on. 'My Michael's got beautiful teeth – go on, son, show Mrs Whatsername.' And I'd have to perform with the big smile. So when I got one knocked out, it was like the end of the world.

When I was in my teens I used to go to the Royal Tottenham on a regular basis with my little firm. I got into a ruck one night with a young geezer. He gave me a shove, so I knocked him clean out. Trouble was, he was on the firm of Dennis Wilde, who was a bit of a big noise in the High Cross area. When he showed up at the dance hall a bit later, I thought I'd better have a word with him, explain my side of what had happened before he heard different and the trouble escalated.

He was a lot shorter than me but big and stocky, but either way I fronted him up. 'Dennis, I want a word about what went on earlier.' He never even answered me, just spanked me straight in the mouth, and the huge sovereign ring on his finger broke my front tooth in half and split my lip. I was knocked arse over bollocks through all these chairs and out on to the dance floor, and while I was getting a good kicking and spinning round on my back, I kept getting flashes up the skirts of girls who were dodging out of the way.

I don't remember it hurting me very much, but what filled me with fear was what my mother's reaction would be. I went round to Uncle Fred's, and when he saw the state I was in he asked me what was the matter. I showed him the gap in my mouth. I said, 'Uncle Fred, I can't go home – Mum will kill me when she sees this.' He said, 'Don't be silly, she'll understand. You're a boy; you've had your tooth knocked out. It happens, no big deal.' I believed him, went home and she went absolutely berserk. She screamed and shouted, and if I hadn't been leaking enough claret anyway, she would have claimed me. Upshot was an emergency appointment first thing and a porcelain crown screwed into my gum.

So apart from that one, every single tooth in my head is my own – and Frank's. So if anyone wants to dig me out with smart-arse remarks I suggest they get their facts right first.

I've already said that the only reason for knocking myself out with work was for the money, which doesn't mean that I ever had the attitude of gimme the wedge and run. I've always put a hundred and ten per cent of myself into whatever I was into and in return, thankfully, I was weighed out handsomely.

I know I keep harping on about the contrast between my early lifestyle and later, but there were times when I just couldn't believe what was coming in. Even today, it's mind-boggling when I consider that my mouth and personality, for what it's worth, has generated between six and seven million pounds. And that's inside twenty-six years.

Not that it all ended up in my pocket, because there was always a number of people having a dip into my wages. Manager, road manager, accountants, and of course, when I made the decision at the beginning of my career to go legit, there was the government bleeding me dry. At one time I was paying out ninety-seven pence in the pound in taxes, and it broke my heart.

I know there's always that argument, and one I probably used myself years ago, that if you're paying that much to the taxman then you must be earning a bloody fortune, so stop moaning. Let me tell you, though, it's a different ball game when you do get into that position. Start turning over a certain figure, and you find that for every thousand pounds you graft your nuts off for, you're allowed to hold on to thirty pounds. No wonder too many successful people go on the fiddle or leave the country.

I've always kept myself straight, though, not because I'm any more honest than some of these others, but I know that one slip-up means the taxman gets on your back and never lets go. I could moonlight for a bit of cash in hand every night of the week, but what would be the point? I did my share of that when I was ducking and diving. I never paid a penny in motor tax, income tax or insurance stamps, but on the other hand, never took a copper coin from unemployment benefit or any other handouts. So I might have got away with murder as a young man, but by Christ I've paid my whack since then – and more.

Still, having complained about what I was paying out, I've got to say an enormous amount stuck to my fingers, and me and Shirl were like two kids in a sweetshop; we didn't know what to go after next.

Between the two of us, we haven't got an ounce of business acumen. Different times we thought we had, then things would go wrong and I'll say it again, if something doesn't work or I'm making an arsehole of it, give it the elbow – move on to something else.

There was a time when I laid out something approaching forty thousand pounds in kennel fees for eighteen pups out of a couple of greyhounds. When I think of what I had to earn just to keep those dogs. It was phenomenal, bearing in mind what I've already said about taxes and so on.

How it happened was down to my love of dogs and a great passion for racing. A guy rang me up to tell me that a friend of his had a bitch for sale. She was over in Ireland, was an open racer and all he was asking for her was seven hundred notes – unseen. I've agreed to buy this Caribbean Cherry, and had her flown to Stansted Airport.

When I got the cage home and opened it up I thought, 'Reidy's done it again.' This supposedly top-class dog was flea-bitten, had mange all down her chest and all sorts wrong with it. Yet once the vet got her sorted out, she repaid us by going round the track like greased lightning.

I stuck her with Dave, a trainer in Walthamstow, and after a while the trophies were piling up. That's the bit I loved, picking up those little silver cups. They were silver-plated and not worth a light, but what they represented meant so much to me.

Three months after I bought this first one, the same guy offered me a dog that was the sister of Caribbean Cherry. No name, good price, so I went for it. I combined my old woman's name with her mate Marge's and called the dog Shirma. She was the equal of her sister, and I was chuffed to bits.

I'm not one of those geezers who think a greyhound is an earner on legs; they were my girls. I treated them with respect and took them all over the place. When Dave heard that I used to take them out in the field to chase rabbits he went up the wall. 'Mike, they're worth a fortune – they could pull a tendon or break a leg.' I just said, 'Dave, if all they've got to look forward to is a quick run round the track then be shut in a cage until the next time, I'd rather give it all up.'

I've always been a sucker for dogs and babies. Doesn't matter how rich you are, if either one doesn't like you, there's nothing you can do about it.

One thing led to another, and I thought I'd get into the breeding game. I mean, if these dogs are worth a mint, what are their pups going to fetch?

First, I sent Cherry back over to Ireland to be covered by this champion whose name escapes me. Cost a bomb, but I thought it was worth the outlay. It was a long time after that I found out my bitch had been served by a ghost. Well, it must have been, because the champion sire had been dead for three years prior to this. Those Irish! Likeable people, but sharp as razors, and knowing how green I was they'd snatched my bollocks off.

Shortly after that I had Shirma put in pup, with the result that I ended up in total with eighteen of their offspring. And from day one they were boarded in kennels until they reached eighteen months, because they can't run to earn a penny until they reach that age. At a score a week each, that set me back close to thirty thousand. On top of that, there were vet's bills for monthly check-ups, inoculations and so on.

When they reached the stage of going out to a trainer, I stopped and told myself, this is absolute nonsense. I'm working day and night to keep all these dogs, when quite honestly the novelty had worn off. I won't say I'm fickle with my interests, but once whatever it is has run its course and I've achieved what I set out to do, I lose interest. And basically that's what happened here.

It was only partly to do with the money. I sold the two bitches back to the people I'd bought them off in Ireland, needless to say at an enormous loss. And the pups, if that's what they still were, I actually gave away to good homes. With what I'd slung at them, plus their pedigrees, they were worth an enormous sum, but I never chase dead money, and once I knew they were going to be looked after I just walked away.

Another time I did the same with a racehorse. It was a big, big status symbol for me, being a bit flash I suppose. Any horse costs a fortune to keep unless they're like the old nags I kept on the marshes. When they're racehorses you can more than treble the cost, day in and day out. I had my fun, played the top owner, then wiped my mouth of it. I learned a lesson there, and I'd never do it again.

My manager Tony Lewis had a lot of dealings with America. He handled top-name people like Shirley Bassey and Trevor Howard, and naturally had made contacts all over the States. I asked him to try and sort out a bit of work for me, because I knew the Yanks just loved a cockney accent. They might not have understood it half the time, as I found on the cruise ships, but nevertheless they had a thing for it. Nothing came of it, but I still fancied going over there, work or not.

I did a stag do at a conference at the Lancaster Hotel in Bayswater, and at the same time in the main hall there was one of those property sales functions that are always advertised in the top papers. After I'd done my bit, I wandered down to have a look and got chatting to one of the salesmen by the name of Charlie Clamp. He gave me a load of spiel about these new houses his firm was putting up in Tampa, Florida, but he seemed genuine enough and got me interested. I had a talk with Shirl and we decided we'd take up Charlie's offer to be flown out there, put up for two or three days and be shown what was on offer.

We flew to Port Ritchie on the Gold Coast, were picked up in a car and showed finished houses, half-finished houses and plans of what we could have, for in the region of thirty-five grand. What we'd get for our money was just incredible, but on top of that we're taken out for meals and on sightseeing tours, and to be honest, we were both knocked out by the potential lifestyle and signed on the dotted line.

I got very friendly with Charlie Clamp and once the house was completed, with him overseeing it, we spent a lot of time together whenever we went out there. He had this wonderful sports fishing boat and he used to let me take it out, a Mako. Top of the range – best in the world, and I wanted it. Jesus, did I want to own it. He didn't want to part with it, but when I told him he could use it like his own when I was back in England, we struck a deal.

The house was out of this world. It was in a complex, but the big garden that was full of palm trees backed on to a lake, and as it matured it was gorgeous. To round it off, I bought a brand-new Rolls-Royce for pottering about in, and things couldn't have been better.

I'm not just trumpeting about my possessions here. This list of bits and pieces that I'd accumulated becomes very relevant later on in my story, same as me making a mention of a fella by the name of Don Milson. This Don was the youngest of a family who'd almost all died young of heart attacks. As he told me, if I'm going to die before I get old, I might as well do it in the sun, so he bought a place just round the corner from me in Florida.

As he was a permanent resident, and obviously I wasn't, I paid him thirty dollars a week to look after my place when I wasn't there. Everybody kept their places immaculate, so with him mowing the lawn and keeping the weeds down I felt I was keeping my end up.

Strangely enough, the place reminded me of London when I was a kid. Well, not the place so much, more the atmosphere of stepping out on a lovely sunny morning and no-one being about.

I love America. I love Americans. I find them friendly, polite and almost without exception, they fall arse over head to try to help you. I remember distinctly those first few weeks when we were there having a constant traffic of neighbours bringing home-made cakes, offering this and that. Please come and join us – Come for coffee – Come for dinner. We were made more welcome by these strangers, culturally speaking, than in some of the villages back home.

When me and Shirl went out there, which was as often as we could, we made an effort to see as much of the States as possible. We'd fly to New York, then drive down the West Coast, or another time the East, then central – and it was magic. We never hung about in New York – that's not America; cold, hard-bitten place. As are Miami, Los Angeles and Las Vegas. They're all, 'Hurry up, give us your money and piss off.' Completely money-orientated.

But the rest's marvellous; wonderful. Unless you've been there, you just can't imagine how big the place is. Going at seventy miles an hour, stopping for a bit of breakfast and lunch, it took us three days just to drive across Texas.

In essence I was totally in awe of America, full stop.

Initially, the whole idea of crossing the pond was in the hope of getting work there, which then leads on to international acclaim, if you like, but it just never happened. As time went on, any aspirations I had in that direction dwindled to nothing.

Now that I'm older, even if I was asked to do a major film over there I'd say no, thanks. It's too late in my career; I'm winding down, and don't want to be involved in all that high-flying stuff.

Different ball game in this country, but I'll cover that later on.

Australia was another place where I eventually fancied dipping my bread, but by the time I got round to it, it was too late. In the early days, just after *The Comedians*, they were screaming for me to go over there. Indeed, they desperately wanted all of us. The other fellas went, but I had more work than I could handle at home, so I gave it a miss.

Years later, when I thought I should give it a go because I was still very popular out there, our wonderful actors' union Equity decided, in their infinite wisdom, that too many Aussie acts were coming to this country and they were going to put a stop to it. They stipulated that the only way to get in and work was if these people were inter-national stars. Tit for tat, the Australian equivalent of Equity said well stuff you lot, the same can apply the other way round. International star I have never been, so that was that.

I've visited the place no end of times, from a boy of sixteen right through, but never been allowed to work there in the show-business sense.

Back home, we'd made a move into the house I'm sitting in right now, and to me it was and is everything I could ever have wished for. It's five hundred years old, beautifully thatched and set in ten acres amongst wonderful rolling countryside. I'm in heaven here – there are literally roses round the door. When we first came, it was a bit of a comedown from what we'd been used to, but then we only paid a fraction of what we had laid out for those other places, with their twenty bedrooms and what have you.

Since then, though, I've spent thousands and thousands getting it just right. Swimming pool, extensions, games room, landscaping until I've got it a real piece. And that's what I had to tell my old woman only the other week. She came out with, 'Mike, I want to move. This place isn't big enough.' I put my foot down, which is something I rarely do. Anything for a quiet life, that's me, but in this case, I said no. Categorically *no*.

I know our kids and the grandchildren practically live here, but at the end of the day there's only the two of us a lot of the time. No: this'll do me until my time's up. This, plus perhaps half a year in Spain, work permitting, and I'll never want for anything else.

There was a time when I wouldn't have gone back to Spain for a million pounds, but thankfully, once the memory of a bad experience there had faded away, I reconsidered a decision I'd made that everything Spanish could fuck off.

It all started with my all-abiding passion for motor cars. I went to see Colin Chapman, who developed and produced Lotus cars, and paid serious folding for a brand-new Lotus Turbo Esprit. When it was delivered I couldn't take my eyes off it – it was gleaming.

Now just to explain something: the lane that leads down to the beginning of my drive is so narrow that if you put a matchbox down, you can't get past. Up until then, I'd never thought this was a bad thing, because no-one could approach our property without being seen by somebody or other. That wasn't just paranoia on my part, because on three occasions I'd been warned by certain connections that I was going to be turned over. Each time I made sure the dogs were wandering the grounds, and I never suffered being robbed.

The same thing had happened when we lived at Crabs Hill House in Hatfield Peverel. Same warning from friends who'd got a whisper – I put the dogs out and nothing came of it. But next door to us lived a greengrocer. A wealthy man, he had a beautiful house in eight acres. In fact, our houses were the only major properties down that lane. The villains came to do me, couldn't get near because of the dogs, so went next door and completely emptied my neighbour's house. Everything, right down to pots and pans.

The best of it was, I watched them do it. I should have thought, what with expecting something to go off, but these geezers looked dead kosher. Sign-written lorry, green overalls. I thought, same as anyone would, that they were moving something in or moving out. This neighbour didn't say too much, but if he'd known about my past, I think Old Bill might have been knocking on my door.

So, this lane – once I'd had my fill of studying this superb piece of machinery, I just had to take it out for a spin. And with only delivery mileage on the clock, I drove out of my gates, went eight hundred yards up the lane and crashed head-on with Mrs Ellis, who lives opposite me. Eighty-five years old, steady driver, she's come round the slight bend and written off my beautiful car with her big old lumpy Austin 18. I'm sure I was polite to the old girl – these things happen – but I must have shed a few tears. Lotus came and picked it up, and I wasn't to see it again for six months.

When I got word that my car was being returned in a few weeks, me and Shirl made up our minds to give it a good run by driving down to Spain to visit her brother Verdi, who lived near Benidorm. I couldn't wait to set off, because in that rare piece of a motor it was going to be a thousand miles of sheer pleasure.

Four miles from my brother-in-law's house, I got pulled over by Spanish coppers on motorbikes. None of us spoke the other's language, but they're the same the world over, so after a load of sign language I realized they wanted me to dig out my documents. I soon realized I had a problem when they started gesticulating at these papers, and one of them climbed into my motor and started it up. I've gone, 'Oi, get out of it. You're not driving this brand-new motor', and I grabbed hold of his shoulder. Not for the first time in my life I got a gun shoved in my back, so I put my hands up and watched him tear off like Nigel Mansell. The copper who was left just grinned and raised his arms as if to say tough shit, gringo, or whatever they called us.

We're hot, tired, pissed off and don't know where we are. So we set off walking until we found a phone box. Got in touch with my brother-in-law's place and his missus Maureen, who could speak Spanish, came out to rescue us.

We went back to where the copper was still waiting, and she found out that I was missing some green card or other, and as far as the law were concerned, I'd nicked the motor. What a carry-on!

I've got the old woman on my ear'ole because she'd put out this piece of paper to be signed weeks before, and I hadn't got round to it. The car was impounded. It took more than a week before I could get my mate George back in England to courier me out the papers, then before I could get my car back I had to pay about five hundred pounds in fines. Those bastards really strapped me up – an absolute arm and a leg.

It was a dodgy old start to our holiday, but once it was all sorted out, we put it behind us and got on with enjoying ourselves.

One night we all went to Huelva for a meal and a few drinks, and I was quite taken by the place. It was lively, and I couldn't help noticing it was heaving with expats. Towards the end of the evening, I said to the others that I thought it would be an ideal place for a nightclub.

How was I to know that that simple statement would remain the scourge of my life for years to come?

With the seed planted, my old woman and the in-laws jumped at it, and I've got to say, the more I thought about it the more smitten I became. Mike Reid – El Patròn! We talked about nothing else for days. By the time we'd kicked it around, my idea of a nightclub had gone out of the window, as I was talked into settling for a club-cum-restaurant. I went along with that, though my dream of a nightclub never really went away.

Most people are the same, but I think I'm worse than anyone. When I want something, I want it, and I don't care what I pay for it, although as this was going to be a business venture with Shirl's brother and his missus, I couldn't go too silly.

We checked out properties everywhere, haunted the estate agents and eventually someone pointed us towards a pizzeria up in the mountains that was owned by a Spaniard. It was run-down, but beautiful. It had stunning views and was well big enough for what we wanted.

The only thing in my defence at the time was that I kept saying it was in the wrong catchment area. I felt we should have looked closer to Benidorm, where all the tourists were. But having found somewhere after so much searching, I was easily talked into it. I'm not saying the others forced my hand up my back – I was as keen as they were – but I had reservations.

Now was the Spanish owner an actor, or what? He actually cried at the thought of selling his place, but he'd no choice – family problems, so he said. Did he give us some old bollocks! He showed us two sets of books that proved the place was a gold mine. Later on, we found they deserved to go to number one in the fiction charts.

We worked out some figures, made a bid that he accepted and weighed him out more than I really wanted to, allowing for the fact that we still had to do the place up. Even then we had a shortfall of about twenty grand, and signed a paper saying we'd square up with him at the end of the year.

We were in business. We pulled in another guy, Paul Howard and his missus Mary, and we all worked our bollocks off to get the club into shape. Nothing was spared, and with my idea of clubs back home, everything was done to West End standards. Flock wallpaper, which was all the rage at the time, chandeliers, loads of marble and painted inside and out from top to bottom. We even power-hosed the roof so it gleamed in the sun. An outside bar with thatched covers over the tables added the finishing touch.

What it all cost was frightening, but we knew we were on to a good thing, and would recoup it in months.

There were seats for four hundred people inside and outside a theatre that would hold as many again. Balconies with marble stairs led up – flowers everywhere. I tell you, it was a piece.

On recommendation I found a chef and offered him a job. He gave me a knock-back. 'No work for you. You gangster.' I think he must have been reading too many newspapers, and thought every Londoner was a bullion robber on the run. I ask you, do I look like a gangster? A raise on the wedge I'd offered and his scruples went out the door. Plus the fact that I said he could hire all the waiters and kitchen staff.

Eighteen in all we ended up with, and no doubt he was getting a cut from every one of them. But that wasn't enough for the greedy bastard. Much too late, I found he was ripping us off for a fortune every week. He wasn't just nicking wine and other bits and pieces; he was charging me top dollar for the very best cuts of meat, then buying in shit to serve to the punters. Cunning, though – he kept a small reserve of good-quality gear so that when any of us had a meal it just melted in our mouths.

Once we got up and running, we did a PR job on the locals to keep everyone sweet. The Spanish revere their old people, and give them a ton of respect. So we sent fruit and turkeys to the local old people's home, then laid on coach trips for anyone over a certain age.

Using my name, which in all modesty I have to say had a high profile then, I got in touch with all the tour companies. Blue Sky, Thompsons, Horizon, and so on, and got us put on the Mike Reid International Tour. People like them get people like us by the short hairs, because in a sense we need them more than they need us.

The deal was that they would bus tourists out to our place for twelve pounds a head. Out of that I would get four pounds a head to feed them, entertain them and give them free wine. The sums didn't add up, but then you don't count up your profits every day, that's a longer-term thing. So initially I thought we were coining it. We were always packed out, and it got so no-one could move outside for cars and coaches.

As an investment, we poured some serious money into getting a two-acre car park laid out on the hurry-up. In came the bulldozers, down came the trees and it was all gravelled and laid with tarmac in no time.

They finished it on the Thursday. On the Friday the local council dug a big ditch right across the entrance for pipe-laying, and nobody could get in or out. I screamed, I pleaded, and all I got was *mañana*.

Complete waste of time. That hole in the ground stayed there until I walked away from the place, so everyone was back to parking in the road.

My brother Brian got involved as resident singer, playing the keyboards and getting everyone up singing and dancing. Primarily, once all the graft was done, my function was to put myself about among the punters and do my comedy routine. But what with the pressure of finance and other aggravation, I caught shingles. The pain was terrible, yet so as not to let anyone down, I forced myself to carry on even though all I wanted to do was lie down in a dark room.

Those package tours were bleeding us dry. Because all the tourist punters had been brought by coach perhaps twenty to thirty miles, just as they were loosening up and ready to start spending a bit on booze, it was, 'Everyone back on the bus'. Remember, they've had a meal with wine on the table, then the agreement was that we gave a free bottle to every couple. I didn't blame the tourists because they did eventually drift towards the bars, and in a different location, from that point on they would've drunk the place dry. But they didn't get a chance, and on a good night I'll bet we weren't selling more than a hundred beers.

I called a meeting with the tour operators and asked for an extra fifty pence per head. That's all it needed to turn the corner, but they told me to piss off – take what you're getting or come off the tour.

I so desperately wanted that place to succeed because it was such a wonderful setting, and all of us had worked so hard.

What had started as a holiday to give my Lotus a burn-up had run into seven months of hard work over there, and the turning-down of very lucrative work back home. And all I can say at the end of that time was it had skint me.

It was getting close to the time when we had agreed to weigh out the balance owing, and what with being robbed by the chef, the overheads and the small profits from the customers, we were in the shit. So I said to my partners, the in-laws, 'Look, I'll have to go back home and drum up a bit of work for myself and see if I can tide us over until things straighten out.'

Me and Shirl drove back to England in mid-September, and two weeks later it all went pear-shaped in Spain. I'd come back to three nights at the Talk of the Town and nothing else. Not even a voice-over or one single stag do. Seven months I'd turned my back on it, not seven years, and it was the old story: 'Mike who?'

I've said to my agent, 'Surely there's something for me to do; the phone never stopped ringing before I went away.' All he said was, 'I warned you six months ago.'

That night the phone rang. It wasn't work, it was my brother-in-law. 'Quick, Mike, we need five grand for wages and the drinks bill.' Oh, hell, I haven't got a brass farthing – I'm totally b'rassic, but you can't rip off Spanish nationals or the authorities have your nuts for castanets.

I was forced to get into the ribs of my manager. If memory serves, this was the one and only time I ever asked anyone for help, but I was desperate. Tony, good as gold, slung me the five as a loan off future work, and I sent it out to Spain. It was like pissing in the sea. A week later Verdi's on the phone again for another three, which I didn't have. On top of that, he reminded me, as if I needed to be, that our contracted final payment was due.

Earlier in the year, the balance seemed nothing. Well, not nothing exactly, but as we reckoned we'd be turning over thousands a month, certainly nothing to worry about. Now, though, on top of everything else, it was an insurmountable problem. My in-laws didn't have a bean because they'd sunk all their funds into the project. So it was down to me as the only one with any assets.

I made a frantic phone call to Charlie Clamp in America. Sell the house, get the best price you can, but it's got to be settled within the month. I told him I didn't mind losing a couple of grand, as long as it was gone in the time. It went – and I lost bundles. A banker's draft came flying over to me, quick turnaround, and equally as fast I turned it round and sent it to Spain. It was a start, but not enough.

My Mako boat was worth a fortune. Not only its own value of $30,000, but the on-board equipment must have been valued at $15,000. There was radar, depth finders, fishing equipment of every description, ship-to-shore radio – it just went on and on. With a bit of luck, the sale would pull us out of the shit.

I got my son-in-law, who lived in America, to pick up the Mako from where it was stored in Texas, and asked him to drive it to

Galveston, where I could expect the best price. He got stitched like the proverbial kipper. He left it with a dealer who showed a bit of interest, then two days later went back to be told the engines had blown up on a trial run. Did they see him coming, or what? Two Johnston 200-horsepower engines, capable of 70 knots – nearly 80 miles an hour – and they've both given up at the same time? Take it off your hands for $5,000.

He rang me in a panic, and I was so sick I just told him to take the cash and forget it. I'd no choice, I needed every penny.

I'd run through a series of expensive motors while I was in America, and at the time I'm referring to I had a rare and beautiful Lincoln Continental. It had hardly turned a wheel, and was worth almost $30,000. Quick sale – $24,000.

I've got to calm myself down a bit, because even now, all these years later, I'm still incensed by how my friend Don Milson turned me over. The loss of the house was business, and I swallowed it. The boat was the same. Dealers, any dealers, get up in the morning ready to turn somebody over. If I didn't like it, it was up to me to get my arse over there and get a better deal. But I couldn't even afford the fare, so it was down to experience. But Milson; the dirty one-eyed bastard was a mate, and a good one, and when I asked him to sell the Lincoln he came back with an offer of $6,000.

I said, 'Don, that motor's only done three thousand miles, it's worth twenty-eight thousand of anybody's money. Try somewhere else.' On the phone again: 'Sorry, Mike, I've tried three other places and the first offer is the best.' I was gutted, on my uppers, and I didn't know where to turn next, so I told him to accept whatever, thinking that every little would help. If he said that's what it was worth, then I'd got no reason to doubt him, because we'd been good friends over the years and I'd helped him out many times. What happened? That dirty bastard sold my car, disappeared and I never saw him or my bit of money ever again. No doubt he got the right price for the motor, but didn't once consider my desperate situation and quite happily made himself twenty-eight grand out of my misfortune. He took me for a mug, no question of it, and I'll never forgive him. My only consolation is that wherever he is, he has got to live with the thought of what he did, to a friend, for the rest of his life.

The cash I was expecting from Milson would only have followed the rest to pay off our debt in Spain, and I don't suppose it would have made a great deal of difference. If I'd had the time to sell off my assets at my own pace, I could have covered what we owed, but time had been against me and now there was nothing left but the house we lived in. I got some people in to arrange a mortgage on our home, and they told me it would take about a month.

I hadn't even signed anything when I got a call from my brother-in-law. The Guardia Civil had turned up at the club overnight and padlocked every door. I'll bet they enjoyed that, and it wasn't the first time.

When we were open and in full swing, one night this geezer came into our foyer which was all decked out with plush seats and flowers, sat for about twenty minutes then disappeared off. Paul's wife Mary clocked him, wondered why he didn't have a drink or anything, then forgot all about him. Next morning when we arrive to open up, it's padlocked all round – same as this time. The Guardia eventually came asking if we had a music licence, which we did. 'Our man came last night, but it was not displayed.' So all that carry on because that arsehole didn't ask to see someone in authority. That was the sort of mentality we were up against all the time.

We were out on our earholes. We'd gone one day over the redemption date, and Spanish law being what it was then, plus the fact that the local magistrate just loved to screw foreigners who take advantage of their own, everything reverted back to the Spaniard we'd bought it off. How lucky was that slippery bastard?

With no argument or process of appeal from us, he's been given back the whole club, lock, stock and barrel. Plus the lion's share of what we owed him, and we couldn't do a thing. He must have thought he'd won the lottery. Same as the chef; 'He no work for gangster', could've given a few lessons in that game himself. Not long after we were thrown out he opened his own restaurant on the beach, and I can only presume that he paid for it with what he'd creamed off our business.

Being the name I was, the whole affair got a good airing in the papers. Remember, I've wiped myself out to pull me and my in-laws out of the shit. OK, they lost their bit of savings and what they'd originally put in, but I lost everything. Years and years of graft down the pan.

I think it was a reporter from the *Sun* who rang me up. He asked me if I had any comment on the allegations made by my sister-in-law. When I asked him what sort of crap he was making up he just said, 'Listen to this', and played a recording of Maureen, one of the family, slagging me off. Coming out of her own mouth was stuff I couldn't believe. She said I'd pissed the profits up the wall; I never worked and spent all my days by the pool and because of me, and only me, I'd ruined them. I think that was the final straw on top of everything else. It totally destroyed me and Shirl with that part of the family.

As for Spain and everyone in it, I just burned with hatred for what its bent laws had done to me, and vowed I'd never set foot in it again as long as I lived.

Why didn't I sell my beautiful, expensive Lotus, which was the only asset I might have had control over? I'll tell you. Our Mark, taking after his dad, stepbrother, brother and even stepsister, decided he'd nick it one night from out the front. I didn't even know it had gone, but the police spotted him, thought he looked a bit suspicious and chased him. Don't ask me why, but he went through Bishop's Stortford at eighty miles an hour in second gear and blew the engine to pieces. With the bumps and knocks it got on the way, by the time it was brought back on a trailer it wasn't worth two bob.

Funnily enough, it was only recently that I found out that my Angie used to nick my motors regularly when she was only fourteen, and I didn't have a clue. What is it with my family and cars? Surely taking without consent isn't hereditary?

The only blessing after that Spain business was that we still had the house, and I didn't become bankrupt. But God, did it take its toll mentally and physically.

I've got to say, and I stick my chest out when I do, that I have this attribute, this inner thing, that won't allow me to be crushed down so far that I can't get up. OK, I was on my arse, but I'd never been shy of a bit of graft and nothing had changed. Cor, did I work – day and night, every hour God gave to pull me and my family back up again. I never asked anything from anyone, and I never kissed arse to get work.

The one favour I had asked my manager Tony for was paid back out of the first few jobs I got in. I can't say that was by choice; I thought he'd nick a few hundred off every bit of work until it was paid off, but not him. He's a lovely man, but on the other hand he's a businessman without too much sentiment. Bang, he took the whole five grand in one hit, leaving me with nothing in my pocket. Still, that's the name of the game. You borrow, you pay back, but I was a bit aggrieved at the time.

One door shuts, another opens. I say it time after time, but it's a fact of my life. It didn't always happen straight away, but without becoming complacent, I knew something would come up to help me turn the corner.

Going all the way back to when I finished *Runaround*, the same director, Colin Nutley, phoned me up to tell me that he had a wonderful script for a sixteen-part serial called *Noah's Castle*. Best of all, he wanted me to play the lead villain. Now this was really my first bit of serious acting, so I put my heart and soul into it. And, like before, this was to pay dividends, though I didn't know it at the time.

The storyline was that somehow the world was devastated by several atom bombs, with the result that essentials like food and this and that cost bundles. My character monopolizes the market and then sells a pound of cheese for a thousand quid. I got bumped off in the end, but without making myself Mr Wonderful, over that four months of half-hour programmes, I made my mark and got noticed.

The writer of the series, Geoff McQueen, was a smashing fella, and a great writer, and he was to become a very dear friend. His talent lay in picking up everything around him like a sponge. We'd be talking and, although it wouldn't be obvious, he'd be picking my brains. I use a lot of terminology that over the years has become my own, if you like, and he'd suck all this out and make a mental note of it. Never moved a muscle, never raised an eyebrow when I threw something into the conversation that he might have thought, 'Cor, I like that.'

The upshot being that when he went away and wrote a cameo role in a new thing of his called *Big Deal*, naturally the part fitted me like a pair of slippers. Well, it would, because he'd used my own personality as a starting point. The series was a massive success, and considering, like I said, that was my first stab at a bit of serious drama,

I must have made a job of it because my cameo stretched to six episodes out of seven.

Exposure is what this game is all about, and Julia Roberts, one of the top people on the very popular soap *EastEnders*, noted my performance. When Dirty Den got laid off and she was looking for a proper cockney to take over the Queen Vic, guess who was top of her list? Yeah, Reidy, and I was absolutely knocked out. What a compliment to me. I went down the studio for a reading, or audition if you like, but it was already in the bag and I came away clutching a script like a dog with two dicks.

Just like before, when I got accepted for *The Comedians*, I drove home with a big grin on my face, I was so pleased.

That weekend sticks in my mind as one of the highlights of my life – my working life, that is. There are three landmarks in that area.

The first was when I thought I was going to be taken into partnership with Benny Palmer. That came to nothing, I know, but nevertheless the feeling of elation and excitement at the time was unbelievable.

The second, and pretty obviously, was *The Comedians*, and the third was *EastEnders*.

The weekend before I was due to do my first scene is as clear today as it was, what? twelve years ago. Me and the family all sat round the pool, and they were all knocking back the turps and having a wonderful time while I studied and studied my script and never touched a drop because it was such a challenge, and I wanted to do the best I could.

My very first scene was with Pam St Clement, where Frank meets Pat on the quay by the *Cutty Sark* at Greenwich. As the script had put over that I was an old flame from years back, the first thing we did was kiss. No dialogue – wallop, straight into a clinch, with us in real life being virtual strangers. So at that first meeting she kissed me like I was a schoolboy, with her lips pursed, and ever since I've called her Lizard Lips. Now we do it every time we meet, just for a laugh.

I should think a lot of people get a surprise when they meet Pam for the first time, 'specially if they've watched her in the soap, because while in that she's very ''ow's yer farver', out of character her real voice is proper cut-glass.

Over the years we've become very fond of each other, and I think the world of her. We went through a lot of storylines together, and the wonderful thing is we seemed to gel lovely, and had this spark between us, which was perfect for what we were doing. I learned so much from her. Not that she sat down and deliberately went out of her way to teach me how to act – I found my own style – but she certainly educated me. She knew I was watching her, so she made a point of showing me all the cunning bits and pieces, like shots and angles that go towards bringing out the best in yourself.

Unlike most of the actors and actresses that got pulled into the soap as new storylines evolved, I never had any problem with nervousness or feeling out of my depth. I had years and years of experience behind me of fronting up big audiences, so I could confidently hold my head high. I'd already made a name for myself, so I was never in the least intimidated by joining this close family.

Believe it or not, the fact that I already had a very successful career caused me a bit of soul-searching. I was very aware that by stepping over from where I was earning extremely good wages into the new venture, I was effectively taking the bread out of the mouth of a paid-up actor.

Take someone like Frank Bruno, for instance. I'm not digging him out in particular because he's a lovely guy. I'm just using him as an example. He's a multimillionaire and he does pantomime, for Christ's sake, and deprives somebody else from earning a crust. What I'd say to him and some others is, why don't you sit at home and count your money? Enjoy yourself, play golf, and leave an opening for someone else to get the chance to pull themselves up.

I tend to run off at the mouth over this business, and yeah, I've got to hold my hand up and say I was equally as guilty, but to redeem myself, I was very conscious of the fact. Though I have to say, that feeling has diminished over the years since I've dedicated myself one hundred per cent to being an actor. I'm always knocking back the cabaret these days. It's become secondary to my acting career, so now I don't think any accusations of nicking other people's work can be levelled at me. I know I might seem a bit pompous going on about this, but we're all individuals, and this just happens to be one of my idiosyncrasies.

When I first joined the cast, I might have been given a big name outside, but it meant nothing on the set. I was welcomed in and made to feel one of the family, if you like. So because of the way I was accepted, since then I always made a point of going out of my way, and have done for years, to make any new people feel at ease. I won't say I become friendly with them straight away – that takes a long time – but then that's my nature.

Nothing to do with thinking I'm better than they are, because regardless of the fact that I've made a name for myself and have earned a few quid out of my chosen game, I never think I'm any better, or worse for that matter, than anyone else. At the end of the day, I'm just a working comic who's had a lot of luck.

One of the reasons I might appear to be a bit distant sometimes is that I'm very sceptical about developing new relationships. Too many times in my life I've given different people a lot of myself, only to end up with a kick in the bollocks or a boot in the arse, so now I keep my distance. I've always been friendly, looked out for the others, but until I felt I could trust them, I suppose I've held myself back – I'm not stand-offish, just a bit reserved.

Strange to think, really, that when you watch the programme we all seem to be in each other's pockets, rubbing shoulders and bumping into each other all over the square. In truth, it's surprising how many of the cast I've never had one bit of dialogue with. Even Wendy Richard, who's been a mainstay since the beginning: I can only remember doing one scene with her in twelve years.

As for getting to know everyone involved, I can only liken it to working in a large factory or a superstore. You're all employed by or involved with the same thing, but your paths never cross. Some of the characters I only ever see if I put on the television in my room and watch the in-house channel direct from the set. Other than that, I don't suppose I've watched the show more than half a dozen times since I started.

The one episode that does stick in my mind was recent, and I only watched that because my missus said I should.

I was staying in my flat at Elstree as I do two or three nights a week, and I committed the unpardonable crime of telephoning the old woman during *EastEnders*. Shirl was crying, not because I was interrupting her viewing, but because of the scene she was watching. I've said, 'OK, ring me later', and put the phone down, thinking, what's that all about? I stuck on the TV and it was Tiffany's funeral, and it was an absolute blinder.

I sat enthralled by the way everyone worked together – they were wonderful. I got caught up in it from a professional point of view, but more importantly, I saw us through the eyes of a punter. It had everything – light, shade, laughter and tears. Nobody could have asked for more.

It was more than an hour before my old woman could pull herself together enough to phone me back. She had three of her mates indoors with her and they were all at it, crying and sobbing. After that, I had a couple of other people ring me up. One of them was a guy, and even he was overcome.

I've always been extremely proud of the show and my own involvement in it, but after watching that one episode, my chest went right out for all of us.

Never ever say to me that soap actors are anything less than the best. And that's the trouble with this country. The media knocks anything that's popular, and anyone webbed up in it gets kicked into the sidelines. The papers never did us any favours with their constant slagging off. It's too drab – too miserable. In the end, people start to believe what they read.

Over the years, on a regular basis, the show's been watched by between fourteen and eighteen million people weekly. Yet no matter who you spoke to, they never watched it. Or, more to the point, didn't want to own up to the fact. That's the power of the press, and we're ridiculous for allowing ourselves to be led by them.

In America it's the complete opposite, and in my opinion, their soaps are terrible. Every actor is handsome, every actress is beautiful and their storylines aren't worth two bob. Yet they get every accolade going, and are fêted around town as big movie stars.

I'm not suggesting we deserve that, but a bit of respect from those within the business would go a long way.

I can remember doing a breakfast show about two years ago, and on the show were two other actors, well-known faces. Those stuck-up bastards looked down on me as though I was a piece of crap. This isn't paranoia on my part – they sneered at me because I worked in a soap. I thought to myself, you haven't got a clue what we have to do. You sit there thinking you're prick the bishop, only you couldn't kiss my arse if you were faced with what we have to achieve.

Major actors have come into *EastEnders* and they've thrown their hands up. Initially I suppose they think it'll be a bit of a holiday, condescending to slum it with people they perceive to be amateurs. Two minutes, and they're screaming. One woman I won't name actually broke down on set saying, 'I can't do this'. They had no choice but to tear up her contract and let her go. And she wasn't alone – there's half a dozen well-known names that I've known couldn't handle it.

I know people will be thinking, 'Go on, Reidy, blow it up so it seems more difficult than it is!' But I'm serious. When I took a break from the show to do a series called *Underworld*, I couldn't believe how easy it was. I got stuck in like I'd been used to doing it for years, and had the director shouting 'No-no-no Mike – slow down for God's sake, we've got all day.' All day, for only a minute's footage sometimes. I thought I was in heaven after all the hurry-up on *EastEnders*.

What I did find, taking things at a nice steady pace, was that my diction improved dramatically. I'm not saying I mumble my way through the soap, but when I can take my time, everything comes out a lot clearer.

It wasn't always as frantic as it is these days. Years ago, we used to rehearse on a Friday and Saturday. In the morning we'd do what they call a producer's run. They'd watch each scene, making notes and what have you – we don't want this, add this, change that, and then pass it on to the director. Come the Monday and Tuesday, we'd go through it all again on the set and put it in the can. Wednesday and Thursday we'd be picking up our new scripts ready for rehearsals the next day. This was week after week. Then, for whatever reasons, the powers that be decided to upgrade and add on another episode. An extra half-hour? it sounds like nothing, but it turned our schedule on its head.

It may have been that our people were keeping up with *Coronation Street*, our only serious rival, or it might have been the other way round. Either way, we came off worst. Without adverts breaking up the length of an episode, in effect we were doing what amounted to almost another episode within these three. So while the other side stretched to what we'd already been doing, we were stretched even further, and everything changed.

To be honest, as far as shooting goes, I actually prefer the way it is today. I never liked rehearsals. The more you mess about with something, the less spontaneous it gets. As it is, I sit in my dressing room quite relaxed, reading through the script. When I get my five-minute call, I get dressed in Frank's clobber, walk onto the set and straight into a scene – no messing. Invariably, it's all done in three or four takes, and if it's not because one of us fluffs our lines or a door bangs or something, we have a laugh then get straight back into it.

With the deadline we work to, there's no time for having a laugh or messing around, and if something does break out, the director's straight in there with, 'Keep it down, keep it down.'

There was a time when I tried to inject a bit of humour into my part, but them above soon made it clear that it wasn't wanted. Perhaps I look at the whole concept too simplistically, but in everyday situations (and that's what we were supposed to be portraying), people crack gags every five minutes. So that's what I thought was required. Not because I'm a comic, but to inject a bit of realism.

Once or twice when an ad-lib one-liner might have got past the director, I blew it by chucking in the eff-word. Hands up, my conversation is peppered with a bit of colour, which is so much part of me I don't even notice, but early-evening TV isn't ready for that yet.

Another thing is eating. Bad manners or not, most people eat and talk at the same time, so when I'm in 'Cath's café' and a breakfast is put in front of me, I get stuck in. I should know better by now, because acting is fraught enough without adding to it by trying to speak a line with a mouthful of bacon. And I've been caught out a couple of times. One of those gets a regular airing on Denis Norden's show, and this is where I'm sitting at the bar in the Queen Vic casually eating cheese. My line came up quicker than I anticipated, with the result that I sprayed most of it over the bar. If I'd been the director, I would have left the scene in and given everyone a good laugh, but if it's not in the script, it doesn't happen.

An instance of that happened in a street party we were shooting. Everybody's out in the road; tables, food and what have you, and a bit of a group playing some music. We shot the piece, something wasn't right, so it had to be set up again. While we're all waiting, one of the musicians started to knock out a tune. The other boys joined in, then the cast broke into a bit of dancing around, so I jumped up on the improvised stage and went into a rock 'n' roll number. The cameras were rolling and I thought, this is going to be wonderful, and it would have been, but it was knocked on the head, which I thought was a great shame.

People often ask me for a bit of inside information or a rundown on whatever's going on. Who's fallen out with who? Is so and so knocking off their screen partner out of the studio? and so on. The simple answer is that I don't get involved. What anyone else gets up to is no concern of mine. I'm there to do a job, and when it's done I'm in the car and on the way home.

More than once the papers have offered me money, and I'm talking thousands in cash under the counter, to give away the storyline on some long-running episode, or they've had a whisper that one of the cast is leaving, and who is it? I'm not so skint that I need to be sucked into all that, and if I was, I still wouldn't have anything to do with it. Without exception, we all find that sort of thing unfair to the viewers, and very frustrating.

Take my missus as an average viewer. She's watched it since day one, long before I went into it, and although she's dying to know what's coming next, she never ever asks me what's going to happen. There are scripts lying about our lounge, and she'd never dream of picking one up to get a preview. That's the build-up to any drama, and that's exactly what we are. Once you know 'whodunit' in a murder book, you might as well sling it away because the whole point has been lost.

Personally, I think it's a deliberate leak from the top to boost the viewing figures of each individual incident, whether it's Dirty Den getting shot or Tiff getting run over. But why? We've got the highest figures of any soap every week of the year, so why spoil the enjoyment of all those regular, loyal people for the sake of dragging in a few extra thousand? OK, a little hint perhaps, but not the how, why and when that happens every time without fail.

Talking about Dirty Den, Leslie Grantham, makes me think about all those faces that have literally disappeared over the years. A lot of youngsters and quite a few of the older people have left the soap hopefully to do greater things. I'm not talking about natural turnover, like when a storyline and subsequently those involved have run their course, but the others who have asked to be written out. I'm not knocking them, because we're all tarred with the same brush, but they start believing their own publicity and want to break out into the big time. I'm going to do this, I'm going to do that. I'm talking a lot of people here, and a massive amount of talent between the lot of them, but with a couple of exceptions, none of them have really been heard of in a big way.

Let's face it, if Leslie Grantham couldn't make it into the big time, who could? He was probably the most well-loved actor in the country – by the ladies, anyway – yet his screen character was an absolute monster. He was a cheat, a womanizer and never slow to hand out a slap, and the female viewers couldn't get enough of him.

I was working down at Canvey Island doing a couple of nights at The King's nightclub. On one of the days I was there Leslie came to the island to open something or other, and they brought him in an open-topped bus. I've never seen anything like it. The women went absolutely mad for him. Hundreds of them started rocking this bus from side to side and nearly had it over, screaming 'Leslie, Leslie', 'Dirty Den – give us one'. Jesus, when a bunch of women get together they're worse than any blokes. And when you think, they all want to be given one not by the actor, but by the horrible character he portrays. It remains a complete mystery to me as to what goes on in the female mind.

Now we've got Ross Kemp doing the same thing when he plays Grant Mitchell. He's like a psychopath, and they love him. When I analyse it, all I can think is that there is a fault in the make-up of most women, and it just doesn't compute with me.

That series Leslie starred in shortly after leaving the soap was a wonderful vehicle for him, and he was great in it. But as *The Paradise Club* had a lot of location filming, it ran into I believe something like three hundred thousand pounds per episode – a great deal of money for a TV show. Trouble was, it didn't pull the viewing figures, and that's what it's all about. So Independent TV dropped it. If it doesn't work, 'Get rid of it'. Not fix it – get rid of it. I think they made episodes that were never even transmitted.

Cindy, lovely girl played by Michelle Collins, is one of the exceptions, and seems to have done very well for herself and I'm over the moon for her. Same as with Nick Berry. He's consistently turned out great performances in the number of things he's been offered. Now Tiffany, Martine McCutcheon, is aiming for international stardom as a singer, and please God she succeeds.

I caught a programme about her where they filmed every step towards the making of her new single and the video that goes with it. Something struck me when one of the producers said they wanted to move her as far away as possible from the character of Tiffany. They didn't want a novelty act of soap star turned singer – they wanted Martine to be totally herself. And in reverse, that's what the producers of *EastEnders* wanted when I first joined them. That's why all my gags and funnies were kicked into touch, because they didn't want Mike Reid the comic, though initially that must have been a bit of a contradiction.

Without putting myself down, I reckon there were bundles of cockney actors who could have taken over the Queen Vic and played the part equally as well as I do, so obviously the producers were trading on my celebrity status to put bums on seats. And no doubt loads of viewers tuned in to see Reidy either die on his arse or give it plenty of 't'rific' and 'wallop' and all that. I like to think they were surprised by my performance.

As time has gone on, Mike Reid has been left behind and I've become Frank Butcher to millions of people. Time after time I meet people and they kick off with, 'Hello, Frank', then get a bit embarrassed and quickly go, 'Sorry, I meant Mike.' And I'm not just talking little old ladies or kids, but right across the board. Far from thinking I've lost my identity, I take it as a compliment that I'm able to play the part so convincingly. I think I'm safe in saying that I know Frank better than anyone else. How he thinks, how he would react to different situations; and it's only in this regard that I ever raise my voice on set.

Over the years we've had a turnover of directors, and they've all had their own ideas of how things should be. They might say to me, 'Look, this is how I want you to handle this scene', or, 'I don't want you to do such and such'. I go, 'Whoa, hang on a minute. Don't tell me. I know this man, I've been playing him for a dozen years. You've just arrived, and right now you don't know nothing about us people.' I don't get backs up or act the prima donna, but I take the part and the character very seriously, and I won't have either buggered about just so a new broom can sweep clean.

Sometimes I take Frank on board too much, like when I went through all that business of having a breakdown. When Frank walked out of the square and me with him, after nearly burning Phil to death, I was extremely tired – physically and mentally knackered. The storyline had dragged on, with me having to play this fella who was permanently down. He was sick, crying, unshaven, and I found it more and more difficult to shake that off when I left the set.

I wanted out, but so my leaving wouldn't make things difficult for the show, I agreed that after six months I would turn up again for three months, so that they could tidy everything away. In my mind was the thought that in the six months I could do a few other things, relax in Spain and then come back refreshed and raring to go.

It didn't work out like that. Though I was well out of it, like they do with a lot of the characters, they kept my name up front. Every other episode it would be, 'Have you heard from Frank?' 'What's Frank up to?' So of course, the public wanted to know what had happened to him. Subsequently, the Christmas I turned up the viewing figures went off the graph. I wasn't looking forward to it, because I knew it was going to he hard, and I wasn't disappointed.

Bang – I'm straight in where I left off six months before – and it was terrible. I thought I'd shaken off the way the part had affected me, but as soon as I picked up on the depression and the downtrodden aspect of the character, I felt myself sinking into a similar feeling personally. Frank was being totally self-indulgent, and gave out that all he wanted to do was curl up in a corner. After six or eight weeks of featuring this strong storyline in almost every episode, I began to get very depressed. Strange, really: I've always been self-reliant and more outgoing than the average person, so I found it hard to believe that I could be affected by something that was total fiction.

Since I was appearing in practically every episode, I never really got a chance to come out of character. I had pages of script to handle, so I was reading and thinking, reading and thinking, doing my bit then starting all over again. My missus often told me that I'd changed, and I wouldn't have it. She said I was miserable, and never said two words if I could get away with one, and when I stood back and analysed the way I felt, she was dead right. After that, I virtually counted the days until the storyline was finished.

Most of the people who leave the soap, whether it's their own decision, they get fired or their contract runs out, whatever, invariably there are tears. Girls especially break down and cry, but I've seen more than one guy with a bit of grit in his eye as he's walking out the door. Me? I ran down the road singing for joy. I was so elated, it felt like a heavy load had been lifted off my shoulders.

Seems an ungrateful attitude considering that it was the massive and wonderful vehicle of *EastEnders* that put me in the public eye, and raised my acting profile higher than I could ever have imagined. But I was then, and still am today, extremely grateful to the soap for what it's done for me.

If I'd never been offered the opportunity to join the cast, and had concentrated solely on plugging away at my cabaret, stag nights and other bits and pieces, the maximum number of people who could have seen me wouldn't have matched the number of viewers who watch *EastEnders* in a single week. I've done thousands and thousands of appearances since I was a young man until today, and if I totalled up the very unlikely figure of two thousand people per venue, it still wouldn't add up to the millions of people that tune in every week. It's absolutely mind-blowing to me, and certainly beyond comprehension that that number of individuals is watching my every move – and those of all the other talented people I work with, of course.

When I do try to imagine the colossal number of viewers sitting in front of the TV, I just have to give up – my brain won't compute it. On top of that, *EastEnders* is shown all over the world, so on any given night it wouldn't be out of the way to double the figures. It's certainly a humbling experience, and I've got to repeat, I can't thank the programme enough.

So when I walked – no, *ran* – out of the studio on that last day, feeling like a prisoner who'd been released after seven years' hard time, I suppose I held the firm and the scriptwriters responsible for how I felt. For a dramatic storyline, they'd written me into a desperate situation, and by virtue of that had totally screwed my head up.

In retrospect, I've now got to admit to myself that there was more to my near breakdown than depressing scripts. While it was four years or so since me, Shirl and the family had been crucified by personal tragedy, in all that time I'd made sure I kept up an outward appearance of strength. But some things just can't be buried, they've got to come out, and all I can think is that the combination of over-work and the storyline was the catalyst that brought everything together in my head, and mentally knocked me on my arse.

CHAPTER NINE

IS THERE A PRICE TO BE PAID FOR REACHING GOALS THAT I'D dreamed of since I was a little kid? To reach celebrity status and financial security that was beyond imagination, while I struggled to make a name for myself? Well, if there is, I paid and paid and paid, when we lost our son Mark at the age of twenty-four.

If it meant that my boy could walk through the door right now with his jokes and his big smile, I'd go back to the coal round in a flash, because all the money in the world can't compensate for having to bury one of your kids. It's wrong, it's unfair and it's unnatural for the offspring to die before the parents, and standing at his grave knowing that my son was under my feet was just too much to bear. The pain was indescribable. It's like having a steel band around your head and chest, and a concrete block in your stomach hour after hour, day after day. I couldn't take in the fact that I'd never see him again. That was it – final – finished.

I'm not a weak man. I've said before, I'm self-reliant, buoyant, ready to face anything – but this crushed me. If it wasn't for the fact that Shirley and the rest of our family turned to me for strength and support, I'd have gone under. When I wanted to crawl into a corner and cry my heart out, I forced myself to be strong so that I could be a leaning post for everyone else. Mark would have been thirty-three in a few months' time, yet he's locked in my head at age twenty-four and will never be anything else.

I haven't come to terms with his loss and today, nine years later with the pain still there and me nearly sixty, I know I'm never going to.

People must see me on the telly, in cabaret or whatever, and think old Reidy had a bit of a rough time of it some years ago, but he's got over it. They see me laughing, singing, cracking gags and imagine that time has healed the pain and the scars. If only they knew.

I said Mark is locked away, and he is – not forgotten, just hidden away in whatever part we keep our private grief, otherwise I couldn't function. And now, for the purpose of laying myself open for this book, I've got to go in there and resurrect all that emotion, and it's hurting me already.

I still smile when I think of being shown that little black baby all those years ago in the maternity hospital. And please God he's alive and well, and his parents haven't suffered what me and Shirl have.

It seems like only yesterday, the kids being born, growing up and all the capers that went with it. All gone in a teardrop of time. I missed out on the first months of Mark's life, what with going away on the day he was born. And hands up, I missed out on a lot of time I would've liked to have spent with him and Michael. But it's the old story. When you're young, you've got to earn a living the best way you can, and in my case that meant working all round the country and missing out on family life.

If you could get your head round the morbid thought that your kid's life might be short, you wouldn't let them out of your sight. You'd never send them out the door with a telling-off or a clip round the ear, just in case it was the last time you might see them. But life's not like that.

Me and Brian were fortunate in that we were able to spend so much time with our dad. His leg injury was a terrible thing, but he was compensated by being with his sons more than most blokes were, while we gained wonderful wonderful memories of the times we all spent together. Not that my boys didn't have that – just not so much of it.

Whenever I could, I took them out bird-nesting or just wandering in the fields, teaching them the same things Dad had taught me. I remember taking Michael and Mark scrumping for apples. Nothing to do with not being able to afford a bit of fruit, because last thing down the market, you could pick up a carrier bag full for five bob. No – this was all about me getting back to, and sharing with them, a bit of my own childhood. And looking back, considering I must have been thirty years old, I was worse than they were. Over fences, sneaking through the grass, climbing trees.

Mark did have a problem, though, and one that we never really got a proper answer to. My very first recollection of things not being quite what they should be was when he was three years old. At that time we were living in Sutton-cum-Launde, and having a bit of land I kept a few chickens. My brother-in-law used to drive for a firm that supplied some fried chicken company with their birds. They were all kept in tiny cages and pumped up with food, so although they weren't very old they weighed something like four pounds.

How he got hold of these things I never bothered to ask – fell off the back of his lorry, I presume – but every now and then he'd give me a crate of live chickens, a dozen, sometimes two. I'd stick them in a pen and they'd sit there for two or three days because they didn't know what their legs were for.

Cut a long story short, when we were having a barbecue or friends in for a meal, I'd neck some of them, hang them for a couple of days and they'd be beautiful. On this day I picked out three, stretched them and left them by the pen while I went in for a cup of tea. I came out ten minutes later and found young Mark chopping them to pieces with an axe. They were still warm, so as you can imagine, there was blood and feathers and guts everywhere. He was covered in it, but didn't seem to notice, he was concentrating so hard on destroying those chickens. I can tell you, it stopped me dead in my tracks. I thought, 'Now hang on – there's something wrong here. This ain't right.'

If memory serves, I don't think we made a big deal of it. Shirl cleaned him up and we put it down to one of those silly things kids do without thinking. I told myself he'd seen me chopping a bird or two, so in his mind he was helping Dad, but at the back of my mind I had this nagging feeling that it wasn't normal behaviour.

I'm not saying that that incident was the beginning of Mark's mental problem. I'm saying that casting my mind back, that is the earliest point in his life when I can put my finger to a day that might have been a beginning. This is in hindsight, because while it gave me pause for thought at the time, I can't honestly say that I felt what he did would lead to anything more sinister. I mean, if a kid nicks a tanner out of his mum's purse, she doesn't think, 'Oh, Christ, he's going to turn into a bank robber', and that's how it was with me. Mental note, then file it away and forget it. And throughout his earlier years it was proved that I had nothing to worry about because, give or take one or two bits and pieces, he was as normal as the next kid.

Ninety per cent of Mark was a mirror image of me. He looked like me and he was buoyant and funny, and he had that loner streak I've always had. Only trouble was, he took that side of him much further than I ever did. He didn't make friends very easily, if at all, and I can't remember him attending a single one of his own major birthday parties – not one.

As we did with all the kids, when they were five, ten, fifteen and so on, we always gave them a big birthday party to note these occasions. With my Mark, it would always be the same. His friends, or more honestly, his 'associates' would turn up, he would show his face, say, 'How you doing – thanks for coming', then he'd disappear until it was all over. And I don't just mean he'd take off and play in the garden or in his room on his own, he'd hide himself away in a cupboard or under the stairs, and when we'd find him he'd be perfectly rational. All he'd say was that he didn't want to be there with all those people.

When he was very young I put it down to shyness. I remembered kids at parties when I was little myself; they had to be dragged in kicking and screaming so they could have a good time. And if you'll remember, when it came to doing a turn, a lot of them were traumatized – so I could make excuses to myself for my boy's behaviour.

But when he got older he'd scream out, 'Leave me alone – please leave me alone', whenever we'd find him behind the settee or wherever he'd hidden himself. And against our nature that's all we could do, because the more we coaxed, the worse he got. The sense of helplessness we felt because we couldn't get through to him hurt me and his mum more than his outbursts.

He was so much like me, but at the same time he was an individual

– his own person, and I accepted that. We were brought up differently. I had to fight for every penny I ever got from an early age, so it forced me to be outgoing and confident and, for good or bad, a right Jack the Lad. Whereas both my boys grew up during the period when their dad was fortunate enough to have bunches on the hip: they wanted for nothing, and so didn't have the need to go out doing what I had done.

As the years passed, me and Shirl ran out of excuses for his behaviour and took him all over the place to try to get the problem sorted. Because by now, he had started what I can only describe as 'going into one'. I could be talking to him about cars or dogs or football, and all of a sudden his eyes would go and I'd think, 'What the hell's going on now?' From being a polite, gag-cracking, normal boy, in the blink of an eye or the snap of a finger he'd shut off and withdraw into himself.

In later years this developed into blind rages. Short in duration, but so intense it was frightening, not only to those involved but to himself, because he didn't know what was taking him over. To try to understand these outbursts, I guessed and likened them to those fits of anger that used to overwhelm me myself. Though in my case, I'd have to be pushed and pushed before I reacted – but even then I could control myself. With Mark, they came from nowhere – nothing was needed to spark them off. And that poor kid couldn't handle it – it terrified him. He was crying out for help, and we could do nothing for him.

Me and Shirl are just ordinary people, we haven't got bundles of O levels between us, so like anyone else we relied on the medical profession to tell us what the problem was, and then deal with it. But it didn't happen. They did this test, that test, sent him to professors and specialists, and in the end they came up with schizophrenia, which put a label on his condition but didn't do nothing to solve it.

To this day I've never understood why they couldn't keep it under control. I knew it couldn't be cured, but thousands of people lead normal lives with this illness, so why were the doctors defeated when it came to my boy?

I'm not saying this thing blew up every day, and at the same time, a lot of the things he got up to had nothing whatsoever to do with his mental state. Like his brothers, Michael and Jimmy, and his dad, he had a thing about motors. Unfortunately half the time they belonged to other people, so Old Bill was no stranger to our place. Now don't think that because I got up to far worse as a young man that I condoned his behaviour: 'Good on you, son – chip off the old block', and all that. I bollocked him no end, and tried to advise him that he was going the wrong way.

I've never laid a hand on any of my kids. Tap on the arse when they were tiny, same as anyone, but I've never held the belief that you can punch your way to respect or authority. So I actually used myself as an example. I didn't make a secret of the fact that I'd been a bit of a toe-rag, nor did I pretend I hadn't spent time behind the door, in the hope that he would sit up and take notice. Of course he didn't. So many things happened as he grew up, and most of them I don't know about even to this day, because his mum protected him and shielded me from the truth.

Like I said, I spent a lot of time away from home, so Shirl took the brunt of the responsibility, in effect, for most of the kids' lives. And I've got to hand it to her; she has been a wonderful mother. I'm not saying this because it will be printed and read all over the place, I mean it. No-one could have been more staunch as far as her kids were concerned.

Because this is my story, when I'm writing about Mark it's all me, me, but my Shirl suffered equally as much as me, and if it's possible, dare I say, much more. She was his mum, and that gave her a special bond that us blokes can't even contemplate. The cord that ties them together is cut at birth, yet there's another invisible one that binds mother and child together that can't ever be cut, no matter what the child does. She went through agonies then, over all kinds of things, and as regular as clockwork she goes through agonies today. And same as with Mark, I can do nothing to help her and it breaks my heart. Like I said, she protected him and at the same time protected me from the aggravation and heartache of what he was up to.

I'll never know why he felt the need to thieve off me, but he did countless times. If he'd said, 'Dad, I'm skint', I'd have given him money. Like all dads I would've moaned, but he'd have got it at the end of the day. Instead of that, he chose to rob me. I might have had three hundred notes in my pocket – next time I look, I'm down to two. At first I'd look at it and think, 'I don't remember spending that', but then what with the casual attitude I have to cash when I'm holding, I accepted that I must have done. He didn't clean me out, and there was plenty more where that came from – not like when I cleaned out my dad's pocket and had his dinner money away. But that was once and once only, and it's caused me mental anguish from that day to this. I don't think Mark ever thought about what he was doing.

When I twigged what he was up to, I took to hiding my bit of cash in the car before I went indoors, but no matter in what devious places I hid it, he always found it. I'd go up the wall and be shouting at him, 'Where's my bloody money?' and he'd just shrug his shoulders. 'Not me, dad.' What could I do?

Another time – and my missus doesn't know to this day that I know what happened to my tie pin. It was a piece and I loved wearing it. It had my initials in the middle, surrounded by two carats' worth of diamonds – beautiful, and worth a fortune. Mark's lifted this off my dressing table and taken it to a pawnbroker who, looking after his own arse, phoned the law, and they've shot down and captured my boy. He told them his dad had given it to him, and I should think they fell about laughing. 'Your dad gave you a two-carat pin so you could flog it? We'll check it out.' They phoned Shirl and she said, 'Yes, his father gave it to him', to keep him out of trouble. Red faces. 'Sorry, madam.' I never followed it up, and I never mentioned indoors that someone I knew was in the shop at the time and gave me the full SP – but it hurt.

I don't want to paint a black picture of our son. I'm just trying to put over that he gave us problems over and above those he couldn't help – or to put it another way, it seemed at the time that part of him just didn't care. He was out to do his own thing, and never mind the consequences.

I put it all down to basically normal behaviour for his age. OK, not so normal for St John's Wood or Hampstead, but where I came from, not out of the way. So though I got bloody annoyed about the things he got up to, I was convinced it was a phase he would grow out of like we all did.

I'll give an example of how reckless he was. If he was coming down the road and got a puncture, he'd look around for a model with the same size wheels, calmly do a swap and drive on his way. He never seemed to think he might get nicked, and if he did he didn't seem to care.

Eventually Mark was diagnosed as suffering from psychopathic schizophrenia. Jesus Christ, what a horrible word to have hung on your own flesh and blood. It conjures up an image of some dangerous maniac, and I never would and still won't accept that our boy deserved that label.

Even though events contradicted the way I thought, as far as the family were concerned, who knew him better than anyone, the only danger he posed was to himself. He might occasionally have raged and smashed things up, but no-one in the family ever had a moment's fear that he might go over the top and harm them.

Not even the time when he and Shirl were talking in the kitchen, when what I describe as the 'blue haze' came over him. In a split second he went from being his normal self to grabbing a knife off the worktop and going for his mother. Midway he stopped, threw down the knife and burst into tears, going, 'Mum, Mum, what's happening to me? I didn't mean it – help me.' That's what still hurts. His cries for help that we couldn't answer, no matter how much we desperately wanted to. That boy was tortured, and he looked to his mum and dad to sort it all out for him and we were both helpless.

Another time, I bought him a car. This was a long time after he'd blown up my beautiful Lotus Esprit. I knew he wanted a motor. I just happened to pull into a garage forecourt as the owner was shaking hands on a deal with a young kid. The boy must have been down on his luck, because this Ford Escort was a piece that he must have spent years doing up. It had everything; racing wheels, flared arches, a wonderful respray and full stereo kit. I said to the geezer, 'How much?' He said, 'Six hundred to you – cash money.' I've gone, 'Bit strong, innit?' But as he said, he's just weighed out five – he can make a oner in two minutes or it could sit there. I dug into the wallet, said, 'Go on, then, you greedy bastard', but I wasn't serious. That car was worth eight of anybody's money.

I got him to drop it up home and gave Mark the keys. Understandably, he was over the moon. 'Thanks Dad, this is fantastic.' The next time I saw the car it was smashed to pieces. Not in an accident but slowly, systematically and deliberately destroyed by my boy. He'd been indoors with his mum and girlfriend Annette, they'd had a cup of tea and were laughing and joking about. Next thing he's run upstairs, picked up a baseball bat, gone out to the motor and attacked it in this terrible rage. All Shirl could do was give Nett a cuddle and wait until it was all over.

He'd smashed the headlights, bonnet, roof, all the windows – everything. Then he climbed into the driver's seat and put his head on the steering wheel. When his mum went out to him he was sobbing his heart out – inconsolable.

Again he begged for help, and again all she could do was hold him until he'd calmed down. No point in telling him off, no point asking why, because he didn't have any answers.

Time after time I asked him how he felt inside. What was the problem, as he saw it? I didn't demand to know what was going on in his head – I never raised my voice, just talked to him, man to man. No matter how bad the rage had been, he was always lucid and rational afterwards.

I remember saying to him, 'Look, son, I don't give a monkey's what you are or what's gone on in the past. You are my son and I love you, whatever. I don't care if you're gay – bent as a nine-bob note. I'm your dad so please, please, help me to help you, and tell me what's troubling you.' All he ever said was that he was sorry, but he didn't know why these things were happening to him. I tried so many times to get through to him, but I think we were all in the dark together. I never walked away from it in despair; I gave myself to him – all the time in the world. He knew I was there for him any time, night or day. Same with his mum. We didn't neglect the others, but in the situation we were in, he got the lion's share of both of us.

The only hope we had was given to us by one of the psychiatrists. He said that as time went on and Mark matured, these attacks would get less and less and, perhaps by the time he was twenty-five, he would most likely outgrow the problem.

We'll never know, because a quirk of fate destroyed the last bit of mental stability he had. I don't believe in God, but I do believe in fate. That in some way, our lives are mapped out for us, and so in a way it was inevitable that throughout Mark's life, he slowly worked towards this terrible event.

As I said, he had no real friends – never had. Plenty of people around him, but no one individual who you could say was a close mate like those I've had myself. So when I talk of his friend Ian, I have to say it was an on-off relationship. They'd be together all day and get on like a house on fire, then all of a sudden Mark would tell him to fuck off – give him the elbow and say he didn't want to know.

Now this Ian had been doing a bit of work at a psychic centre not far from here, part time gardening and labouring, I really can't remember. While he was there somebody told him that the near future held some danger for him, so be careful. Pretty bloody stupid thing to say to a young kid, because it worried him and made him think. Days later he was riding along on his moped when he went into a skid, came off the bike and a lorry missed him by an inch. This is only conjecture on my part, but I have to think that he must have been extremely relieved that the premonition was put to rest, and that he'd come through it without any injury to himself. Days later, our Mark shot him dead.

I remember I'd gone out that day – a bit of work, business. I don't exactly remember why, but I'd left them in the garden doing some work for me. They were at a loose end so I said, 'If you both want to earn a few quid, there's paint in the garage. Give the snooker room a couple of coats.' 'Oh yeah, great.' And that's how I left them. But as soon as Dad was out of the way, they decided shooting birds in the garden would be more fun, and they both knew that I would never have allowed that if I'd been around. It wasn't that I didn't approve of them messing about with guns, because Mark had been conversant with firearms since he was a kid, but I didn't agree with using live creatures for sport and target practice.

What really happened next we'll never know for sure. But my theory is that the tragedy came about through a combination of accident and deliberate intent on the part of Mark. Saying that if I hadn't had guns in the house it wouldn't have happened is like saying that if there weren't knives in the kitchen he couldn't have gone for his mum with one. So in that respect I've got no guilt. Him and Michael had handled guns since they were dots. I'd laid down certain rules and made sure they stuck to them religiously. Never carry a gun with one up the spout; never point it at anyone. I mean, there was a long list, and as far as I was concerned, they never broke my rules because they became second nature. Which is why I think Mark knew what he was doing when he aimed the gun at Ian.

Shirl won't agree with me. No-one will agree with me, but I think they've gone back to the snooker room, had a few words and the 'blue mist' came down. I've got to add that the shotgun had a very light-weight trigger, and in my honest and true belief, Mark's gone to scare his mate by firing at the wall beside him, but instead shot him point-blank in the heart. The shooting might have been intentional, but the terrible end result wasn't.

The rest is a nightmare where all the details are mixed up in a blur, not only on that day but for months and months after.

I know he was clear-headed enough to ring his mum, wherever she was, then go back to Ian and try to staunch the blood with towels, but it was no use because that poor kid must have been dead before he hit the ground.

I was contacted on my mobile, and by the time I got home I couldn't get down the lane for police cars. They were everywhere. They were only doing their job, but it struck me that they seemed to be treating this accident as though it was murder, and that all came together when that's what they charged our son with.

Like dropping a pebble in a pond, the ripples from that one tiny jerk of a finger stretched out and touched so many people. Me, Shirl and all our family were devastated and traumatized, but we still had Mark. Ian's parents and family had lost that young boy, and though eventually I would understand the heart-stopping pain of what they went through, at that moment in time all I could do was imagine with horror what they were suffering. Yet not once did they point a finger at our son and hate him for what he'd done. In their own grief they found time to tell him to his face to try and put it behind him, because it was an accident.

Everyone told him that – even the judge, when Mark was brought to court and the verdict was read out as misadventure. The only one who blamed him for the shooting was himself.

Going back to my theory, did he and only he know something in his heart that no-one else did? He never ever came out of those hazes going, 'What happened? Where am I?' He always knew what had gone on. He hated it, it tore him apart, but he was powerless to stop himself. Did he know it wasn't the accident we all tried to convince him of? Whatever, from that day on he was finished. And in the same way we lost, or began to lose, our son from the moment he pulled that trigger.

For so long afterwards that I lost track of time, I'd be in bed and I could hear him crying and crying in his room. It's no good asking anyone to try to imagine what that did to me and Shirl. That broken and tortured boy through the wall was our child. Didn't matter that he was in his twenties, he was still our child, and his pain was ours. I wouldn't wish it on anyone.

As time went on, it began to appear that Mark had got it in his head that as he'd caused so much suffering to others, he should inflict as much on himself as possible.

First of all, he swallowed a mouthful of paraquat crystals. This is a weedkiller, and one of the deadliest poisons the layman can get his hands on. Once ingested, there is no hope of survival, so it had to be some kind of miracle that he pulled through. After twenty-four hours it attacks the liver and kidneys, and nothing can be done. He was taken into hospital and the doctor told me he couldn't understand why he wasn't dead, though he did warn us that the next twelve hours would be critical, and to prepare ourselves for the worst. It never happened, and he walked away with no after-effects.

Mark wasn't a fool. He knew what paraquat was all about, so was that his intention, to die in the most horrible manner he could think of at the time?

Over a period of three years it was one thing after another. He slashed his wrists. He slashed his neck with a Stanley knife. He ploughed into a wall with his car, and got out without a scratch. And each time after the depression had worn off he'd say, 'God, what have I done?'

We thought he might have been able to achieve some sort of breakthrough when he was sent for therapy sessions. This was where a group of people with similar problems could be encouraged to unburden themselves to each other under the supervision of a psychiatrist. Whereas he couldn't, or wouldn't, tell us what his problem was, we felt that he might be able to open up with strangers. And as far as we know he did just that. Though exactly what he came out with we don't know, as this sort of thing is supposed to be confidential.

Supposed to be. Some dirty bastard within the group got in touch with the papers, and tried to sell them every word that Mark had poured from his heart. The first we heard of it was when a reporter rang us, told us what was going on then reassured us that they wouldn't touch it. I've got to say that restored a little faith in the press, and showed they can't all be judged by the few.

Mark was totally gutted, and understandably refused to go back. So what might, just might, have helped him was kicked out of the window because of one person with the morals of a rat.

The trouble with trying to put over Mark's mental state and the problems he had is that it becomes a list of negatives, as though he put himself and us through hell every day. It would be wrong to give that impression. There were long periods when nothing out of the ordinary happened. He held a job down, set up home with his girl-friend Annette, and they were extremely happy. They had a son named Lee, and when Mark was twenty-four and told us she was expecting twins and that they intended getting married in the July of 1990, we really did think the doctors had been right and he'd finally outgrown whatever was inside his head.

We had a wonderful start to the New Year, when Michael and Kirsty Anne were born towards the end of January. Like two peas in a pod and they were absolutely beautiful. I've got photographs of me and Mark holding these tiny little babies, and we're both grinning from ear to ear. He was the proud dad, and I was the very, very proud grandad. What a present, six days after my fiftieth birthday.

Being a grandad wasn't a new experience for me. I got that title when Jimmy's boy Scott was born. Trouble was, I was only thirty-five, and if memory serves, I wasn't too impressed. It was as though it made me old before my time. No reflection on the boy, I just had this silly idea that you had to be an old man to get called that.

With these two it was no problem, and I preened. I was working on *EastEnders*, plus I had quite a heavy workload of cabaret and other bits and pieces, and to be honest I was tired. So when the opportunity for a short break came up, I snatched it with both hands. It was only a long weekend, so I planned to fill it with everything I loved. Good food, a nice drink, plenty of golf and some quality time with my wife.

We set off to Chepstow, just over the bridge on the River Severn, to stay at a beautiful golfing complex called St Pierre.

I'd been a fanatical player since the first day I'd sliced a clean shot down the fairway back in the seventies. Up until that point I was a film buff. I could've gone on *Mastermind* with film for a subject, because doing the club circuit and being away from home, I filled my days by going to local cinemas, often twice a day. That was until somebody suggested a round of golf with them. I wasn't too keen, didn't have any gear, and went along expecting to be bored out of my head.

The first few times I was rubbish. I couldn't hit that poxy ball, and when I did it rolled about two yards. I was shown how to stand, how to grip the club, how to follow through – then it happened. I connected face-on with the ball and watched in amazement as it soared away to land somewhere near where I'd intended it. That's all it took to turn me into an addict.

On my top-ten list of loves of my life, golf sits just below my family. It's taken me all over the world. I've played with most of the top names in the game, and many times the pure relaxation of it has kept me sane. Eventually I got Shirley involved and, same as with me, as with anyone who cares to try it, after that first magic stroke there was no looking back.

So we were both looking forward to this weekend in beautiful surroundings. We arrived, got unpacked and without wasting a minute we both went out on the course. We had a light lunch – bottle of Chablis – nap – golf again – lovely dinner at night, then retired to our room overlooking the green. And that was it for the rest of our stay – absolute heaven, with all our problems and worries forgotten.

On the Sunday we'd had a brilliant day, came back to the hotel, went upstairs, got showered and changed and then went down to dinner. I ordered the meal for both of us, and had just got started on a bottle of wine when a waiter came over and discreetly said that the police wanted to have a word with me. Unlike anyone else might, I didn't immediately think that somebody had dented my car in the park outside, or that we might have been burgled at home. I knew straight away that it was something to do with Mark.

I'm being honest here, even though it hurts me to think what went through my mind then. I was annoyed – no, I was seething with anger – and as I walked out to the foyer I could've wept with frustration that he wouldn't even allow me and his mum to have this desperately needed holiday without spoiling it. In hindsight, people will think that's terrible. How could I have thought like that? But I'm only human – I'm not a saint, and I really did have it up to here with him. At the same time, I couldn't have dreamed of what lay ahead of me and Shirl.

I went up to the copper and said, 'Well, what's he been up to now?' I think he was a bit thrown by my aggressiveness, so he hesitated. 'Er – I – I – he . . .' I've gone, 'What's wrong?' but as I said it I could feel the blood draining out of my head. 'I don't know the details, Mr Reid, but your son is in Colchester Hospital – I believe it's serious.'

We were out of the hotel in one minute; just slung everything in bags and tore out of the gates. I won't say I drove like a maniac because I knew how to handle a motor, but from Chepstow to Colchester I never dropped below 110 mph. Straight through Bristol, right across country, I passed Old Bill no end of times, and not one of them gave me a pull. I wouldn't have stopped anyway. Shirley was in a state, and all I could do was try to convince her that 'serious' could mean he'd cut himself again, and like every other time, a number of stitches would put him right and he'd bounce back.

That was for her benefit. Inside, I was frightened of what we'd find out once we arrived.

We reached the hospital just before midnight, and rushed up to the room he was in. Some of the family were in a side room, and they went straight for me as though just by being there I could make things right. Shirl went through to Mark, while I hung back for a moment to make sense of what had happened and to pacify the others. They were crying and saying, 'Oh Dad, he's dying – he's dying.'

As Shirley got to our boy and held his hand, he opened his eyes, looked at his mum, then gave a sigh and died. I heard her scream out, and flew in to be with her, but it was all over. We like to think that he waited for us – that through all his pain he hung on until his mum and dad could be with him, and I'm sure we're right.

I haven't got the words to describe how we felt, and if I did they wouldn't be necessary, because anyone who has ever loved someone has only got to put themselves in that situation, then double the pain to encompass the way that poor kid took his own life. Because that's what he'd done, and in the most horrible way you could imagine.

If I live to be a hundred I'll still be asking why, when he appeared to have so much to live for. His lovely Annette, the boy, those beautiful babies – surrounded by people who loved and cared for him. And what a cruel irony that he chose Mothering Sunday to end it all. No, chose is the wrong word. I don't suppose he even considered what day it was, but every year when that day stares off the calendar, it's a reminder we could do without.

When I pieced together the details, it made even less sense because it appeared that he'd seemed as normal as could be. In some way, I could understand it if he'd gone into one and grabbed the first thing available to harm himself. But I spoke to the man who must have been the last to speak to him, and Mark was full of himself, or, as the bloke in the corner shop put it, 'As bright as a button'.

He'd gone into the shop to buy some bits and pieces, and while he's looking round he was cracking jokes and larking about. Because when he was on top, that was the sort of personality he had, same as Michael – a great sense of humour and a very funny boy. As an afterthought he said to the guv'nor, 'Oh, give us a bottle of that barbecue fuel,' and paid up. 'Tara, mate. See you soon.' He went home, took himself into the garden, then poured this stuff all over himself and struck a match.

The mental picture that forces itself into my head totally crucifies me. Then the questions came. What if this? What if that? What if we hadn't gone away that weekend? The answer's always the same – I don't think there was anything we could have said or done that would have changed anything in the long run. He was the boy that cried wolf. He was always in trouble, and I'd go flying round to his place and he'd be as right as rain. Or I'd get a call that he was out of control, get home and find him perfectly normal. 'Sorry Dad, I don't know why that happened.'

If we'd been home that weekend, perhaps he would have come to us and talked it through and things might have been different. But there would always be another time, because he had a seed planted in his brain that to this day his mum is convinced was the catalyst that made him take his life.

A hypnotherapist that was treating our boy told him that there were two Marks, and that one of them was in a coffin. And if Mark took that on board, and Shirl feels that he did, that man might as well have handed him the box of matches. Because in effect, he set him on the path to his own destruction.

It's all academic. Whatever fingers are pointed or questions answered nothing, nothing, will bring our boy back. And as we stood at his grave, knowing that our sensitive, funny, wonderful son was lying under our feet, the only tiny consolation we could squeeze out of his death was that his troubles were over. All the pain and torment he'd suffered was washed away and he was at rest.

But us left behind were totally, totally bereft – destroyed. My missus just cried and cried, and nothing I said or did could console her. I honestly don't know where I got the strength from to support her and the others, because I was near collapse myself, but couldn't show it. They all looked to me to hold them, be strong, be stalwart and do everything to get through it. I did it and I did it willingly, but when I looked behind me, there was no-one there for me to lean on. It was hard. Jesus, it was so hard.

When the others weren't there and Shirley would finally drop off to sleep, I'd escape to my room, pull the duvet over my head and cry for hours. I wanted to run away, bury my head in the sand – in fact, just give up and let the grief take me over. But I couldn't. I had a commitment to my family and commitments outside that couldn't just be brushed aside, even if I'd wanted to.

It was nothing to do with money, and nothing to do with trying to lose myself in work, but two nights after that terrible thing happened, I had to do a pre-arranged stag do. I stuck myself on automatic, put my Mark to one side and went out and did it. The gags, the blue jokes, everything, and afterwards the audience gave me a standing ovation.

I mean an absolute standing ovation that just went on and on. What were they applauding? My act? Or what they perceived as my bravery? I wasn't brave, I was horribly empty inside, but I owed it to myself, my family and even to Mark, that I couldn't allow my emotions to destroy what I'd worked for all my life.

The following night, and my Mark wasn't even buried yet, I was due to make my very first video. Johnny Hamp, who I mentioned before was Executive Producer of *The Comedians* and indeed Head of Light Entertainment for Granada TV, had gone freelance. He'd organized this video through Tony Lewis, but instead of producing it in London, he insisted it was done in Manchester so he could use all the gear from Granada. So this was all arranged when I phoned him up and told him I couldn't go through with it. I said, 'Johnny, please. I'm just not able to carry it off. I haven't got the strength. You know what's happened, and my wife is crying twenty-four hours a day – I've got to be with her.' His reply was, 'Mike, you've got to be a pro.' How easily that slips off someone else's tongue. I'm not criticizing the man, but he couldn't have had any comprehension of what it would cost me emotionally to be 'a pro'.

Jumping forward, I've got a tour of the country coming up, and two places that won't be on my itinerary are Liverpool and Manchester. I can die on my arse anywhere, but those two cities are guaranteed. They've seen everyone and his uncle, from Frank Sinatra to Harry Bolt – they've heard every gag in the book, and on top of that I'm a flash Londoner. So what happens? Johnny Hamp sticks me in a two-bob piss-hole of a club and expects me to work miracles.

Eleven o'clock at night, and all the punters are pissed out of their brains. The cameras were focused on the people at the front, and the crew were geeing them up to clap and cheer, which they did reluctantly because they didn't give a monkey's about me. Shouting, belching, talking, 'Aye oop, Harry – do yer wanna pint?' 'Cold one tonight' – beer, beer, beer. Be a pro? I was sweating cobs, and I might as well have been talking to the wall. Sweat? I've never leaked like I did that night, before or since. I wore a brand-new white silk dress jacket and it was ruined. I had it taken to the cleaner's days later, and they told me to chuck it in the bin.

I didn't go out there expecting sympathy, which was just as well, because the general attitude was that none of the audience would've pissed on me if I'd burst into flames. Although I was in pieces, I went out there to do my bit for a video that would be a first of its kind. Everybody does them now, and have done for a few years, but right then it was an innovation to package up a comic like that. It was crap, and I still feel Johnny Hamp made a bad decision not only with the venue, but to have insisted I do it against my will. They packaged it, tried to sell it, but like me, it fell on its arse because it was devastatingly bad. I swore then that I'd never touch another one. Forget it – I'd steer well clear in the future.

Obviously I changed my mind on that score, as thousands and thousands of my fans will testify. Every video since has been an unmitigated success, but I still think anyone who picked up that first one should've had their money back, because it didn't do me any favours.

Driving home that night, tired, depressed and sick inside, a picture of Mark popped into my head and I burst into tears. I must have driven a hundred miles blinded by tears until I had to tell myself, 'Come on, come on – pull yourself together before you get home,' because no way could I let Shirl see me in that state. Not that she wouldn't have understood or have expected otherwise, because she knew all our kids were my life, same as her, but I had this male thing that forced me to be strong so that they could gain strength from me. So I did most of my grieving in private.

Again, not long after, I was driving to a club over in Surrey to do a show. I set off fine. I felt calm and ready to work, and then one of Mark's favourite songs came on the radio and I lost it completely. I just couldn't stop myself sobbing. It started in my stomach, welled up in my chest and just kept bursting out, making me shake from head to foot. It was uncontrollable, and I was still blubbering when I pulled into the car park of the club.

Within half an hour I was due to be the funny man – knock the punters out. 'Whaaaay', 'T'rific', 'Fucking 'andsome', and all I could do was sit in that dark car park with my head on the wheel and tears rolling down my face. In the end I got angry with myself, jumped out of the motor and took a number-seven iron out of my golf bag. I didn't stop to think, just smashed myself on the instep – crash.

The pain was incredible, and as it washed over me it overtook the pain inside. It got me out of that terrible feeling, and I managed to grab a pair of sunglasses and limp to the men's room and straighten myself up.

I did the show more or less balancing on one leg, but I did it and was proud of myself. I never had to hit myself again or anything like it, but it wasn't the last time grief took me over. I never spoke of it to anyone, not even Shirl. I suppose from the outside it must have appeared that I was coping better than could be expected, but really all I was doing was taking every day as it came – trying not to look back, and certainly not looking forward.

July the fourth – Independence Day – is another date I can't bear to look at on the calendar. I don't want to hear it mentioned, I don't even want to think about it, because four months after losing our Mark, part of his legacy to us, little Kirsty Anne, died in her sleep. That beautiful, beautiful baby girl was taken from us before she was even six months old – a victim of cot death. I can picture her in my head now. Healthy, chubby-cheeked, laughing when you tickled her tum – and next thing we're at Mark's graveside again as her tiny white coffin was gently placed beside her dad's. Together for ever.

After that, I never wanted to go to Little Easton churchyard ever again, because I knew it would destroy me. Shirley goes there often, and it's the best-kept grave in the whole place, so in a way she's much stronger than I am. It's nearly nine years now, and only once have I forced myself to go because I felt I owed it to Mark and Kirsty Anne.

We were going to Spain for a holiday, and I suddenly had the urge to go and talk to my boy – virtually hours before we caught the plane. I went and it tore me to pieces, turned me inside out, so much so that I cried all the way to the airport and onto the plane. I've told Shirl, and she understands; that I will go back when the time is right, whenever that might be, but I'm in absolute fear of what it will do to me.

I can go to where my friend Ted is buried, same as I can with my mum and dad. Of course, it upsets me when it comes home how much I miss them and others that have gone the same way over the years, but it doesn't devastate me to the degree of barely being able to stand. I certainly don't need to go into a churchyard to be reminded of my son, because his essence is around us every waking hour. We're surrounded by memories. There's his guitar; he played football on that bit of lawn; this was his favourite food; this was his favourite TV programme; it goes on and on and on.

Like I said, I put on a brave face for everyone, but my missus, who's always been so open with her feelings, was either totally numbed by it all or constantly tearful. When I had to go to work, it practically took a general anaesthetic to get her out of my arms. What could I say? I knew myself that words couldn't make it better; nevertheless I tried. I used to point out that what we were suffering, and often worse, happened every single day. I'd pick up the paper and read of eight kids dying in a house fire, or five in a bus crash, and every one of them had mums and dads and families. But it was no consolation to her, or to me, or indeed all those other parents.

I said the same thing over and over again, thousands of times but in different ways, because I didn't know what else to do. And slowly, slowly, slowly, there would be maybe two hours between these emotional breakdowns, then four, then ten – until days passed at a time and she seemed to have it under control. Not accepted, or come to terms with it, because neither of us have – not even today, but under control.

How Shirl did it is only for her to say, but for myself, I immersed myself in work. I was in *EastEnders* before it happened and right through. I didn't take time off, I just locked myself in my dressing room and studied and studied my scripts. Everyone there – cast, crew, directors – everyone was a wonderful support to me. They gave me my own space, but let me know they were there for me if I needed them. I won't forget that, but like I said, I preferred to shut myself away and learn my lines over and over again. It was difficult though, because Mark's face kept getting between me and the pages.

When I was at home I discovered a therapy that, in a nutshell – and I can't put it any other way – saved my sanity. I was sitting in the garden, thinking and thinking, and I spotted a few weeds in the flowerbed. I reached over and started pulling them out, and for half a minute the pain went away. Over a period of time, as I got more and more engrossed in gardening, I found that it was slowly healing me. If I try to say that the mass of blooms in the beds all round our grounds are down to me, Shirl will crack up laughing, because I'm as good at growing things as I am at DIY. But in my own way I found that whatever I was doing was immensely therapeutic.

Another thing that crept up on me was my relationship with every living creature I came across. This is a man who spent his childhood and youth killing pheasants, rabbits and what have you. After Mark and Kirsty Anne, I unknowingly developed a profound respect for life. Didn't matter what it was. I'd step round ants on the path and carefully scoop butterflies off the pond. I didn't do it consciously at first, but obviously something inside me was telling me that I'd suffered enough from death, without adding to it needlessly. Sounds a bit slushy, but no-one can judge how other people react to certain situations unless they've been there themselves.

CHAPTER TEN

So I TURNED MY BACK ON *EASTENDERS* WITH A RELIEF THAT AT the time was overwhelming. All I wanted to do was take a holiday, rest and recuperate my strength. And apart from my own back garden, there was only one place in the world where I could guarantee I'd have all my problems washed away, and that was Spain.

Bit of a contradiction, to my way of thinking, when I'd turned my back on the place years before, totally ruined and facing crippling debts, down to that club. I'd managed to dig myself out of the mess that experience had got me into and clawed my way back up financially, but even years later I still blamed the country, its laws and the people in it – right or wrong, that's how I felt.

Three or four years prior to my leaving the soap, I'd put in for a break. I think I had to give them a month or so notice so that the scriptwriters could fit my absence into the storyline; Frank taking a holiday or going away on some business or other. They agreed, and it was all laid on. As I said, it was only going to be a short break, so any holiday we planned didn't want to be too far, but above all, wherever it was it had to be warm. My Shirl, who obviously didn't bear the same grudge as I did, jumped straight in with, 'Let's go to Spain.' I've kicked that straight into touch with, 'No way. Sweetheart, stick a pin in the map, anywhere you like as long as it's not there.' So we left it at that.

In the meantime, I was playing a golf tournament for the Variety

Club at, of all places, St Pierre in Chepstow, which as you can imagine, brought back memories that I'd buried as deep as I could. I was on the practice ground and got talking to Mike England, Captain of Tottenham and Wales – nice fella. As we're putting around chatting about this and that, he brought up the subject of Spain. I'd already mentioned I was taking a holiday soon, so he said, 'That's where you want to go, Mike, it's beautiful, it's warm and there's golf courses everywhere.' I knew all that anyway, but he wasn't aware of the problems I'd suffered down to that country, and I didn't think that was the time to go into all the ins and outs. All I said was that I'd had my fingers burned and I thought the place was a piss-hole.

He was like everyone else who falls in love with the country. It's not enough to enjoy the place themselves; they've got to sell it to anybody who's got two minutes to listen. I'm the same myself now, but then I just let it go in one ear and out the other.

Eventually he got round to the fact that because he was too tied up with work in this country, he was selling a villa he owned down at San Pedro – about an hour from Malaga. Now, still selling the country like he was on a percentage from the Spanish Tourist Board, he said, 'Look, Mike, it's sitting empty. Take your wife over there, you'll find it's all changed. It won't cost you a penny, so what can you lose.'

It wasn't the money, but time was running short for booking somewhere, so I said to Shirl, 'OK, it's only for ten days, we've nothing to lose so we'll give it a go.'

Revelation – absolute revelation. We both fell in love with the place all over again. I don't know who gave the Spaniards a kick up the arse, but Mike was right, it had changed. Their attitude to everything was different, particularly to foreign tourists. As for the villa, I had to drag my old woman out when it was time to go home. If it was just another place to stay, it might not have had the same effect, but because she knew it was on the market, she made our mind up that we had to have it.

I'd hardly unpacked my case when she had me on the phone to Mike in Wales to say we'd have it. By this time I'm a bit excited myself, because once I've made my mind up about something I want it there and then. Never mind tomorrow – now, whatever the cost. I was gutted when he told me he'd just taken an offer and a cash deposit off some old rich woman.

It wasn't Mike's fault, because I'd never said I was interested, but I was bitterly disappointed, and so was Shirl. What's meant to be is meant to be – it's all laid down, as I've said before. Five days later he rang me up to tell me the sale of the villa was a bit of a farce. It had turned out that the old woman was not only very wealthy, but at the same time very eccentric, and what she did to fill in her last years was travel all round the world putting her name down on properties. She wasn't knocking anyone, and no doubt the sales would've gone through if it wasn't for her family following her round cancelling these deals as soon as she made them. Upshot was, me and Mike shook hands, if you like, over the phone, and we had ourselves a villa.

Now while we were in the villa for that first holiday, according to my missus it was total perfection – everything was just right, and all we had to do was move in and put our feet up. Two minutes and she had other ideas, with the result that over six or seven years it's cost me in the region of sixty grand to get it the way she wants. Extra rooms built, this pulled out, that stuck on – right down to altering the doors. I mean, a door's a door, but no – she had to have the frames arched and the regular doors replaced with natural pine ones. No wonder she's got a black belt in spending. I'm not really having a dig, because at the end of the day she's made it lovely, and I'm totally in love with the place.

All I need to do to get away is pick up the phone, book a flight, grab my passport and I'm off. Everything I need is waiting for me. Everything from toothpicks to two beautiful cars.

So early February 1996 I left England with my shoulders slumped. No question about it, I was depressed. I don't have to explain it to anyone who's ever been through it. You feel terrible all the time, but you can't take a tablet for it like a headache or toothache. You can't get rid of it, and it stays like a knot inside you. I'm just as human as the next person. I have my ups and downs, but that depression – that dark cloud hanging over your life – must be one of the worst feelings, and it's something I've gone through twice, maybe three times, maximum four, and it has never got any easier to bear. Funny thing about that state of mind, you can tell yourself time and time again that everything is going great, and look at all the positive sides of your life, but the brain just won't compute it.

The only answer, as far as I could see, was to take myself out of the environment where everything was bearing down on me and get away from it all, so I headed for what I class as Utopia – our villa.

It worked its magic within two minutes of driving out of Malaga Airport. It's difficult to describe the feeling, but as I sat back in my beautiful Camero that I'd arranged to be waiting for me, a feeling of relaxation just washed over me from head to foot, and I knew I was going to come out the other side.

I think Shirley knew I had to get this beaten on my own, so she'd stayed at home to keep things ticking over. We spoke on the phone two or three times a day, but as for my taking off without her for a few months, it never gave her or me a moment's thought. That's a nice state to reach when you're pushing on in years and have been together for a long, long time. In essence, you can lead separate lives, yet be closer than you ever were.

At one time we always went to bed together. In fact, it didn't matter what time I came home from work, she'd be waiting, just so we could have that bit of togetherness. Over the past ten years or so, things have changed. Shirl's become a night bird, while come eleven o'clock, I'm nodding off in the chair. There's nothing I can do about it – I just have to go to bed. On the other hand I'm up early, and she can still be in her bed at half past ten in the morning. So as regards our sleeping habits, our lives have become separate. And in a lot of other ways, that can have a knock-on effect. But – and a very big but – we have an extremely comfortable relationship.

Being madly in love, like you are when you first meet and for some time afterwards, is a wonderful feeling, and I've got to say there's nothing like it at the time. What no-one realizes while they're in that romantic state is how much better it can become the longer you are together. And after nearly thirty-nine years, being very comfortable with each other is the word that sums it all up. You can't buy that – it only comes with pure, unadulterated one hundred per cent experience of what the other person is all about. And that's what me and Shirl have got. It's terrific.

I don't want anyone else, and I wouldn't insult this lady who's stuck by me through thick and thin by even considering going over the side. And thankfully she knows it. I say thankfully, because if it was down to the newspapers and the pieces of shit that keep their copy flowing in, our marriage could have been destroyed more than once. The papers have rarely done me any favours, but then if you put your name up for a bit of fame, they presume you're asking to be shot down in flames and gladly oblige.

As I said before, I do not give a brass monkey's what goes into print about my life, as long as it only concerns me personally. I'm too long in the tooth for anything to worry me like I might have done years ago. But when it involves my family, that's a different ball game, and I get very angry. I do have to say that when our Mark died the press were extremely sympathetic – they really were. They poured themselves over me and my wife, and we were very grateful for the comfort they gave us. But that could never make up for all the times they gave us a knock-back.

Because he was my boy, and for no other reason, Mark made head-lines with 'Mike Reid's son has sex with twelve-year-old girl', like he was some perverted paedophile. For Christ's sake, he was a young sixteen-year-old, and her with all the make-up and big tits, looked and acted like she was eighteen. I'm not making excuses because he's dead and gone, but they did sling it at him and he was hurt for himself and for me, because he said over and over again, 'Dad I'm sorry, I've let you down.' They dug him out a number of times over bits and pieces that they wouldn't have touched if he'd been anyone other than my son, and it didn't help his mental state by a long run.

I was saying about my old woman and trust, and what I'm getting round to is that during the year prior to me leaving *EastEnders*, they gave Shirl a smack in the face by headlining that I paid for one off the wrist in a Spanish massage parlour. Now if it had been true and taken place, as they spread all over the paper, I think right now I'd keep my mouth firmly closed, because it's old news and long forgotten. If I'd been caught bang to rights I'd have wiped my mouth and suffered the aggravation. But it wasn't true, and I never got the chance to put my side of it.

In brief, I was having a few days in the villa and spending most of the time playing golf with Bill Reilly. I was getting out of the bath one morning, put a soapy hand on the end and bosh – I've gone down on my side. When a guy my weight drops his ribs on a thin, rounded edge something's got to go, and I really thought I'd hurt myself badly. I stood in front of the mirror breathing in and out to make sure I hadn't broken anything, and within three minutes a bruise started coming out from my armpit to my waist. What a state I was in – and me looking forward to a few rounds.

I'd arranged to meet Bill at his place around eleven, so on the way I slipped into Rascal's, a little café in Benahavis, for a full English breakfast. It's only up the road from San Pedro, so it wasn't out of the way. By the time I got to Bill's I was as stiff as a board, could hardly turn my neck or lift my arm. His idea was that I had a good soak in a hot bath. I told him to forget it, saying that if it wasn't for the poxy bath I wouldn't be in this mess. After a bit, with the pain creasing me up, I decided the only answer was to get myself a sauna, so we jumped in Bill's motor and shot off down to Marbella.

We found the sauna place, parked up and went in. The woman at the desk was on the phone so we stood there, and while we were waiting this English-looking geezer rushed in, looked at Bill, looked at me, then rushed out again. All I thought was, 'What the hell's up with him?' and then forgot it. Five minutes later I was in the sauna and I steamed the pain away for about an hour and a half – it was wonderful. While I was stretched out on the bench, some bird came in and asked Bill if we wanted anything else. He politely told her no thanks, and that was that.

We went back to Bill's place, I picked up my car, said I'd see him later and set off home. On the way I noticed I was being followed. When I slowed down, so did the other motor. When I speeded up, it kept right up my arse. Just before you get to my place there's a little cul-de-sac, so I shot in there, pulled into an alley and waited. Sure enough, in came the car. Whoever was driving didn't know where they were; I pulled out and blocked the road. I carefully climbed out, walked over and pulled the door open – and the two fellas inside shit themselves. They didn't know that with my ribs done in I couldn't have punched a hole in a paper bag, so they think they're down for a good hiding.

Straight away they're both giving it, 'Sorry, Mr Reid. Sorry, sorry.'

The back seat was covered with cameras and bits and pieces so I said, 'Ten seconds to tell me what's going on, or I fill you both in.' I wouldn't have done, but I looked as though I meant it and they couldn't tell me quick enough that they were press, and all they knew was that their editor wanted a few photos. Load of bollocks. If they'd asked me, I would have obliged them with the big grin. Anyone knows that I've never been so much up my own arse that if a reporter is reasonable and gives me a bit of respect, I'd never stop him or her from making a living.

Now when the papers are going to stick it to someone or expose them, they usually have the decency to ring up the night before to tell them they are going to be dropped in the shit the following day – have a good night's sleep. In my case there were no phone calls – nothing. This was Saturday. Next morning, right across the Sunday paper was, 'EastEnder Mike caught in brothel'.

Nobody knew I was going to that sauna, not even me until I got to Bill's, so they must have been setting me up for something because I had been tailed from my villa all the way to Marbella. I know that, because in black and white was every movement I'd made, even down to the egg, bacon and fried slice I'd eaten at Rascal's.

What story they would have made up if I hadn't conveniently gone into the sauna, I don't know. As it was, they had a field day. They even had a photograph of me walking out of the place counting my money from a wallet. Anyone who knows me could tell you that my cash comes out of my hip pocket loose, and that in fact I was rolling a cigarette from a tobacco pouch.

But who gives a shit? I shouldn't have to justify myself, but that rag has put me in the position of having to. If there was a case to answer, and I assure you there wasn't, who really cares? The public? No. They'd be giving it, 'Reidy – whey-hey, get in there, son.' My boys? No – don't give a monkey's. But to my old woman it was a terrible effrontery. Thirty years ago she might have thought some-thing of it, but with me at age fifty-five and her knowing me inside out, she never once questioned those allegations, and I love her for that.

What hurt her was the fact that to sell a few newspapers those reporters were quite happy to try to stick a great wedge in our relationship, and with a couple less secure with each other, it might have worked.

Worse, though, was what my little grandkids had to go through at school. Their little mates would listen to talk indoors, then come out with, 'Your grandad's a dirty old man.' 'We can't play with you because your grandad's a pervert.' At the end of the day, I told myself that this wasn't so much a personal attack on me but, as usual, a dig at *EastEnders*. As I said, the papers have never treated the soap too well, yet they're perfectly happy to boost their circulation by using its name in a headline – never mind what shit they put under it.

Look what they did to Gillian Taylforth – Cathy. They hung her out to dry over something or nothing that was only between her and her husband. Another time she got the headlines when some distant relation was accused of selling walk-on parts in the show. It was nothing – nothing to do with her, but she got the brunt of the publicity. It's the price we pay for the success of the soap, but when will they realize they're hurting the innocent? Or do they know it already, and just don't care about people's feelings as long as they can sell a few more papers?

Is it any wonder that I'm not the same character I used to be years ago? Instead of the outgoing Jack the Lad I'm subdued, and, yes, wary of new people I meet and of situations where whatever I do might be misinterpreted.

Just take the other night, for instance. I dropped into the Moat Hotel, which is just up the road from the studio, to get myself a sauna. When I got inside the sauna it was empty, but within minutes a couple of young ladies had come in and I was out like a shot. I waited until a group of fellas turned up, went back in and had my steam bath. That newspaper article was four years ago, and I'm still paying the price – frightened to death of going about my normal business, in case someone's waiting to fit me up. It's totally repressed the real me, bordering on the paranoiac.

To give you an example, me and Bill Reilly were having a couple of lunchtime beers by a pool in Port Andalucia. It's a beautiful day and we're chatting away when he said, 'Hold up, hold up', and put his finger to his lips. I've said, 'What's up now?' because he gets as paranoid as I do, what with being included in that sauna piece. He said, 'That geezer over there, he's watching us and listening to us.' I looked over, and sure enough the bloke was reading an English paper with his ear cocked towards us. Yeah, definitely a reporter.

Just then a young girl stopped and asked me for my autograph, and I nearly shit myself. She must have thought I was a bit rude as I signed her bit of paper and got shot of her without the usual banter.

We kept our eye on this fella and after about half an hour he got up, walked over to where the cars were parked and ducked down behind one of them. I said to Bill, 'When that snake pops up with a camera, we're out of here.' Next thing I see is him cycling past us without a second glance, cycle clips firmly round his ankles. He's been bending down putting them on. We cracked up. But then there was the more serious side of how we should never have been made to feel the way we did.

Anyway, that was all past by the time I left *EastEnders* to relax in Spain, sort myself out and enjoy my retirement.

One of the first things I wanted to set in motion was something that had been in the back of my mind for a long time. And that was to give my Shirl the wedding day of her dreams that she'd missed out on all those years ago. In essence, I proposed to her all over again and we retook our vows in Little Easton Church. What a contrast to ten minutes in Redbridge Registry Office, then a skinful of vodka.

This time Shirley turned up in a gleaming white Rolls-Royce wearing an ivory chiffon dress and silk jacket. She looked a picture. And when I repeated those vows after the vicar, I meant every word of them. There was a tinge of sadness, knowing that our Mark and little Kirsty Anne were lying nearby in the graveyard, but we kept it to ourselves, knowing they were both beside us in spirit if not in the flesh.

The papers gave it a lot of coverage, and one in particular gave it plenty of 'Mike this, Mike that'. 'Good old Reidy, much-loved comic.' Three months later I was back to square one – relegated to plain old Reid as those same papers slagged me off on the word of one of the biggests rats I've ever been unfortunate enough to be associated with.

I've already said give me five minutes and I'll have anyone sussed. So, when it came to this particular piece of crap I'm referring to, that extra sense didn't let me down because I had his number straight away. Unfortunately I was a mug, stupidly ignored my inner feelings and allowed myself to get sucked in.

If you get a thorn in your foot or finger and can't get it out, a callous grows over it until it's buried and doesn't hurt. In the same way, any pains I've suffered over the years have been covered over and had the edge taken off them. But for the purpose of this book, I've had to strip away layer after layer and expose myself to painful memories and grief that I'd rather forget. The Nottingham business, Milson and the Lincoln, Mark and Kirsty Anne – each time resurrecting either pain or extreme loathing. And that's what I'm feeling at this moment, as I start to think about how that rat tried to destroy me and my family.

I first met this rat through a friend of mine, Freddie Smith, who's dead and gone now. I don't trust easily, and if it hadn't been for Fred, I honestly don't think I would have given him the time of day, because he came over as a slippery bastard. But with him being backed up by a very dear friend I went over the top, like I do, and did everything I could to help him on the way up.

He had a bit of a business going, and on at least two occasions, when he moved into new premises, I'd turn up as Mike Reid the personality to open the shops and draw the punters in. Didn't cost him a penny, and at that time my manager Tony Lewis could pick up four figures easily for a job like that.

Later on I introduced him to the Lady Ratlings through Shirl, who's a member herself. This is a charitable organization, made up entirely of show-business people or their family, and is affiliated to and the female equivalent of the Grand Order of Water Rats, which has raised millions over the years for children. Although I came to regret it, with my help he got a lot of business put his way, and he could've made himself a fortune if his slippery side hadn't taken over, but I didn't find that out for a long while.

One way or another, I bent over backwards to help him because he was a pal – or to repeat, more accurately a friend of a friend. He had nothing I wanted, and I never asked him for anything because that's the way I am. Then, for reasons known only to himself, he turned on me, sold a load of rubbish to a newspaper and turned my life on its head all over again. In a massive headline he had me down for arranging parts in *EastEnders* for young birds in return for sexual favours. How green would I have to be to fall into something like that?

Remember, I was ducking and diving when I was just a dot. I understood human nature by the time I was fifteen, and by twenty-five didn't have much more to learn. So is it feasible at an age more than twice that, I would lay myself wide open to exposure for the sake of a quick leg-over? God forbid, but if I fancied a bit of extramarital excitement I could get it every day of the week. I wouldn't have to pay for it, and I wouldn't have to make wild promises.

Let's be realistic. The power that TV screen gives us so-called celebrities is awesome. I could snap my fingers and birds would be lining up. Not to jump into bed with Grandad Reid the person, but so they can say Frank Butcher gave them one. To reiterate that I like to think I understand human nature better than most, why, why, why would I take the risk? But that's exactly what the papers had me down for.

When muckrakers like him go to work, they always make sure there is a kernel of truth as a starting point – it gives their story credence. And this little bit of truth was the fact that I'd got a day's work on set for a young Australian girl.

This sort of thing wasn't out of the way for any of the actors in the soap, or indeed any like it. I suppose in the twelve years I've been doing this, I've helped someone no more than four or five times, and three of them were fellas. The powers that be don't even concern themselves, because it means nothing.

I can still remember when I was a star-struck kid. So when I've been asked by some young hopeful to please, please get them two seconds on screen, for the sake of my scribbling their name on the first assistant's list I can give someone a dream come true – that's all it takes. I'm not being Mr Wonderful, but I get touched like anyone else. And that's what happened with this girl.

This bloke put her on to me, and when I met her she told me she had a serious stomach complaint and was soon going back to Australia for hospital treatment. That was an aside, not a lever for me to do her a favour. She asked me if I could arrange a walk-on so she could dine out on her fame back home where the soap is absolutely massive. No problem: I did the business and never saw her again, not even her few seconds of glory on screen.

The next time he caught up with me I had left the programme. He said, 'Remember the Aussie girl?' I said, 'Yeah, nice kid – the one with the stomach problem?' He said, 'Well, she wants to get back in again.' All I could say was that I was out of the soap, but that if I was to go back and she was still around, I'd try to help. There was more, though. He told me he knew three really horny girls who would do anything, with much emphasis on the anything, to get on the show. He drooled down the phone, the dirty git. 'You'll love 'em Mike. Blonde, big tits, the works.' I didn't get the hump, just laughed and told him, 'I'm not interested in that sort of lark, and never have been.'

I'd had a long day, was extremely tired and all I wanted to do was get rid of him and get my head down. So I told him that as a favour, if I were to get back into the soap, I would try to fix something up for them, but I wanted nothing in return, and I stressed *nothing*. In essence, that was the sum total of the conversation, and I thought no more of it.

Not long after that I distanced myself from him, not from anything that affected me, but because I'd been getting whispers concerning various dodgy areas he was getting himself into, and other kinds of stuff that, to be honest, I didn't approve of. Sounds a bit pompous coming from Reidy the ducker and diver, but that's the way I felt at the time.

Like I said, I let things cool off a bit, then he phoned me up and asked for a loan of ten grand. I didn't even think about it, just said, 'Sorry, no can do.' He kept on, 'Mike, I need ten thousand now.' I told him I wasn't even going to ask why he wanted the money, the answer was no. He said, 'OK, fine', but real slow, with an inflection in his voice that was saying something else.

First thing next morning he's back on. I said, 'What do you want?' and all he said was, 'Mike, those three birds won't wait.' Now I do think something's going on, and I said, 'I don't know what you're up to, but I've got a feeling you're trying to fit me up, so fuck off!' and I slung the phone down. A bit later a reporter rang me, introduced himself and asked me if I knew an Australian girl, such-and-such name. Caught me on the hop really, so I thought and said, 'Yeah, vaguely.' Quick as a shot he said, 'Thank you, Mr Reid, that's all I want to know', and put the phone down.

Sunday morning I'm spread all over the paper as some sad, dirty old bastard accused of group sex and gaining sexual favours by offering parts in *EastEnders*. All down to the word of one man, no-one else. No pictures, no statements from girls – nothing.

On the one hand, it was a compliment to me that they thought I was worth the front page of a national Sunday paper. On the other, once again, my old woman and grandkids were put through the wringer big-time. Though once again Shirley stood firmly beside me and never once questioned if there was any truth in the accusations thrown at me. If she'd had to think about it, it would have made those vows we'd made three months earlier worthless. But she was as staunch as ever.

Going against the respect for all life that grew in me after we lost Mark, here was one man I could've killed stone dead for what he'd done. Not the reporters, they were doing the dirty job they were paid to do, but this man was supposed to have been a friend. He kept his head well down, so in a way I was held back from doing time, but I wasn't going to let it go.

I approached a lawyer to sue for the sake of my family's good name. He was the biggest litigation lawyer in the country, so he knew all the ins and outs. He took one look at the article and told me that without question I'd win hands down. I'm going, 'Yeah, great, wonderful', and he's going, 'Whoa. Whoa.' Then he told me the score. First and foremost I'd have to lay out fifty grand up front and lodge it with the courts or whatever. The case could then take up to three years to be heard, and in the meantime the paper would stick every cub reporter on my back to watch my every move. When it finally got to court, I'd have to suffer four or five days with my whole life splashed across the headlines. The good news was that I'd win the case and walk away with two or three hundred thousand, and that fact wouldn't trouble them one bit because they've covered themselves by selling that amount of extra papers.

He also told me to bear in mind that the owner of the paper is a powerful man, and if it came to it he'd throw ten million against me on principle, and to him it would be like sneezing. So, using my own terminology, the lawyer suggested I wipe my mouth and forget it.

I was gutted. Not because I wanted their poxy money, that was never an issue. It was the fact that I didn't have a voice to put my side of the story with.

As I was leaving the office he said, 'Mike, I want you to think about what I'm going to say, and this applies to anyone in a public position. Be careful of putting yourself in any situation that leaves you open to misinterpretation. For instance, if a girl stops you in the street and asks for your autograph, and you oblige her plus a few words, she can go straight to the phone and tell the papers that Mike Reid has just propositioned her in the most awful way. As long as she's prepared to put her name to the allegation, they can print it and as you've seen, you will have no redress. It's her word against yours.'

And that bit of advice brings me right back to what I was saying about the personality change I've gone through. What am I supposed to do when a female fan approaches me? Allowing that these people have put me in the very comfortable position I am in today, should I blank them, turn my back and walk away unless I'm surrounded by witnesses? Perhaps I should, but I never will, even though I'm terrified of being vilified in the press over nothing.

While I was climbing the ladder towards success, I thought everything would be roses once I arrived. I never imagined that me and my family were going to suffer some of the shit we've had thrown at us.

Another time the papers got it wrong it was annoying but amusing at the same time. I was in Spain, and I picked up an English newspaper, and there in banner headlines was 'Frank Butcher nicked at 100 mph'. What had happened was that a traffic policeman had given a pull, then rushed off back to the station full of himself and waving this bit of paper. 'Guess who I nicked today? Frank Butcher.' He must have looked a right lemon when it was pointed out to him that outside the soap, Frank doesn't exist. Either way, the papers got hold of it and stuck me up as a danger to the public. If it was true, so what? I could paper a room with the amount of speeding tickets I've been given over the years, but as I hadn't even been in the country when this was supposed to have happened, it got up my nose.

I phoned them up to put my side and asked for a printed apology the following day. I was told it couldn't be done, though they were prepared to send me a personal letter saying they were sorry. I told them to stick it up their arse. I said to them, 'You lot have dug me out in big print, so now have the courtesy to do the same when you're in the wrong.' Waste of time, because in the end I got neither and it left me fuming at the injustice of it.

On another of the many occasions when I was pulled over for speeding, I was driving an American car and happened to be wearing a Stetson. I'd probably just come back from the States or whatever. I mentioned before that I can knock the corners off my voice as easy as breathing, so when this copper starts giving me some, I went into a Texan drawl. 'Ah'm sorry, sir – ah jest ain't gotten used to your wonderful, wonderful freeways.' He stood back, looked at me and said, 'Fuck off, you're Mike Reid. I saw you at a stag do a couple of weeks ago.' I got away with it, though.

That year after leaving the soap was one of great highs and equally great lows. Surprisingly, once the pressure of work was lifted off my shoulders my old buoyant self bounced back. Spanish sunshine and golf – wonderful therapy. I was retired, or should I say semi-retired, because while I was taking it easy, I was still open to offers for bits and pieces of work as long as I didn't get involved to the degree where it was taking my life over.

While I was relaxing on the veranda of my villa with a nice drink or two, back home I was appearing on the screen in a short series I'd knocked out before leaving. If you didn't catch it at the time it was called *The Terrace*, a DIY programme fronted, if you will, by ten-thumbs Reidy. When I first got the offer the actual details were a bit thin, and when I told Shirl she just collapsed laughing saying, 'I hope they don't ask you to build a serving hatch.' Fortunately I was there as linkman with all the gags and banter. It was a bit of fun, and was filmed in no time and without any pressure. It put a few quid in the bank, and kept my face in the public eye. Which is when I came to the conclusion that life could be so much easier for me if I went down the road of doing a bit of work here and there instead of full-time. I could spend four months at home, four months in Spain and the remainder keeping a bit of wages coming in.

The wonderful writer Geoff McQueen came up with a series

specifically written with me in mind, and without exaggerating, I was absolutely knocked out. And more so when I found that the other main character had been moulded to fit Bob Hoskins. The basic premise was that me and Bob would play two rival villains – east and south, if you like. They both get thirty-year prison sentences, and it's after they're released that the dramatic storyline comes into play.

I was so excited about it, and told Geoff I thought it was an actor's dream. Bob had been sent a script, so I said to Geoff, what did he think of it, is he up for the part? He said, 'He likes what he's read. Why don't you give him a call and talk about it?' I don't want to labour the point, but in my own mind I'm just plain old Reidy, doing a day's work to the best of my ability. But Hoskins – I was in total awe of that man. He was top of the tree. I mean, *The Long Good Friday* – his performance was out of this world. I said, 'Geoff, I can't go ringing up somebody of his status for a chat.' He said, 'Don't worry, Mike, he's expecting to hear from you.' OK – in for a penny, and I phoned him up.

I fell short of calling him 'sir', but it was close. 'Mr Hoskins?' 'Yeah?' 'I understand you've had a script from Geoff McQueen.' 'Mmm.' 'I've got to say I admire your work very much.' 'Mmm.' 'The script. Did you like it?' 'Mmm.' I've never been an arse-kisser and I wasn't then, but I was extremely polite out of respect, but this geezer was giving me the hump with his negative reaction. 'Mr Hoskins, I've got to say you're making this conversation very difficult for me.' For the first time he opened his mouth. 'Whaddya want me to say?' I said, 'Say? Say? I don't want you to fucking well say nothing', and I banged the phone down. I sat in the chair and fumed, I was so livid. Needless to say, that project was kicked out the window, for the time being anyway.

Later on I was in Marbella with some of the Foremans – a very strong family – and I happened to mention this story. Greg, I think it was, went apeshit. 'Gimme the phone, I'll have that Hoskins, the jumped-up prick, who ain't even a real cockney.' I'm saying, 'Please, just leave it – it doesn't matter.' 'Don't matter?' he said. 'How dare he treat one of his own like that – he's bang out of order.' In the end I had to hold onto the phone until Greg calmed down, because I didn't want any trouble.

As far as that wonderful script is concerned, it's still lying in Geoff's office, because sadly he died before anything further could be done with it. His wife Jan, who was totally immersed in him, has left all his things just as they were because she can't bear to sort through them, and I can understand that. But when the time is right, I would love to put it through my own production company with, if he was up for it, Billy Connolly as the other lead. He's not only the cleverest comedian I know, but also a great actor who I have the utmost admiration for. And in a commercial sense, the bringing together of Scotland and London would work even better on screen.

As usual in my life, one door closes and another opens. The writer Andy Hamilton got in touch with the script of *Underworld* – a real solid drama. There was a part in it for me as Graham the cabby, a fella who acts as an enforcer and killer when he isn't driving his cab. I snatched at it with both hands, because a quick read-through told me this was right up my street. On top of that, it would allow me to work with talented people like Annette Crosbie, Alun Armstrong and David Troughton.

I loved every minute of that part, and made up my mind that this was the direction I wanted to go in – gritty drama that didn't tie me down. When I mentioned this earlier, I said how I couldn't believe the pace of productions compared with *EastEnders*. And with this in mind, I could see that if my future plans materialized, I wouldn't have to graft my plums off for the best part of the year.

During the latter part of my eighteen-month exile or semi-retirement, whatever you want to call it, I was asked on several occasions to go back to *EastEnders*, but I always said no. I kept hearing on the grapevine that casting directors, and indeed other actors like Ross and Steve, wanted me to sign up again because things weren't the same without me. I could only assume that they meant it had gone a bit quiet without me singing around the place and making them laugh. I was touched, but at the same time I don't think any of them realized just how much I'd been affected by those scripts, and as much as I missed this other family, I wasn't prepared to put myself through all that again.

Even Barbara Windsor tried to talk me round every time I saw her.

She pointed out, as if I didn't know, that when we worked together the whole action was lighter and much easier. Also, as she put it, 'If it wasn't for you, Michael, I wouldn't be in the show. I get nice and settled, then you walk out.' She was right. I was instrumental in getting her recognized by the casting director, and had been happy to do so. But this was no string-pulling on my part – I haven't got that much clout.

Once I'd brought the two together, everything after that was totally down to her own personality and talent. I've known Windsor for thirty years, and first met her through our mutual friend Anna Karen who I mentioned earlier. It was when she and Barbara were in *The Rag Trade* that Anna introduced me to this little blonde, her best friend. Since then, she's always been close to me and my family.

Early in 1994, and me and Shirl and Barbara were having dinner with another mutual friend, Gina, who lives in Spain. We were kicking the conversation around when Windsor said to me, 'Do you know what, Mike, I'd love to get a part in *EastEnders*.' I had to agree that she was prime for some sort of role, but didn't tell her that I'd already been making overtures to Casting for them to consider her. My suggestion was knocked back every time. 'No, she wouldn't fit in. She's the *Carry On* girl – all that bubbly blonde silly stuff just wouldn't work here.' I wouldn't let it go, and fortunately a chance came up where I knew she could put herself forward.

I was having a party at my place for some occasion that escapes me, and a lot of my colleagues and their associates were coming. As it happened that most of them were from work, it basically turned into an *EastEnders* night. Now this wasn't arranged, it just came about. But I knew one of the casting executives would be turning up, so I rang Windsor and told her that no matter what she might have arranged for the following Saturday, to drop everything and make sure she got herself over to my place. She did, and spent the whole evening talking to the casting woman. I don't know what they found to talk about, but in the November she made her first appearance in the show and has never looked back. I'd even go so far as to say that she has been the best thing that's ever happened to the soap.

Like myself, she joined the cast as a celebrity in her own right, but I think she would agree, those first appearances were nerve-racking, wondering how the public would accept her. She needn't have worried. Everyone took to her instantly, and since then she's just grown and grown. Remarkable, considering that this was the first real drama she'd ever taken on.

The public still wants to see that giggling *Carry On* girl, and away from the serious storylines of the script, she still gives them what they want. But if you get to know her like I have over the years, you'll find that there is a depth and sensitivity that's just crying out to be channelled in the right direction. I'll stick my neck out and say that in four or five years' time, when producers and directors take note of the stunning performances she consistently turns out, then there's no question – absolutely no question – that she'll be up for serious drama roles outside the soap that will earn her the respect and awards that she's deserved for a long time. Only recently she picked up the Best Actress award for her faultless work in *EastEnders*, which just backs up what I'm saying.

End of the day I'm very fond of Barbara, and bless the day when them upstairs saw the light and turned her into Peggy Mitchell. Not only for her sake but mine as well, because in terms of our screen performances, we sparkle together and bring out the best in each other.

Having said that, no matter how much I missed working with Windsor and all the others, when I did cave in and agree to return, my reasons were mercenary ones. In essence, I talked my future through with my mate Bill Reilly and decided, with retirement on the horizon, that I should raise my profile to its highest limit. I would do a national tour – video – book – all promoted by Frank Butcher. I might be the old man, dad and grandad indoors, but outside I'm a product that has to be sold like anything else.

I had meetings with Mel Young, Head of Drama, and Matthew Robinson, Executive Producer, and they both enthused about wonderful future storylines. I went away, chewed it over, then arranged another meet where I told them I'd love to come back, with two or three conditions attached.

First, I don't want to work so hard, so I want at least three months off a year – no problem. Frank has a business in Manchester, or he could be buying cars abroad. Second, because I've done a few

well-recognized roles outside the soap, I'm now getting regular
enquiries as an actor. I want you to look favourably on any requests
I make to take up these offers and with notice, give me time off – no
problem. Last, but most importantly for me, is that Frank must never
get into that down and depressed mode for months on end. I've been
down that road with him, and I don't want to go there again – rest
assured, that will never happen. OK, thank you. We shook hands on
a two-year deal.

I started back on 16 March 1998, and by the time we packed up for
a Christmas break on 20 December, I'd had twenty-six days off, and
that included Sundays. I was gutted.

During that same period I was asked to do three movies, one
in particular with Michael Caine. Another film company was so
desperate to get their hands on me they virtually offered my manager
Tony Lewis a blank cheque, and the agreement that they would shoot
round me at my convenience. That's unheard of in the business –
nobody does that. I'm not blowing my own trumpet here, just stating
the facts. I approached the powers that be and their answer was,
'Sorry, Mike, but the schedule is so tight we can't allow it.' So in less
than a year everything I shook hands on went out of the window,
because next thing I heard was that I was going to kill the much-loved
and very popular Tiffany.

I said to Shirl, 'If I've got to suffer all that depression shit, cranky
letters and abuse in the street, I just can't do it.' I don't usually look
on the black side; I'm normally very much the optimist and that
should have guided me, because as it turned out, the storyline wasn't
half as bad as I'd imagined.

I'll put it another way. Yes, the storyline was everything I
imagined, but I played against the script and turned it all around.
Same words, but an inflection here and a facial expression there can
change the concept completely. I played it for all it was worth for
sympathy, and that's what I got from the audience, by the sack-load.
It was so different from the time before, when most people said they
were glad to see the back of me because I was a miserable bastard. It
was a very strong plot, but fortunately done and dusted in just over a
month, without it affecting me emotionally.

After that, me and Windsor were thrown together in practically every episode as we acted out the trauma of Peggy's breast cancer, followed straight off with our getting married. And thank God for the honeymoon, because it allowed me to take a break of about a month and I was off to Spain like a shot.

So where do I go from here? By the time my contract runs out with *EastEnders* I will be sixty, and I've always said that's when I'll retire. Maybe I will, unless circumstances dictate otherwise. Though having said that, I would prefer to dictate my own future. I want to slow down now, start thinking about winding down but not winding up completely. Ideally I want to keep the same standard of living that me and Shirl enjoy now, but without grafting my plums off eleven months of the year. What I don't want, and this is presuming I don't renew my contract with *EastEnders*, is to get webbed up in something else that would take up just as much time.

Over the past three years or so I must have been offered in the region of a dozen West End shows. I'm talking leading parts here, and I've turned them all down flat. In the main because I was tied up with the soap, but at the same time I couldn't even project them into the future.

Some of these offers came from a mate of mine, Dave Benison, who's not only a director of Spurs football club, but an entrepreneur when it comes to show business. At the moment he's got *Seven Brides for Seven Brothers* doing the rounds of the provinces, and another show, *Saturday Night* – and I was initially offered the lead in both.

Something else he had written specifically for me is a musical he asked Johnny Speight to write. If that wasn't enough to guarantee a success, he got Chas and Dave to compose the music. I went over to Dave's house, listened to the tapes and music, went through the scripts and found I couldn't be anything else but enthusiastic. He offered me a fortune and a percentage of the gate if I'd take it on. But in the back of my head was the thought of having to get a flat near the West End, leave my old woman stuck at home for four or five nights every week, plus I would be totally committed for every week of the run. Did I tell him that? No. I said, 'This sounds great – right up my street.' Bill was with me and he chipped in, 'Mike, what is the fucking matter with you? You keep talking about knocking it all on the head and retiring, yet you're sitting there raring to go and commit yourself to years of work.'

He turned to Dave and said, 'There's no way Mike can do this.' Bill said what I wanted to say, but couldn't bring myself to put into words and let Dave down. I understand he's got Dennis Waterman in the part now, and as far as I'm aware it's going very well. But I do think that Dave is expecting me to take over when Dennis is finished, and as much as it grieves me, I know I never will.

I say grieves me, because a trait of mine, and one that has been a cross all my life, is that I never, or rarely, let anyone down. It's just not in me, and it's something I'm very proud of. I'm never late, and in a professional career spanning thirty years or more, only two occasions spring to mind where I didn't turn up for a booking. Two out of thousands – no wonder I can stick my chest out.

One of these was back in the late seventies, when I was to do a stag function for Old Bill at Chigwell Police Sports Club. Why I didn't show escapes me, but when you consider that I went on stage days after losing my boy, my reasons then must have been a bit special.

There was no excuse the other time, and that wasn't many years ago. I was having an early night, dozing off nicely, when Shirl brought the phone in. Some geezer was screaming in my ear, 'Mike. Mike. Where are you? Have you had an accident?' I said, 'Not that I'm aware of – I'm in bed.' It was a club manager, and I should've been on stage an hour past. I sincerely apologized, and though my schedule barely allowed it, put in an appearance a few weeks later. But honestly, I was gutted for not only letting all those people down, but myself as well.

Funny really, I've been in the game since I was a teenager, and I think you'd have to go a long way to find anyone less 'showbiz' than me. I'm not sure if that's a virtue or not, but I can't be any other way. Basically, I've never forgotten my grass roots, if you will. I'm no better than anyone else; it just happens that my job puts me in the public eye and gives me what you might say is an enviable wage at the end of the day.

Going back to that chat show I mentioned where the other two actor guests looked down on me while they were pontificating about their work this, their work that, I thought at the time, These two wankers wouldn't know a proper day's work if it crept up on them. OK, we've all got to hang a label on how we earn our bread, and I use the term myself. But c'mon, this business isn't work in the sense of what millions of ordinary people have to do every day to keep their head above water. It's just a game we all play.

My mum's attitude changed once I became a success, but before that, when I was struggling to get recognized and skint most of the time, she would say, 'Michael, why don't you get a proper job?' And I suppose that's a general perception of what the public think about people in show business. So there's no excuse for any of us to put ourselves on pedestals and look down on the people who put us where we are today.

I'm proud to say I'm not guilty of that. I don't shut myself away in some ivory tower; I go up the local pub, and I'm no more a celebrity than the village chippy or bricklayer. And when I'm at the studio and need a bit of shopping, I walk out to Borehamwood High Street knowing that I'm going to be stopped every five yards by fans of the soap, and I don't mind at all. 'Hello, Mike', 'Hello, Frank, how's it going?' I see it as all part of the job. As long as I'm not ridiculed or pulled about, I'm perfectly happy to shake hands up and down the road.

Another thing is that every other day I get invites to premieres, shows, this lunch, that lunch, and give or take one or two that might be particularly special, I just don't go. And, digging myself out, I'm totally out of order. I've no excuse, because it's my business to be seen and see what's going on in entertainment. When I do make the effort to show my face, people come up to me and introduce themselves as this director or that producer, and I should be able to say, 'Oh, yes, you did such-and-such a show', but I don't know them from Adam, and that's wrong. But I've always been the same, and I'm not going to change now.

It's like when I'm at the studio. Come the end of the day, I'm very tired. OK, I haven't been humping bags of coal around, but the hanging about and the mental pressure of studying scripts can knock you out just the same. All I want to do is get in the car, get home and go to bed. I can hear Windsor singing in the dressing room next to mine. I stick my head round the door and she's all done up to the nines, ready to go off to some function or other. She's done a hard day's work and she's full of it – bubbling, because she loves every minute of going out and mixing on the celebrity circuit. Good luck to her. But me, who's a few years younger, wants nothing more at the end of the day than to be indoors with my missus whenever I can.

Yet that's another thing. I fly home, then we spend the evening in separate rooms. She loves the telly, while I've got lines to learn. So apart from meeting over the odd cup of tea, we don't have too much contact. But I know she's there, and she knows I'm there.

It goes back to what I was saying about being comfortable in a relationship, and personally I think that's a truer test of love and togetherness than clinging to each other every minute. Not that I want to give the impression that we don't spend time together. I make a point of taking Shirl out for a meal every week without fail. It doesn't matter what work pressures there are, our night out is carved in stone. We relax, enjoy ourselves and talk about family business – and especially now, what we see us aiming for in the future.

That's when it comes home to me that I could walk away from my career at the drop of a hat and put those plans into action. People don't believe me when I say that, but in honesty I almost dread going on stage as a comic now. It's become hard work, and I suppose that's only natural at my age.

Once I'm up and running, I fall into my routine and no-one gets short-changed, but that moment before I go on I have to take a couple of deep breaths and psych myself up before I bounce into the 'Heeey – Mike Reid – good evening.'

The acting side of my life is different, and even after twelve years or more in the soap, I still get excited about a fresh script. And this is why I think that when I do pull the plug on everything, that's what will drag me out of retirement – a meaty drama. That's my one final ambition – to show what I really can do with a role that will stretch me to the limit.

Failing that, I'm quite happy to sink into oblivion surrounded by my family. They are what has driven me on all these years. They've been my incentive to raise myself up so that I could give them all the things I had to struggle for myself in the early days. And I've been repaid a hundred times over by being on the receiving end of love and respect from every one of my kids. That's not what I would like to think – it's a fact. We have the sort of relationship where, at different times, each one has come to me and told me how they feel. And that being the case, I feel that my worth as a father has been proved, and it makes me very proud.

It's funny how I refer to them every time as kids, when Jane and Michael are in their late thirties, Angie's in her early forties and Jimmy's pushing fifty. All of them are well-balanced adults with kids of their own. And these kids are a wonderful, wonderful bonus to me at this time of my life. I don't care if 'Grandad' makes me sound like I'm ninety – I love it. It's a bit of a change of attitude from what I felt when Jimmy presented us with Scott and Claire, but I was a young man then, with a completely different outlook on life.

Michael has Amy, who's a little darling, same as all of them. Jane has Lilly, Lucy and Jade, who at seven has suffered more than she should have in these early years of her life. She was born with Prada Willy Syndrome, which means absolutely nothing to anyone if I bring it up in conversation, which I do at every opportunity in the hope that it will raise people's awareness of this illness. In essence, this syndrome is an eating disorder. It's not life-threatening, but having said that, because the sufferer will eat anything – and I mean anything, whether it's soap or wallpaper – it could leave them wide open to ingesting something harmful. Another downside, and a pretty obvious one, is the unnatural weight gain. Fortunately for her and for all of us, she's only a borderline case. For that we're extremely grateful, but my heart still goes out to any other child with the disease, and I pray that sometime soon some doctor or research establishment somewhere will take this illness on and find some cure or prevention.

Trouble is, we live in a world ruled by finances, and with so few people with this disorder there's no great name or fortune to be made out of investing in it. Please God someone out there reads this, and a seed is planted. Not just for our Jade, who hopefully will grow out of it as time goes on – but for all the others as well.

Another point here is that none of us know what's going on in the background of other people's lives when we first meet them. Because of the publicity it received, I found that when we lost Mark and Kirsty

Anne, everyone was aware of our double tragedy and treated me and Shirl with the utmost kindness and sympathy. But there can be other, smaller tragedies, just as painful but not headline stuff. So it's always worth remembering that when someone's performance is not all that, or there seems to be a bit of indifference when getting an autograph signed, allow that me or whoever might have the flu, have had a row with their partner, or are worried sick over a grandchild that's fighting for its life.

That's what me and the rest of the family went through not too long after the pain of our other losses, when Angie's baby boy was diagnosed with a heart problem. She was in America then, as she has been for many years. Little Billy had one operation, but was almost immediately taken down again when complications set in. It was touch and go, and we came within a hair's breadth of losing him. Thankfully he pulled through, and to look at him now, at nearly nine, you'd never have known what he's been through.

Which leaves Mark's Annette, who has become another daughter to us. Their boy Lee is a young man now at nearly fifteen, and little Michael is just like his dad was at ten years old. Occasionally when I look at him little memories come to the surface, and I wonder, 'What if?' I try not to dwell on the past and raise all that pain again – but I don't forget.

So that's my family, who, as I've said before, are my whole life – which brings me about as far as I can go in letting those who are interested see what led me to where I am today, and what makes me tick.

Out of respect for anyone who picks this up, I've been totally honest. Sometimes a little bit too honest as I've laid out my faults and failings, but right or wrong, I'm not ashamed of anything I've done over the years. Yeah, I've done some silly things in my life, and even now at this age there's still room to make a few more mistakes before I'm finished, but as far as that's concerned, I'm no different from anyone else.

What I am proud of, having just scrutinized my life from the year dot, is that I have never knowingly hurt or abused anyone on the way. Everything I've achieved has been without asking for help or taking handouts from anyone. It's taken loads of graft, and at times a lot of courage to keep going. But with a few exceptions, I don't think I'd change the way my life has been even if I was given the chance. I've had my Shirley right beside me all the way, sharing the ups and downs, and without that I honestly don't think I would have gone as far as I have. Any regrets I do have are ones that have been completely outside my control, so in a sense I shouldn't regret anything that it wasn't in my power to change.

If I do make up my mind to retire and sink into oblivion, I like to think I'll be remembered with affection by people I've touched over the years. On the other hand, that special script with my name on it might drop through the letterbox, and I'll shoot off in another direction. Who knows?

INDEX

INDEX

INDEX